The new
iPad
FULLY LOADED

Alan Hess

WILEY

John Wiley & Sons, Inc.

The New iPad® Fully Loaded

Published by
John Wiley & Sons, Inc.
10475 Crosspoint Boulevard
Indianapolis, IN 46256
Copyright © 2012 by John Wiley & Sons, Inc., Indianapolis, Indiana

Published simultaneously in Canada

ISBN: 978-1-118-25216-1

Manufactured in the United States of America

10 9 8 7 6 5 4 3 2 1

For general information on our other products and services or to obtain technical support, please contact our Customer Care Department within the U.S. at (877) 762-2974, outside the U.S. at (317) 572-3993 or fax (317) 572-4002.

Wiley publishes in a variety of print and electronic formats and by print-on-demand. Some material included with standard print versions of this book may not be included in e-books or in print-on-demand. If this book refers to media such as a CD or DVD that is not included in the version you purchased, you may download this material at **http://booksupport.wiley.com**. For more information about Wiley products, visit **www.wiley.com**.

Library of Congress Control Number: 2012934982

About the Author

ALAN HESS

Alan is a San Diego-based commercial photographer and author specializing in concert and live-event photography. He is the author of four Digital Field Guides and the iPad Fully Loaded series of books.

Alan is currently the house photographer for a large concert venue in Southern California and when he isn't out shooting concerts, he is writing books or checking out the newest gear at the local Apple Store. You can follow Alan on Twitter at ShotLivePhoto or check in with him on his website at **www.alanhessphotography.com.**

Credits

Acquisitions Editor
Courtney Allen

Project Editor
Jennifer Bowles

Editorial Coordinator
Carol Kessel

Technical Editor
Garth Murphy

Editorial Director
Robyn Siesky

Business Manager
Amy Knies

Senior Marketing Manager
Sandy Smith

Vice President and Executive Group Publisher
Richard Swadley

Vice President and Publisher
Barry Pruett

Graphics and Production Specialist
Erik Powers

Acknowledgments

I could not have written this book without the support of my family. Working on the tight deadlines to get the book out soon after the new iPad was released meant very long days immersed in a world of Apple, iPads, and not much else. Thank you for your patience.

This book was produced by a team that worked incredibly hard to meet some of the most insane deadlines ever. Courtney and Carol over at Wiley who kept the ball rolling on the project; Jennifer, the new-comer to the series, kept the whole project running smoothly; Garth, who double-checked my work; and Erik, who makes everything I write look better. You guys are awesome and I couldn't do it without you.

Thank you to Patrick, who has more artistic talent that I could ever imagine. Your insight into painting on the iPad was invaluable.

A big thank you goes out to all the people who have bought the previous (and current) version of this book. Without you I would not be able to do this. I thank you all from the bottom of my heart.

And as always, a huge thanks to my wife for putting up with an author husband. I keep crazy hours and tend to mumble to myself about apps, updates, and screen resolutions. Thanks for putting up with the crazy times.

For Nadra

Contents

PART 3: WORK AND SCHOOL 119

Chapter 8: Your Portable Office 121

Chapter 9: Education 139

PART 4: PHOTO AND VIDEO 151

Chapter 10: Photography 153

Chapter 11: Video 179

INTRODUCTION

The iPad has really changed my life. It changed the way I check my e-mail and browse the Internet; it changed the way that I show off my photos; and it changed how I read books. And I am not alone. The iPad has changed the way a lot of people do a lot of things.

In the fourth quarter of 2011 Apple sold 15.4 million iPads. That is a lot of devices out there, most of them being used everyday. There are now three different iPad models. The original iPad was released back in 2010 and discontinued in 2011 when the iPad 2 was released. The iPad 2 was a faster, thinner version of the original iPad, and added two cameras and support for cellular data networks other than the original AT&T. In March 2012, Apple released a new iPad and called it—the new iPad. At the same time, they dropped the price of the iPad 2. That means that there are two different models currently available, each in two colors and three capacities on a variety of cellular networks. In Chapter 1, I break down all the choices for you and clear up any confusion that you have over the different iPad models available.

Behind the really great iPad hardware is the iOS operating system that controls the device. The iOS is the brains behind the beauty and Chapter 2 covers the ins and outs of the operating system and your Apple ID, including Facetime, Twitter integration, and the really important Setting app.

Getting the most out of your iPad has never been easier than with iCloud. The iCloud service gives you e-mail, calendars, contacts, cloud storage, and automatic sync. Chapter 3 covers this and the alternatives for those that don't want to go the Apple iCloud way.

The iPad is not only a great way to deal with your e-mail and calendars, but is also a great way to browse the Internet with the built-in Safari browser or other alternatives, all of which I cover in Chapter 4.

iCloud also allows you to download any of your Apple iTunes purchases at any time, and iTunes Match enables you to not only download purchases, but also provides you access to all your music.

Chapter 6 is all about music, television, and movies. With the release of iOS 5.1 you can now re-download all your past music, TV shows, and movie purchases that you made in the iTunes Store. This is a huge leap forward since it means that you can free up space on your iPad by deleting content at will and just re-download it anytime over Wi-Fi.

There is a good chance that you are reading these words on an iPad in the iBooks app. The iPad is a great eBook reader and Chapter 7 covers the iBooks app and both the Kindle and Nook apps, along with the Newsstand where you can subscribe to your favorite magazines and other periodicals.

Chapter 8 is for those road warriors out there who want to use the iPad for business or just use it on the couch to update any document or spreadsheet. Learn how to sync using Dropbox and check out the Office suite alternatives.

There is a huge push by Apple into the education sector, including new multimedia textbooks and a whole new iTunes U app. Chapter 9 covers the new education offerings from Apple.

I take a lot of photographs and the iPad is the perfect device to use to show them off. With the new higher resolution display, the new iPad is even better at displaying your work. The new iPad comes with a higher resolution camera, and there are also some really great apps for photographers on the iPad, including Apple's new iPhoto app and Adobe's Photoshop Touch app. Chapter 10 is all about photography.

Apple has improved the video camera in the new iPad, and at the same time they have improved the iMovie app to make editing your videos even easier. Chapter 11 walks you though video creation and sharing. Talking about sharing, Chapter 12 deals with social media, including the way Twitter is integrated right into the iPad operating system. It also covers Facebook and the new Google + network.

There are a lot of different types of apps available for the iPad. As of March 2012 there were 585,000 apps, with 200,000 of those created specifically for the iPad. In chapter 13 I cover a few of the apps used for finance and one of my favorites for small business (the Square app used to take credit card payments.) After the seriousness of the Finance apps discussion, Chapter 14 covers the fun side of the iPad—games, art, and music, including the newly updated GarageBand.

The original iPad changed the way I do things, and the new iPad continues to push the capabilities of tablet computing. Hopefully this book will allow you to get as much out of the iPad as I have.

PART 1

Your iPad and Apple

Specifications, Carriers, and Data Plans

The Skim

The Differences Between the iPads
Wi-Fi vs. Wi-Fi + 3G — and Now 4G LTE • Data Carriers and Plans
Memory Storage Sizes — 16GB, 32GB, and 64GB
Screen Size and Resolution • Cameras

With the various iPad models and options available now, picking the right one for you can be a little tricky. Since the iPad was released in 2010 there have been 42 different models released. That might seem like a lot, but when you take into account storage, color, and 3G or 4G carrier, there are a lot of options. Let's start with the differences between the basic units.

THE DIFFERENCES BETWEEN THE iPADS

The original iPad was announced by Steve Jobs on January 27, 2010, and shipped on April 3, 2010—the longest 66 days ever. It changed personal computing forever. I have an original iPad and still use it, and most of the information in this book can be applied to the original iPad. That original iPad came in two different models: a Wi-Fi-only version and a Wi-Fi + 3G version. The original iPad came in black, and the data plan for the 3G version would work only with AT&T. Each of these models came with 16GB, 32GB, or 64GB of onboard memory; a USB cable; and a power adapter.

Figure 1-1
The original iPad, the new iPad, and the iPad 2 (from left to right).

In 2011, Apple released the thinner and lighter iPad 2 and discontinued the original iPad. There were still only two models available: Wi-Fi-only and Wi-Fi + 3G. With iPad 2, though, you had a choice of colors (black or white), the data plans on the 3G models were available on AT&T or Verizon, and it came equipped with two cameras. It still came with your choice of 16GB, 32GB, or 64GB of internal memory.

On March 7, 2012, Apple announced the new iPad and to make matters a little confusing, the name is the iPad or the new iPad. In this book, the original iPad is referred to as the original iPad, the iPad 2 still goes by the iPad 2, and the newest iPad is referred to as the iPad or the new iPad.

The new iPad is roughly the same size as the iPad 2, but under the hood the new iPad is all new. New screen, new cell service, new cameras, and a new battery that still gives the device 10 hours of power (9 hours when using the new 4G/LTE cell service). The new iPad comes as Wi-Fi-only or Wi-Fi + 4G/LTE capability and in the same three storage sizes as the original iPad and the iPad 2—16GB, 32GB, and 64GB. And like the iPad 2, the new iPad comes in your choice of color—as long as it's black or white.

WI-FI VS. WI-FI + 3G— AND NOW 4G

Much of the functionality of the iPad is tied into its ability to connect to the Internet. To check e-mail, browse the Internet, shop the iTunes store, and take advantage of the new iTunes Match, the iPad needs to connect to the Internet. There are two ways to connect—either via built-in Wi-Fi, or the cellular network available on the 3G or 4G versions.

Let's look at the pros and cons of the different ways of connecting to the Internet with an iPad:

- **Wi-Fi:** This term is used to describe devices that can communicate wirelessly over a computer network. It can be a wireless home network or a public Wi-Fi spot. There are no limits on the amount of data that can be transferred over the Wi-Fi connection on an iPad, and all iPads come with Wi-Fi capability.

- **3G**: 3G, or 3rd Generation, mobile telecommunications is a set of specifications for mobile phones and other mobile telecommunication devices. The 3G service was the standard offered on both the original iPad and the iPad 2. Only iPads that have 3G capability can be used on a 3G network.

- **4G**: This is the 4th generation of the mobile telecommunications specifications and is faster than 3G. The new iPad can use the 4G network with gives it a faster connection to the Internet over the cellular network than the previous iPads.

- **LTE**: This term refers to 3GPP Long Term Evolution and is a newer generation of wireless hardware, which offers increased speed over the older 3G service. In fact, according to the Apple keynote, the LTE service has a maximum theoretical speed of 73 Mbps, which is really fast. The new iPad has the capability to use these networks while the original iPad and iPad 2 do not.

LTE Coverage

Even if you get the new iPad with the ability to connect over the LTE network, it does not actually mean you will be able to connect at those promised speeds. The reason for this is that the LTE network is not available everywhere. In fact, at the time of the new iPad

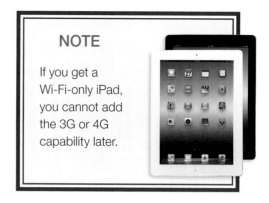

NOTE

If you get a Wi-Fi-only iPad, you cannot add the 3G or 4G capability later.

release, AT&T has full LTE service in only 28 markets—which means if you live in Oregon or Washington or anywhere other than the 28 cities with LTE coverage you are not going to get those promised speeds. Verizon has more LTE coverage, but only one city in Oregon and nothing in some other states.

So if your reason for wanting the new iPad is to have faster Internet speeds over the cellular network, be sure that you live in an area that has LTE coverage.

Carriers

There are two cellular providers that provide data plans in the United States: Verizon and AT&T. If you have a Wi-Fi-only iPad, then this section does not apply to you. If you are planning on purchasing a Wi-Fi + 4G-enabled iPad, you have to decide which carrier you want to handle the data plan before buying the device. The Verizon iPad does not work on the AT&T network, and the AT&T iPad does not work on the Verizon network.

So which one is better? That is a subjective question, but the answer is probably the carrier that has the best 4G service where you plan on using it the most. For me, that happens to be AT&T, but for you it might be Verizon; it all depends on the service available in your area.

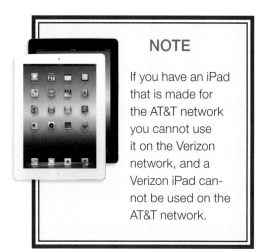

NOTE

If you have an iPad that is made for the AT&T network you cannot use it on the Verizon network, and a Verizon iPad cannot be used on the AT&T network.

Data Plans

AT&T and Verizon each have data plans for the iPad, which are actually very similar. The iPad data plan is not a long-term contract—it is a monthly plan and you pay only when you activate the service. For example, when I travel I buy a month of data, but when I am at home and using a Wi-Fi connection I don't need the cellular service, so I usually only buy two or three months', worth of data plans a year. Now for the actual costs for the data:

AT&T data plan:

- 250MB per month is $14.99.
- 2GB per month is $30.
- 5GB per month is $50.

Verizon data plan:

- 1GB per month is $20.
- 2GB per month is $30.
- 5GB per month is $50.

As you can see from these plans, AT&T offers the smallest data plan and both top out at 5GB.

16GB, 32GB, OR 64GB

All of the iPads come in three storage sizes—16GB, 32GB, and 64GB—with an increase in price as the memory increases. The question is now, How much memory is enough? That all depends on what you do with the iPad, and the size and format of the content you want to work with. Here are some things to keep in mind about the types of files you may want to keep on your iPad:

- **Movies:** The iPad can play movies in a variety of formats, including H.264 video up to 30 frames a second with 48KHz stereo audio in the .m4v and the .mov file formats. What that means to you and me is that you can play HD movies with great sound on your iPad, but these movies take up a lot of space. For example, the movie *The Expendables (Extended Directors Cut)* is 3.9GB in the HD format and 1.69GB in the SD format. That means that the SD copy is less than half the size of the HD copy.

With this you should keep two things in mind: The first is that if you want to carry around HD movies, you'll need more space; the second is that when you buy an HD movie from Apple, you also get the SD version and can keep that version on the iPad and the full HD version on your computer.

- **TV shows:** You can purchase TV shows in both SD and HD formats. The difference is that with the iCloud service you can download an already-purchased show anytime, and when done, you can delete the show and then redownload it again as long as you are connected to the Internet via Wi-Fi. This is covered in more detail in Chapter 6.

Figure 1-2
I keep a lot of content on my iPad, as you can see from the usage bar.

- **Music:** All music that you purchase from the iTunes store is available there at all times, so your music doesn't need to live on your iPad all the time. If you add the iTunes Match service, you can access all your music all the time from the iCloud, which frees up space on your iPad. More on that in Chapter 5.

- **Books:** Regular ebooks are actually quite small. For example, the Stephen King novel *Under The Dome* is a huge book at 4.3MB, while the smaller novel *Taken*, by Robert Crais, is 867KB—but most eBooks books fall somewhere in the middle. This enables you to keep a wide selection of books on your iPad without taking up much space. The really cool thing is that eBooks that are purchased through iBookstore are treated like apps and if you delete a book, you can just go download it again from the iBookstore anytime.

- **Textbooks:** Electronic textbooks are much, much bigger than most regular ebooks. According to Apple, eTextbooks are supposed to be 2GB or smaller, but some of the first eTextbooks available are bigger than that. What this means for you is if you need to keep a lot of textbooks on your iPad, you had better make sure that you have enough capacity to begin with.

- **Magazines:** The size of a Magazine app is usually pretty small, but the size of the actual individual issues can be rather large.

If you start to run out of space and have a lot of magazines on your iPad, you might want to look at archiving the older issues, which deletes the issues from the iPad. Each of the Magazine apps has a different way of archiving older issues but they all let you download the archived issues at any time.

- **Apps:** Apps come in all sizes, from really small to quite large. The smallest app on my iPad right now is the game Black and White that comes in at a measly 848KB, and the biggest app is also a game, Batman, that comes in at a whopping 1.2GB

- **Photos:** Photos can take up a lot of space depending on the size and resolution of the images.

You can check exactly how your iPad memory is being used at any time. This can help you figure out what to delete to free up space, and the best part is that you can actually delete apps right from this view.

1. Turn on the iPad.
2. Tap on Settings.
3. Tap on General in the left column.
4. Tap on Usage in the right column.
5. Tap on Show apps at the bottom of the apps list to see the space usage of all the apps. See Figure 1-3.

You can now tap on any of the apps to see how much space each is taking up and you can also delete the app right from there, as shown in Figure 1-4.

Figure 1-3

It's easy to see how much space each app takes up on your iPad.

Figure 1-4

You can easily delete any app that you feel is being a space hog.

SCREEN SIZE AND RESOLUTION

The original iPad and the iPad 2 both had the exact same screen size and screen resolution. The screen is a 9.7-inch diagonal LED backlit glossy screen with a resolution of 1024 x 768 at 132 pixels per inch.

The new iPad doubles that resolution to a whopping 2048 x 1536 at 264 pixels per inch. This display is so sharp and clear that you can't see the individual pixels at a regular viewing distance. The Retina display, as Apple calls it, is one of the biggest differences between the new iPad and the first iPads. It is made up of a total of 3.1 million pixels, which is a million more pixels than a HDTV, all in a 9.7-inch display.

iPAD CAMERAS

The original iPad did not have a camera. The iPad 2 has two cameras, as does the new iPad. One of the biggest differences between the iPad 2 and the new iPad is the quality of the camera on the rear of the device.

Let's look at the iPad 2 cameras first. The two cameras are not the same: the rear-facing camera can record 720p HD video and audio up to 30 frames a second. The front-facing camera is a much lower resolution than the rear and records video only in VGA mode at 30 frames a second

Now the new iPad cameras take that up a notch, giving the rear camera a real boost. The front-facing camera is still a lower resolution than the rear camera. The front camera is now called the FaceTime camera and is a VGA-quality photo and video camera that records up to 30 frames a second. The rear-facing camera is now a 5-megapixel iSight camera that records in HD (1080p) at 30 frames a second and has built-in video stabilization.

Figure 1-5
The iPad 2's built-in camera was good, producing files of 720 x 960 pixels.

Figure 1-6
The new iPad's camera is even better and produces files of 1936 x 2592 pixels—a huge jump in resolution.

IN A NUTSHELL

When Apple released the new iPad in March 2012, they did not discontinue the iPad 2. It is still available from the Apple store, but at a reduced price.

The iPad 2 now comes in black or white, Wi-Fi or Wi-Fi + 3G, and in 16GB only. The new iPad comes in black or white, Wi-Fi or Wi-Fi + 4G, and in 16GB, 32GB, or 64GB. The Wi-Fi + 3G and the Wi-Fi + 4G tablets can be purchased to run on either the AT&T or the Verizon network.

There you have it, all the specs that you could possibly want.

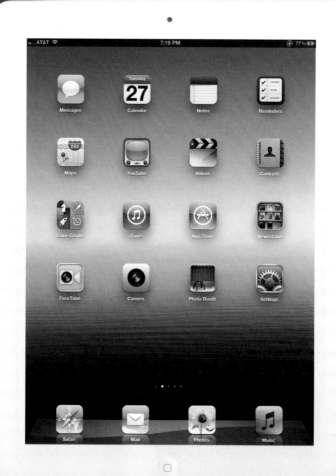

iOS and the Apple ID

The Skim

The iPad's operating system, called iOS, controls its core functionality. The same iOS controls the iPad, the iPhone, and the iPod touch. Apple periodically updates the iOS to add functionality to the devices and fix any bugs. Since the release of the iPad, Apple has added built-in apps and functions tied to the iOS. With iOS 5, Apple introduced a new Notification Center, a message system, updated photo editing functions, AirPlay Mirroring, and Twitter integration, and it removed the need for the user to have a computer to use the iPad.

That's a lot of functionality and if we go by history, Apple will not rest on its laurels and will continue to improve the functionality of the iPad with periodic iOS updates. Before looking at the new and improved functions, let's go over the basics of using the iPad.

THE APPLE iPAD OPERATING SYSTEM

The iPad is really easy to use thanks to technology controlled by the operating system; just use your fingers to navigate around the screen. While the iPad is pretty intuitive to use, knowing a few specific things will make it easier and hopefully less frustrating.

Gestures

Controlling the iPad is done by making gestures with your finger on the touch screen. Want to run an app? Just tap on it with your finger. On a screen where you need to type something? The keyboard slides up into place. Reading an eBook and want to turn the page? Just swipe from right to left. The gestures are very intuitive and usually perform exactly like you would expect them to.

There are also some special gestures that you can use to control the iPad. These special gestures are available in iOS 5.1 and can be turned on and off as desired in the Settings app. These gestures are:

- **Pinch to go the home screen.** Place all five fingers on the screen and pull them together. This closes the app you are using and opens the home screen.

- **Swipe up.** Slide four fingers from the bottom of the screen toward the top to open the multitasking bar. I still find it easier

to double tap the Home button, but this works well if you have a problem with the timing of the double tap.

- **Slide between the apps.** This is a neat way to switch apps; just slide four fingers from right to left to go to the next app or from left to right to go to the previous app.

Multitasking

The iOS allows a form of multitasking, which you can control with the multitasking bar. This bar gives you access to the apps that are running, the brightness and volume controls, and the playback control for the music player. You can also control the Rotation Lock here. To access the multitasking bar, just tap the Home button (that's the only button on the front of the iPad, located at the bottom just below the screen) twice in quick succession. The multitasking bar slides up from the bottom of the screen.

When the multitasking menu slides up from the bottom, the first thing you see are the

Figure 2-1
Double tapping on the Home button opens the multitasking bar, showing the most recently used apps.

Figure 2-2
Swiping across the multitasking bar from the left to right brings up the controls for locking the Rotation or Mute buttons, the brightness slider, the media playback controls, the AirPlay button, and the Music app.

most recently used apps. You can now swipe your finger across the bar from left to right, which brings up the Rotation Lock or Mute, depending on what was set up in the Settings app. To set up what that button does, you need to set the function of the side switch in the Settings app, which is covered a little later in this chapter. My preference is to set the side switch to Mute, which makes this button the Rotation Lock. Tapping the Rotation Lock button locks/unlocks the automatic orientation of the device. When the orientation is locked, it doesn't matter what way you turn the iPad, the screen orientation stays the same. Unlock the rotation and the screen switches between portrait and landscape automatically as you move the iPad.

Next is the brightness slider that controls the brightness of the screen. Just slide to the left to dim the screen, to the right to make it brighter. Up next are the Previous, Play/Pause, and Next buttons that control the music playback. The Next button is the AirPlay button that appears if you have AirPlay devices on the network. Tap the AirPlay button and the devices that are AirPlay-enabled are listed; just tap a device from the list and the output from the iPad streams to that device. Next is the volume slider; just slide to the left to reduce the volume, to the right to increase the volume. The final button is the music source and this defaults to the iTunes player. If you use a different music player like the Pandora Music app, then this will show that app icon.

Moving Apps

When you purchase an app and download it to your iPad, the app is loaded in to the first empty spot on the iPad, starting on the second page. You can move it, though. What if you want the app to be on another page or

Figure 2-3

When you hold your finger on an app it starts to wiggle—now you can move it. Notice that the apps that can be deleted have an X in the top left corner.

grouped with other apps that share a common theme? It's really easy to move apps on the iPad. To do so, follow these steps.

1. Hold your finger on the app that you want to move until it starts to wiggle.

2. Drag the app to where you want it. You can move the app from page to page just by sliding it to the edge of the page until the page changes.

3. Once you've moved the app to where you want it, tap the Home button once and the apps are now locked into place.

Deleting Apps

You may not want to keep every app you download. Thankfully, deleting apps from your iPad is really easy; just do the following:

1. Hold your finger on the app that you want to delete until it starts to wiggle.

2. Tap the X on the top left corner of the app.

3. You may see a warning that you are about to delete the app and all the data associated with it.

4. Tap ok to delete the app.

That's all there is to it. The best part is that once you purchase an app, you can always download it again anytime.

Folders

Apple has made it easy to group apps together by allowing you to make folders to store them

Figure 2-4

This folder has apps that are all related to photography, so I named the folder "Photography," allowing me to find them all quickly.

in. All you have to do is move one app on top of another and a folder is created automatically. Here's how you do it:

1. Hold your finger on one of the apps that you want put into a folder until the app starts to wiggle.

2. Slide one app onto the top of the second app and a folder appears with the two apps inside it.

3. You can now name the folder in the title spot, as shown in Figure 2-4.

4. You can move other apps into the folder and move the folder around the same way as you would an app.

There are a few things that are different with folders compared to apps:

• You cannot delete a folder; you have to remove or delete the apps within it and then the folder vanishes.

• You cannot have an empty folder.

• You cannot put the Newsstand app into a folder.

• You can have a maximum of 20 apps in one folder.

To access an app in a folder, just tap on the folder to open it, then tap on the app you want to launch. When you are done with the app, tap on the Home button to close the app and you will see the open folder. To close the folder you can either tap on the Home button, tap on the folder icon, or tap on the screen anywhere outside the open folder.

Periodically I like to go through my iPad and make sure that the apps are sorted in a way that makes finding then easier. For example, I like to play games on my iPad once in a while and so I like to keep them all together in one "Games" folder.

Figure 2-5
You must agree to the Terms and Conditions before you can use your iPad.

NO COMPUTER NEEDED

When the iPad first came out, you needed to have a computer running iTunes to be able to use the tablet. When you first turned the iPad on, the first thing you had to do was attach the iPad to a computer and sync it with an iTunes account. With the release of iOS 5, this is no longer the case and the device can now be used by anyone, whether he has a computer or not.

Turn on your iPad for the first time and you no longer get a graphic that tells you to plug it into a computer running iTunes. The first screen asks you to slide your finger across the Unlock button to set up the iPad. The next screen asks you if you want to turn on Location Services, which allows the maps and other apps to gather information and use data indicating your approximate locations. If you disable Location Services you can always turn it on later.

It's now time to connect to a Wi-Fi network, and the iPad shows you a list of the available networks. Pick yours and enter the password. Then, you get to set up the device up as a new iPad or you can restore from a previous iCloud backup or iTunes backup. Now, enter the Apple ID you use for the iCloud. If you don't have an iCloud account, you can Create a Free Apple ID here and I suggest that you do.

The next step is to agree to the Terms and Conditions of the iOS. Feel free to read the fine print but if you Disagree you can't use your iPad, so I suggest that you just tap on the Agree button on the bottom right. That's it, your iPad is now ready to use.

WI-FI SYNC AND BACKUP

With the release of iOS 5, Apple introduced Wi-Fi syncing and backup of your iPad. This enables you to sync your iPad to your computer without having to plug the iPad into the computer. You can transfer your apps, music, movies, TV shows, and photos from the computer right to the iPad over the Wi-Fi network. Now, although this doesn't require you to plug the iPad into the computer, you still have to plug the iPad into a power source.

For Wi-Fi sync to work you must be running iTunes 10.5 or later and iOS 5 or later, and you need to attach the iPad to the computer at least once to turn Wi-Fi sync on. First, you need to set up the sync on iTunes, and then you need to set up the sync on the iPad. Just follow these steps:

1. Turn on the computer.

2. Launch iTunes on your computer.

3. Turn on the iPad.

4. Connect the iPad to the computer using the supplied USB cable.

5. On the computer, select the iPad from the Device list in the left window in iTunes.

6. In iTunes, click on the Summary tab at the top of the window.

7. Scroll down and click the checkbox "Sync with this iPad over Wi-Fi" in the Options menu.

Now that the device is set up on the iTunes side, it's time to set up the iPad side of things:

1. Disconnect the iPad from the computer.

2. Plug the iPad into a power supply.

3. Turn on the iPad.

4. Tap on the Settings app.

5. Tap on General.

6. Tap on iTunes Wi-Fi Sync.

7. Tap on the Sync Now button to wirelessly sync the iPad to the computer.

That's all there is to it. Your iPad will now sync with your computer's iTunes every time the iPad is plugged into a power supply.

If you run into problems with the wireless sync, here are some things to try:

1. Make sure that you are using iTunes 10.5 or later.

2. Quit and relaunch iTunes.

3. Restart the iPad.

4. Make sure that the iPad and the computer are on the same Wi-Fi network.

If all of these troubleshooting ideas fail to fix the problem, connect the iPad to the computer and make sure that the Wi-Fi Sync box is checked, as outlined earlier. At times there seem to be gremlins that come around and

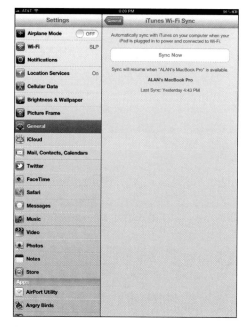

Figure 2-6

The iTunes Wi-Fi Sync menu in the Settings app. Just tap the Sync Now button to sync your iPad with your computer's iTunes.

uncheck those boxes, at least they do on my computers.

Since the iPad syncs wirelessly, it also backs up wirelessly, and you can decide if those backups are stored on the computer or in the iCloud. I talk more about iCloud in Chapter 3, but if you have the iCloud service (and there is no reason not to) then you can back up your iPad data to the cloud.

To determine where your iPad backs up, turn on the computer your iPad syncs with, open iTunes, select the iPad from the device list on the left, and click on the Summary tab. Check the Backup menu and pick either Back up to the iCloud or Back up to This Computer. You can also encrypt the backup if you want.

Figure 2-7
The Apple ID page where you can create an Apple ID, manage your account, reset your password, or just find out if you already have an Apple ID.

YOUR APPLE ID

The Apple ID is the key to getting the most out of your iPad and your Apple account. The Apple ID is the user name that allows you to purchase items from the iTunes Store, and log into iCloud and iChat. The most important thing to know is that purchases are tied to your Apple ID and at this time Apple IDs cannot be combined. That means you need to make sure you are always using the correct Apple ID.

To set up an Apple ID, check to see if you have one, or manage yours go to appleid.apple.com. This site allows you to manage your account, reset your password, or check to see if you have an Apple ID with a simple tap.

The following are places that you need to enter an Apple ID on your iPad.

The Apple ID and Your Purchases

Any content you purchase from the iTunes Store is tied to an Apple ID. This is both really useful and really restrictive. It means that if you purchase an app for your iPad and want to have that same app on your iPhone, then you need to use the same Apple ID in the Store settings on both devices. This also works

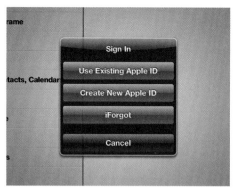

Figure 2-8
You need to sign in using an Apple ID. If you don't have one yet, Apple gives you the option of creating one right here.

for when you have more than one iPad in a household (or business). For example, both my wife and I have iPads and we want to be able to load the same apps (and movies, music, books, etc) onto both iPads without having to purchase the content twice. Now, I have a different e-mail account and iCloud account than my wife does, but both of our iPads use the same Apple ID in the Store settings for content purchased from the iTunes Store.

To enter the Apple ID you want to use for purchases in the Store settings, just follow these simple steps:

1. Turn on the iPad.

2. Tap on the Settings app.

3. Tap on Store in the list on the left side.

4. Tap on Sign In at the top right corner of the screen; a Sign In screen opens.

5. Tap Use Existing Apple ID or Create New Apple ID as needed. If you forgot your Apple ID, then tap iForgot.

6. Enter the required information and tap Continue.

Figure 2-9
The Home Sharing sign in page in iTunes.

Figure 2-10
You can sign in to Home Sharing on the iPad in the Music settings within the Settings app.

Make sure that this is the Apple ID that you want to use to purchase content with. If you want the content to be on other iPads, you will need to enter the same Apple ID in this spot on all the iPads (and iPhones and iPod Touches).

The Apple ID and Home Sharing

Home Sharing is awesome because it allows you to access the content that is in your computer's iTunes library from your iPad (and iPhone and other computer) as long as the computer and iPad are on the same Wi-Fi network, you have Home Sharing turned on, and are using the same Apple ID.

To turn on Home Sharing on the computer in iTunes:

1. Open iTunes.

2. Click Advanced > Turn on Home Sharing.

3. The Home Sharing window opens.

4. Enter the Apple ID and Password.

5. Click on Create Home Share.

There are two places in the Settings app—Music settings and Video settings—where you can turn on Home Sharing on your iPad. When you enter the information in one spot it is automatically entered in the other.

Follow these steps to turn on Home Sharing in the Music settings on your iPad:

1. Turn on the iPad.

2. Tap on the Settings app.

3. Tap on Music in the list on the left.

4. Enter the Same Apple ID and Password that you entered in the computer in the Home Sharing settings.

You can follow these same basic steps to turn on Home Sharing in the Video settings, too.

That's it. Home Sharing is now turned on. You can now access the iTunes library on all computers and devices that have Home Sharing enabled and are on the same Wi-Fi network.

Apple ID and FaceTime

For the video chat FaceTime software to work, it needs to be associated with an Apple ID. This does not have to be the same ID that you use for purchasing from the iTunes Store and Home Sharing. For example, the Apple ID on my wife's iPad in the FaceTime application is different from the Apple ID used for app purchasing and Home Sharing since she doesn't want to get calls meant for me.

To set the Apple ID and the e-mail associated with the iPad FaceTime software, go to the Settings app and tap on FaceTime on the left, and then enter the required information on the right. Simple as that!

The details on using FaceTime are covered a little later in this chapter.

iMESSAGE

Apple has created a messaging service that works between devices using the iOS 5 or later operating system and with Apple computers running the OS 10.8. This messaging system works on the iPad, iPhone, and iPod Touch. iMessage works on Wi-Fi and 3G or 4G, and allows you to send texts, photos, videos, and map locations.

To set up iMessage on your iPad, go to the Settings app and tap on Messages. This is where you can turn on messaging and specify which e-mail account you want to use to receive the messages.

Figure 2-11

The iMessage screen showing a text conversation. It look just like a text message conversation on an iPhone.

Figure 2-12

The iMessage setup screen allows you to specify the e-mail account you want to use for iMessage.

Figure 2-13

The notifications show Google+ updates and Twitter mentions.

NOTIFICATION CENTER

Many of the apps on your iPad send you alerts when something happens. This includes new text messages, e-mails, mentions on Twitter, and just about anything else. In the past, these alerts would come up in the middle of the screen and pause whatever app you were currently using, interrupting your iPad usage. With the release of the Notification Center in iOS 5, that has all changed. Now, alerts don't pause the currently running app. And instead of showing up in the middle of the screen, alerts now show at the top of the screen and last a few seconds before disappearing automatically. They are easy to check by just swiping down from the top of the screen.

You can customize the Notification Center in the Settings app, where you can choose which apps to include in the Notification Center and what they show. To access the Notification Center settings just turn on the iPad, tap on the Settings app, and tap on the Notifications tab.

The first option you choose is whether the apps are sorted manually or chronologically. Just click on your choice and it's set. Then comes the fun part: setting up the notifications for apps on your iPad. Each of the app's notification choices has a series of choices that includes if the app shows up in

Figure 2-14
The Notification panel for my e-mail accounts. I have turned off the View in Lock Screen setting so that new e-mails are not visible when my iPad is locked.

Figure 2-15
The Notification panel for my Calendar has fewer choices than the one for e-mail accounts. I allow these notifications to show up on the locked screen since they remind me of appointments.

the Notification Center, what type of alert style is used, and any other options available.

The Notifications app is now part of the OS X 10.8 on Apple desktop computers, bringing this functionality to the desktop.

FACETIME

FaceTime is the video chat service that runs on Apple products including the iPad 2, the new iPad, the iPhone, and the full range of Apple computers. FaceTime works only on iPads that have cameras, so it won't work with the original iPad. You also must have a Wi-Fi connection to use FaceTime.

The first time you run FaceTime on the iPad 2 or the new iPad, it asks you to sign in with your Apple ID or create a new account. After you have signed in you are asked to specify an e-mail address for people to use when they call you. This e-mail address doesn't have to be the same address that you used for the Apple ID.

Now, this is important: If you have multiple devices that have FaceTime capability and you want them all to ring when called, then you must use the same e-mail on each one. If you have multiple devices but want them each to be considered separate then you

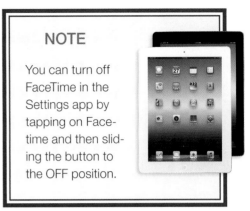

NOTE

You can turn off FaceTime in the Settings app by tapping on Facetime and then sliding the button to the OFF position.

Figure 2-16

When you launch FaceTime for the first time you are prompted for an Apple ID and password. It remembers this info so you don't have to enter it again.

must use a different e-mail for each one. For example, I have a MacBook Pro that has FaceTime installed and I have an iPhone 4 with FaceTime installed. If my wife wants to call me on the iPhone 4 then she calls using the phone number. If she wants to call me on the computer, then she uses my main e-mail address. So when I got my new iPad, I set it with the same e-mail and Apple ID as my computer. I wanted it to ring when someone called the computer so that it didn't matter if I was at my desk or sitting on the living room couch with my iPad.

If your computer and iPad are using the same Apple ID but different e-mails, here is how to

change the Caller ID in the Settings app so that they both ring when one e-mail is called:

1. Turn on the iPad.

2. Tap on the Settings app.

3. Tap on FaceTime in the list on the left. You will see:
   - You can turn FaceTime on or off here, in case you don't want to be disturbed.
   - Your Apple ID account e-mail.
   - The e-mail that you entered as the e-mail to use to call the device, along with a button to add another e-mail.
   - If there is more than one e-mail entered here, there is also a Caller ID field. You must set this field to the e-mail you want for the iPad.

4. Tapping on the Caller ID field allows you to pick from the e-mails listed on the iPad for the one to use as a unique identifier.

Once you have FaceTime set up, all you have to do is use your contact list to call someone. If someone calls you, FaceTime will ring even if it isn't currently running, and then it is just a matter of tapping the Accept or Decline button on the bottom of the screen. The video quality is pretty good, but like all live video over the Internet it is dependent on the

Figure 2-17
The FaceTime
app contact list.

NOTE

FaceTime does
not work with
other video
services like
AIM or iChat.

and by tapping Clear on the top right you can clear all the recents.

To mark a contact as a favorite:

1. Open FaceTime.

2. Tap on Contacts on the bottom right.

3. Tap on the contact you want to add as a favorite.

4. On the bottom of the Contact Information there are two buttons: Share Contact and Add to Favorites. Tap on Add to Favorites. A pop-up menu appears asking which of the contact's phone numbers or e-mails you want to add.

5. Tap on the contact info you want added as a favorite.

To remove a favorite:

1. Open FaceTime.

2. Tap on Favorites on the bottom left to open the Favorites list.

3. Tap on the Edit button in the top left of the Favorites list.

4. A white – sign appears next to each entry; tap on the sign next to the contact to delete the entry.

5. Tap Done when you are finished.

connection speed. The better the connection and the higher the speed, the better the quality of the video.

When using FaceTime it is possible to switch between the front-facing camera and the rear-facing camera just by tapping the change camera button on the bottom of the screen.

The FaceTime interface uses the whole screen when on a FaceTime call, but when you start the app you see a list of contacts on the right side. You can easily add a contact by tapping on the + sign at the top right. Any contact you enter here appears in your address book on the iPad. If you look at the bottom of your contact list, there are two other options: You can view a list of Recent Calls and a list of Favorites. The Recent Calls list shows all the calls or just the missed calls,

AIRPLAY AND AIRPLAY MIRRORING

The AirPlay technology allows you to stream media on your iPad to other devices, the most common being the Apple TV. You can stream music, photos, and videos over Wi-Fi to an AirPlay-enabled device.

Connect the Apple TV to the television set and connect it to the same Wi-Fi as the iPad. Then, the iPad will be able to stream the content playing on the device to the TV, and with the Airplay Mirroring the content still plays on the iPad at the same time. The most important thing to know to get this to work is that the Apple TV and the iPad need to be on the same Wi-Fi network. The iPad will automatically see the Apple TV and the AirPlay button will appear in the controls. So you can be watching a movie on your iPad, walk into your living room where the Apple TV is connected to your television, and start to stream the movie from the iPad to the Television with just a tap.

TWITTER INTEGRATION

Social media is everywhere these days and Apple has integrated Twitter right into the iOS of the iPad. Chapter 12 covers social media and how the integration with Twitter enables you to Tweet from inside other apps, including the Photo app and Safari.

REMINDERS

Reminders is a simple to-do list. This app is a great—especially for people who have multiple iOS devices—since the Reminders are shared over the iCloud service, which means that when you enter a Reminder on your iPad it shows up on your iPhone. Create a shopping list on your iPad at home and it is with you in the supermarket on your iPhone.

Figure 2-18
The Reminders app has a simple interface, making it easy to start entering to-do items.

The Reminder app looks very simple at first glance but it has a lot of power. When you first open the app, you see two columns: On the right are your Reminders and on the left is where you organize the Reminders. You will see two lists already there—a Completed list and a Reminders list. You can easily add more lists by just tapping on the Edit button on the top left, which allows you to Create a New List or delete the lists that you have already entered. I like to add lists for work and home, and for any books that I am writing.

Now just pick a list by tapping on it and then enter a Reminder by tapping on the + in the top right corner. Once you have typed in the Reminder, tap return and you can add another Reminder, or you can now tap on the Reminder you just created to add alerts, priority, change the list, or add a note. You can also delete the Reminder if needed here.

If you need to set a Reminder for a specific date, you can do that as well and just as easily. On the top left part of the screen you can look at the lists in List view or in Date view. In Date view, just tap on a date to see what is due that day or enter a Reminder for that day.

GAME CENTER

The iPad is a great gaming device. I know that I use it to play games once in a while and have spent (wasted) a lot of time making sure that the Angry Birds beat the egg-stealing pigs.

Game Center is a place to find and launch the games installed on the iPad. It doesn't matter what folders or pages the games are on, Game Center allows you to launch them from inside the Game Center app. It also allows you to play games with friends and share your accomplishments and scores to make your gaming a little more social.

The most important part of this app is the menu bar across the bottom where you can see your friends, the games you have installed, and any friend requests. Tap on the Games button to see a list of all the games installed on your iPad. Tap on any of the games and you can see the Leaderboard, Achievements, and any Players that you have played the game with. You can also launch a game just by tapping on the Play Game button.

THE SETTINGS APP

The Settings app is the control panel for your iPad. It is here that you can control just about all the settings for your device. This is also the spot where a lot of apps put their settings

Figure 2-19
I have quite a few games loaded on my iPad and can access them all from the Game Center app.

as well. The Settings app is the most important app on the iPad and the first place to check if things are not working the way you want them to.

The Settings app is divided into two columns, with the Settings list on the left and the corresponding settings on the right, as shown in Figure 2-20

The basic Settings list that comes on your iPad is a follows:

- **Airplane Mode:** When turned on, Airplane Mode turns off the following services on your iPad: cellular service data (for those devices that have it), Wi-Fi, Bluetooth, GPS, and Location Services. This makes your iPad comply with airline regulations. Some airlines now allow Wi-Fi

Figure 2-20
The Settings app.

and/or Bluetooth to be turned on for parts of the flight. You can do this by tapping the Wi-Fi setting and turning it on, and then selecting an available network. To turn on the Bluetooth service, tap on the General setting, then Bluetooth, and then turn it on.

- **Wi-Fi:** This is where you turn Wi-Fi on and off and pick a Wi-Fi network to use. Slide the Wi-Fi button on to see a list of available networks. Tap on the network you want to use and enter the password if needed.

  Next to each available network name are three icons: the first is a lock that shows if the network is password protected, the second shows the signal strength, and the third is a button that opens the

information panel for that network. Tapping on that third little blue arrow icon opens a page that shows technical info about that network, including the IP address, the Router address, and the very useful Forget This Network button. If you joined a network by mistake, just tap this button to stop the iPad from joining it again automatically.

On the main menu, there is also a menu choice that allows you to turn on and off the Ask to Join Networks ability. The iPad will join networks it already knows, and if there are none known available it will ask about other networks in the area as long as this is turned on. If it is off, you have to manually add any new networks.

- **Notifications:** This is where you control how the notifications work on your iPad. It was covered in detail earlier in this chapter in the Notification Center section.

- **Location Services:** This is where you can turn the Location Services on or off, or just turn the service on or off for individual apps. There are some apps that need to have Location Services turned on to work properly, but with others (such as Twitter and Facebook) I make sure they are turned off. I do not want my location tied to my Tweets or Facebook updates. The Location Services allow the location-dependant apps like the Maps app, the built-in camera, and Safari to use the data from the Wi-Fi and the GPS.

- **Cellular Data:** If your iPad has 3G or 4G capability then you have this option. You can turn the Cellular Data off and make the iPad use only Wi-Fi. This is also the place where you can view your data account and turn Data Roaming on and off. If you are traveling, you need to turn Data Roaming off or it is possible to run up a massive bill with your data provider.

- **Brightness & Wallpaper:** You can adjust the brightness of your iPad screen here and turn the Auto Brightness on or off. I have never seen a difference between having this function turned on or off. You can also set the background wallpaper for both the lock screen and the home screen here.

- **Picture Frame:** Your iPad can act like a digital picture frame. You can set the transitions to either dissolve between frames or transition using Origami, a cool way to see your photos. You can also set the length of time to show each photo, turn shuffle on or off, and pick which photo album to use.

- **General:** This is the most used and useful set of tools in the Settings app. The General settings are covered in detail right after this section.

- **iCloud:** This is where you can turn on and off the individual parts of the iCloud service, including:
  - Mail
  - Contacts
  - Calendars
  - Reminders
  - Bookmarks
  - Notes
  - Photo Stream
  - Documents & Data
  - Find My iPad
  - Storage & Backups

- **Mail, Contacts, Calendars:** This is where you can add or edit e-mail accounts on your iPad. You can also adjust the way e-mail is shown, the order and sorting of the contact list, the calendar information, and set the reminders information.

- **Twitter:** This is where you can add your Twitter info and decide which apps can use the Twitter information.

- **FaceTime:** This is where you turn Face-Time on or off and enter the Apple ID and e-mail associated with the service.

- **Safari:** This is where you can set up the Safari preferences, including which search engine to use. These settings are covered in greater detail in Chapter 4.

- **Messages:** This is where you turn on the iMessage service, which allows messages to be sent between the iPhone, iPad, and iPod Touch. You can also turn on the Send Read Receipts here, which shows the sender when you have read a message. Since the iPad does not have a phone number, you need to set up which e-mail account to use for the messaging service.

- **Music:** The iPad has its roots in the iPod, and that device was all about playing music. This is where you can turn on the new iTunes Match service, decide if you want the iPad to use Cellular Data to download music (if you have a cell account), and Show All Music, which is both the songs on the iPad and those in the iTunes Match cloud. You can also turn the Sound Check on or off, set the EQ, set the volume limit, and group the songs by album artist. You can also enter the Apple ID and password for Home Sharing here.

- **Video:** The iPad is a great video playback device. This is where you can set the videos to start playing from the beginning or from where the video left off the last time it was played. You can also set the Apple ID and password for Home Sharing. If you change the Home Sharing Apple ID here, it automatically changes it in the Music settings.

- **Photos:** You can turn the Photo Stream service on or off here. For more on the Photo Stream service, check out Chapter 10. You can also set the slideshow duration, repeat, and shuffle here.

- **Notes:** I don't use the Notes app much on my iPad, but it is nice to be able to change the fonts here.

- **Store:** The iPad allows for automatic downloads, which means that any music, apps, or books that are purchased using your Apple ID can be automatically downloaded to all your devices. This is where you can decide which of those services are turned on or off and if the downloads can use the Cellular Data (if the device has a 3G or 4G capability). There is also a list of magazines and the ability to turn on or off automatic downloads when on a Wi-Fi network.

- **Apps:** This list is dependent on the apps that you have installed on your iPad, but some of the more common ones include the following:
  - **iBooks:** This is where you can set the Justification, Auto-hyphenation, and what happens when you tap the left margin. You can also set up the Sync Bookmarks and Sync Collections here so that the iBooks app looks the same on all your devices that are under the same Apple ID.
  - **Keynote:** Set the app to use the iCloud service and turn on the spell check here.
  - **Numbers:** Set the app to use the iCloud service for the Numbers app here.
  - **Pages:** Set the app to use the iCloud service for the Pages app here.

The General settings tab has so many important settings that it deserves further explanation. This is where you get to set up everything from Bluetooth to the keyboard options. It is also where the Accessibility options are, which are very important for those that have difficulty with using the iPad in its standard configuration.

The General settings offer you the following information:

- **About:** This shows you all the info about your iPad, including the number of apps, songs, videos, and photos loaded on it. It shows the serial number; Wi-Fi address; and all legal notices, licenses, and regulatory notices.

- **Software Update:** In the past you would have to plug the iPad into a computer to get software updates; now all you have to do is tap this button. The iPad does need to be connected to a power supply for this to work.

- **Usage:** Curious as to what is taking up space on your iPad? Here you can see exactly what is using the space. It also shows the iCloud storage settings, and the amount of data sent and received over the cellular network if applicable.

- **Sounds:** At the top of this menu is a volume control slider. It also allows you to pick the sounds for the Text Tone, New Mail, Sent Mail, Tweet, Calendar Alerts, Reminder Alerts, Lock Sounds, and Keyboard Clicks.

- **Network:** This is a setting for more advanced users as it deals with VPN settings. VPN stands for Virtual Private Network, which is a service that provides remote access to a central computer system. If your business uses VPN, ask the IT

Figure 2-21
The General tab.

department for the settings needed here. This menu also shows you the Wi-Fi settings, which is the same information as the Wi-Fi menu discussed earlier in this chapter.

- **Bluetooth:** Turn Bluetooth on or off here. When it is turned on, a list of available devices appears. Tap on the device you want to connect to.

- **iTunes Wi-Fi Sync:** You no longer need to attach the iPad to the computer to sync with iTunes. The iPad automatically syncs with the iPad when it is plugged into a power supply, but you can sync anytime you want (as long as it's still plugged in) by tapping the Sync Now button located here.

- **Spotlight Search:** This is where you pick what is included in the Spotlight Search on

your iPad. Swipe from left to right on the Home page to access the Spotlight Search. This search page allows you to quickly search the whole iPad. If you don't want the Spotlight Search to use certain information, just tap to uncheck. You can also adjust the order of the searched items by holding a finger on the three stripes on the right of the name and sliding the whole bar up or down.

- **Auto-Lock:** If the iPad is left unused it powers down and needs to be unlocked again. The amount of time it takes is set here—from 2 minutes to never.

- **Passcode Lock:** The iPad can be locked so that you need a passcode to use the device. There are two types of passcodes: a simple passcode that consists of 4 numbers and a more complex passcode that can use numbers and letters. You can also set the iPad to erase all the data if someone enters the wrong passcode 10 times.

- **Restrictions:** Here you can restrict what the user of the iPad has access to. This setting is for all users on the iPad. This is very important for using the iPad in schools, or if you have children or employees, and you need to restrict what they can or cannot access. Tap Enable Restrictions and you are prompted to enter a 4-digit passcode. This passcode must then be used to disable the restrictions when needed.

You can now disable access for: Safari, YouTube, iTunes, Ping, Installing Apps, and Deleting Apps. You can also set the Location, Accounts, and Find my Friends apps so that they allow or don't allow changes. You can set the Ratings, Music and Podcasts, Movies, TV Shows, Apps, In-App Purchase, and how long you have until the password is required (either 15 minutes or immediately). You can also turn on or off the ability to play multiplayer games and add friends in the Game center.

- **Side Switch:** There are two options here for the control of the side switch on your iPad. The switch can be used for either locking the rotation or as a mute switch. Just tap on the one you want to assign to the side switch.

- **Multitasking Gestures:** You can turn the multitasking gestures on or off here.

- **Date and Time:** This is where you set the time zone, 12-hour or 24-hour time, and if you want the iPad to set the time automatically.

- **Keyboard:** The built-in keyboard has options that can be set here including Auto-Capitalization, Auto-Correction, Check Spelling, and Enable Caps Lock. You can also add shortcuts here.

- **International:** You can change the language of your iPad here and set up different keyboards, including British, French, German, and Dutch ones, among others. You can also set the region format and the type of calendar used.

- **Accessibility:** There are three types of settings here: Vision, Hearing, and Physical/Motor settings.

  - **The VoiceOver:** This tool speaks the items on the screen. When you turn on VoiceOver, the iPad reads aloud whatever you tap on the screen. And with VoiceOver activated, instead of single tapping to open an app you must double tap, and you use three fingers instead of a single finger to scroll.

You can also turn on the Speak Hints option, which gives you voice directions for most situations. You can even change the rate of the speech, have the voice give you typing feedback (it speaks out the characters and words as your type), use phonetics, and change the pitch of the voice. This menu also lets you add Braille devices, and it controls the Web Rotor and Language Rotor.

- **The Zoom:** This allows you to magnify the whole screen. When turned on, a double tap with three fingers zooms in; a second double tap with three fingers zooms back out. To move around the zoomed-in screen, just use three fingers to navigate. To change the amount that the screen zooms, just double tap the screen with three fingers, and then drag up to zoom in or down to zoom out.

- **The Large Text:** This option makes the text appear larger in Mail and Notes. You can pick between 20pt, 24pt, 32pt, 40pt, 48pt, and 56pt text. This is great for those folks who find it tough to read the default size of text.

- **White on Black Text:** This changes the whole look of the iPad by reversing the colors, making the text white and background black. This high contrast is meant to help people with vision problems. This can also make apps look weird, since it reverses all the colors making everything look like an old film negative.

- **Speak Auto-text:** This setting speaks auto-corrections and auto-capitalizations.

- **Mono Audio:** This changes the audio output from Stereo to Mono.

- **Adaptive Touch:** This is one of the cooler things that I have seen on the iPad—or any device. It allows you to use the iPad with adaptive accessories and create custom gestures.

- **Triple-Click Home:** This setting allows you to decide what happens when you triple click the Home button. The options are:
  - Off
  - Toggle VoiceOver
  - Toggle White on Black
  - Toggle Zoom
  - Toggle AssistiveTouch
  - Ask

- **Reset:** This gives you the option to Reset All the Settings on your iPad, Erase all the Content and Settings, Reset your Network Settings, Reset the Keyboard Dictionary, Reset the Home Screen Layout, and Reset the Location Warnings.

PRELOADED APPS

Your iPad came preloaded with set of apps that can get you started using your iPad right out of the box. These apps cannot be removed from the iPad.

Camera (iPad 2 and the new iPad): The built-in Camera app allows you to take photos and videos with your iPad. This app is covered in more detail in Chapter 10.

FaceTime (iPad 2 andthe new iPad): The video chat application that is covered earlier in this chapter.

Photo Booth (iPad 2 and the new iPad): This app allows you to do funky stuff using the built-in camera. Add some color effects or special effects and just have fun.

Messages: This app allows you to send and receive messages and is covered earlier in this chapter.

Calendar. The Calendar app helps you to keep track of your important stuff. It syncs with the calendar on your iPhone and computer using iCloud or Google services.

Notes: The note-taking app is probably the least-used app on my iPad. I actually can't remember the last time I used it. The app allows you to take notes, and the notes can sync between different iOS devices.

Reminders: The Reminder app is covered earlier in this chapter.

Maps: This is the Google Maps app and it is really cool. It allows you to look at four versions of a map—a standard version, a Satellite view, a Hybrid view, and a Terrain view. You can also place a pin on the map and look at the traffic. When the map is open, just tap on the page curl on the bottom right of the page to open the Settings panel.

YouTube: You can access YouTube on your iPad right here.

Videos: Use this app to play videos. It is covered in greater detail in Chapter 6.

Contacts: Your address book is stored here.

Game Center: This is where you can sign in to the Game Center and launch those games that are Game Center–enabled.

iTunes: This is where you buy music, movies, TV shows, audiobooks, and podcasts, and where you can access your previously purchased music, TV shows, and movies.

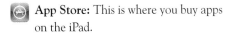 **App Store:** This is where you buy apps on the iPad.

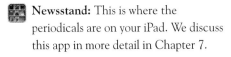 **Newsstand:** This is where the periodicals are on your iPad. We discuss this app in more detail in Chapter 7.

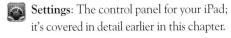 **Settings:** The control panel for your iPad; it's covered in detail earlier in this chapter.

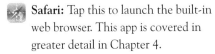 **Safari:** Tap this to launch the built-in web browser. This app is covered in greater detail in Chapter 4.

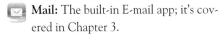 **Mail:** The built-in E-mail app; it's covered in Chapter 3.

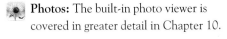 **Photos:** The built-in photo viewer is covered in greater detail in Chapter 10.

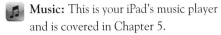 **Music:** This is your iPad's music player and is covered in Chapter 5.

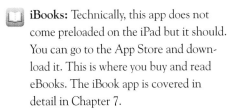 **iBooks:** Technically, this app does not come preloaded on the iPad but it should. You can go to the App Store and download it. This is where you buy and read eBooks. The iBook app is covered in detail in Chapter 7.

DICTATION

There is one feature that the new iPad has that none of the previous generations had, and that is the dictation ability. You can speak instead of type, and your spoken words become written words. This functionality is system wide, so it not only works with the built-in apps but with third-party apps as well.

To access the dictation function, tap on the Microphone button that appears on the bottom of the keyboard to the left of the space bar. This is easy to use and works surprisingly well. For example, to use the dictation to write an e-mail, just do the following:

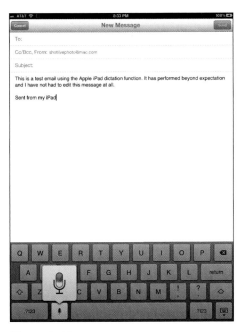

Figure 2-22
When you tap on the Microphone button you can dictate your e-mails. It works really well.

1. Tap on the Mail app.

2. Tap on the New Message button.

3. Enter the recipient and the subject, and then place the cursor in the message box.

4. Tap on the Microphone button.

5. Speak your message.

6. Tap on the Microphone button again to stop recording and your message appears in the message box.

7. Check the spelling.

8. Send the message.

This dictation technology works amazingly well. I plan on using it to take notes on my iPad from now on.

THE MOUNTAIN LION CONNECTION

Apple is starting to make the desktop operating system OS X and the iDevice operating system iOS look the same. The latest version of the desktop OS, called Mountain Lion or OS X 10.8, brings many of the iPad apps to the desktop, including versions of Messages, Notes, Notification Center, Twitter, Game Center, Reminders, and AirPlay Mirroring.

There is a real push to have the iPad experience on the desktop, which will mean tighter integration for iPad owners who also have Apple computers.

3

The iCloud and You

The Skim

It seems that everywhere you turn today people are talking about cloud computing as if it is the answer to all computer and technology problems. The idea is that instead of keeping your information spread out among a variety of devices and then trying to make sure that they all talk to each other, the information is stored somewhere on the Internet and is automatically updated from and to all of your devices, so the info on each of your devices is always up-to-date.

In theory this sounds like a great idea, but there are a few things to keep in mind to make it work. The first is that to access your information, you must be able to connect to the Internet. So if you are traveling or not connected by Wi-Fi, you need an iPad with a 3G or 4G chip and a data plan. That means extra costs, and since you will need to use more data sending and receiving info from the cloud there is a chance of higher data plan fees. The second thing to keep in mind is that if there is a problem with the cloud service, you are at the mercy of the service until it's back up and running.

The Apple cloud service used to be called MobileMe but was recently changed to iCloud.

Figure 3-1
You can access your data stored on the iCloud not only from your iPad, but at the website as well—www.icloud.com.

The single most important part of the iCloud service is that all your purchases made in the Apple Stores are available to you at all times. That means that every movie, TV show, song, app, and eBook that you've purchased can be downloaded to your iPad anytime you are connected to the Internet. This is a win-win for everyone since it gives you real incentive to buy your content through Apple and it makes Apple want to offer as much content as possible. You will see mention of this over and over in this book. It is one of the best things to happen to the iPad because it allows you access to your purchased content any-where, anytime.

iCLOUD VS. MOBILEME

iCloud is *not* MobileMe. It is a replacement service and if you have MobileMe you need to transfer over to iCloud by the end of June 2012. The good news about this is that the process is pretty painless and because the iCloud basic service is free, you will also be saving money. That is one of the biggest changes to the service—the cost. The MobileMe service cost $99 a year, but the iCloud basic service is free.

So what are the differences between the two services? The iCloud service no longer offers iWeb publishing, iDisk service, or the online Photo Gallery service. The core functions are still available, meaning that Mail, Contacts, Calendars, Bookmarks, Notes, Find My iPhone (iPad), and Back to my Mac are all still there. And there are five new features: iTunes in the Cloud, Photo Stream, Documents & Data, Automatic Downloads, and Backup and Restore in the iCloud. Don't worry; we will go over all of these features throughout the book, especially as they apply to the iPad.

SIGNING UP FOR AN iCLOUD ACCOUNT

Before you can use an iCloud account, you need to sign up for the iCloud service. If you previously had a MobileMe account, it's easy—just sign into me.com and follow the directions to transfer your account to the iCloud service. The good news is that your e-mail will stay the same and the Apple ID will be your old MobileMe e-mail.

The key to the iCloud service is the Apple ID. If you do not have an Apple ID or want

Figure 3-2
The Apple ID web portal where you can set up an Apple ID and edit the information associated with that Apple ID.

to edit the e-mail address that is tied to your Apple ID, go to appleid.apple.com. Once you've set up your Apple ID, you can turn on the iCloud service on all of your devices.

TURNING ON THE iCLOUD SERVICE

It's easy to sign in to an iCloud account on your computer or your iPad. To set up an iCloud account on your iPad, just follow these steps:

1. Turn on the iPad.

2. Tap on the Settings app.

3. Tap on iCloud in the left menu.

4. If you need to set up the service and have an Apple ID, then sign in with the Apple ID and go to step 5. If you don't have an Apple ID, then tap on "Create Free Apple ID" and follow the instructions.

5. Tap on Use iCloud.

6. Tap on the On/Off switches to enable the various parts of the service, which include Mail, Contacts, Calendars, Reminders, Bookmarks, Notes, Photo Stream, Documents & Data, and Find My iPad.

You can now set up the iCloud service on your computer, which will automatically sync the information from your iPad.

To set up an iCloud account using your Mac computer, follow these steps:

1. Turn on your computer.

2. Check to make sure that you are running the latest version of the operating system (10.7.3 or later).

3. Click the Apple icon on the top left corner of the screen.

4. Choose System Preferences.

Figure 3-3
The iCloud settings on the iPad showing where you can turn on and off the individual parts of the service.

5. Click iCloud.

6. Enter your Apple ID and password.

7. Select the services that you want to enable.

To set up an iCloud account on your Windows computer, follow these steps:

1. Turn on your computer.

2. Download the iCloud Control panel from support.apple.com/kb/DL1455.

3. From the Windows Start menu, menu choose Control Panel > Network and Internet > iCloud (or Control Panel > iCloud, depending on the version of Windows you are running).

4. Enter your Apple ID and password.

5. Select the iCloud services you want to use. (Outlook 2007 or 2012 is required for accessing iCloud e-mail, contacts, and calendars, while Safari 5.1.1 or Internet Explorer 8 or later OS is required to access your bookmarks.)

Setting up the iCloud on all your devices and computers allows automatic syncing of your data and, even better, you can access it anytime from the Internet at www.iCloud.com. You can enter your Apple ID and password to access your e-mail, contacts, and calendars.

E-MAIL

I am addicted to checking my e-mail on the iPad. It's fast, easy, and the size of the iPad screen makes it perfect for tasks like this. Like many people, I have multiple e-mail accounts and I can check them all on the iPad at the same time. Now Apple would love for you to use the iCloud service for e-mail but the iPad can deal with many different e-mail services, including the ability to access enterprise e-mail, which means that it can send and receive your work e-mail.

First let us go though setting up the iCloud e-mail, and then we'll add other accounts. When you first tap on the Mail app it brings up a list of eight e-mail providers that you can use to set up your e-mail. Your choices are: iCloud, Microsoft Exchange, Gmail, Yahoo, AOL, Microsoft Hotmail, MobileMe, and Other. Tap on the e-mail provider and follow the steps to set up your e-mail. Let's walk through setting up the iCloud e-mail.

1. Tap on the Mail app.

2. Tap on iCloud.

3. Enter your Apple ID and password.

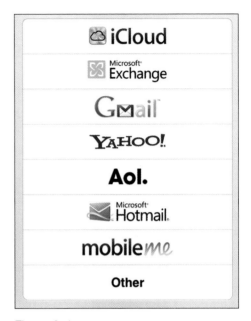

Figure 3-4
There are eight different e-mail account templates that you can use to set up your e-mail account.

That's all there is to it since the e-mail account is tied to the Apple ID.

Setting up the other e-mail accounts is a little more complicated and you need to have some information about your e-mail service. To set up your iPad to access your Microsoft Exchange e-mail, just follow these steps:

1. Tap on the Settings app.

2. Tap Mail, Contacts, Calendars.

3. If there are already Mail accounts set up then tap Add account...

4. Tap Microsoft Exchange.

5. Enter your full e-mail address.

6. You may need to enter domain information. This can be a variety of things, but here are a few to try:

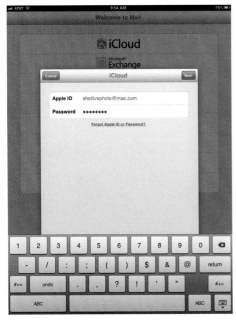

Figure 3-5
Setting up your iCloud e-mail is simple.
Just enter the Apple ID and Password.

- Leave it blank. The information is most likely going to be found by the program automatically.

- Ask your IT department what the company domain is. (This is your best bet.)

- Try the Internet domain of your company's website—both with the ".com" part and without it.

7. Enter your Exchange username, which is usually the first part of your e-mail address (the characters that come before the "@" symbol).

8. Enter your password. This is the same password you use at work to log in and check your e-mail.

9. Enter a description for your account. This is especially important if you plan on checking multiple e-mail accounts on your iPad.

10. Tap Next.

11. The iPad tries to verify the account information. Be patient, because this can take awhile.

If your Microsoft Exchange server does not allow for auto-discovery, you will get an error message and will need to enter the rest of the information manually. If you need to add the server data manually, the best bet is to ask your work IT department for the information and enter it in the Server field. If this request confuses the tech, just ask him for the information he would use to set up a Windows Mobile smartphone; it's the same info.

One of the most popular e-mail services is Gmail, the Google e-mail solution—it is free and easy to use. If you used your Gmail account as the e-mail for the iCloud account and set up the iCloud e-mail, you cannot access the Gmail here as well because the iCloud e-mail is already being used. To sign up for a Gmail account, just go to gmail.com and tap CREATE AN ACCOUNT. To read your Gmail on the iPad, set up your e-mail as follows:

1. Tap on the Settings app.

2. Tap Mail, Contacts, Calendars.

3. Tap Add Account if you already have an e-mail account set up.

4. Tap Gmail.

5. Enter your name.

6. Enter your full e-mail address.

7. Enter your Gmail password.

8. Add a description for your account. This is especially important if you plan on checking multiple e-mail accounts on your iPad.

9. Tap Next.

10. You can now decide if you want to have the iPad get the Mail, Calendars, and Notes associated with the account.

It's that easy! The other e-mail services are just as simple to set up—that is, except the Other e-mail account. The Other e-mail settings are for those of us who don't have one of the previous types of e-mail.

These "Other" e-mail accounts are usually accounts that you have from an Internet service provider (ISP), the phone company (e.g., AT&T), a cable company (e.g., Comcast), or as part of your own website (e.g., www.ipadfullyloaded.com). Setting up these types of e-mail accounts on your iPad requires that you do a little research. You'll want to make sure that you have the information you need to enter in to the e-mail setup menu.

The first thing you will notice here is that the setup looks just like the menu for any of the other e-mail account setups. When we set up the other accounts, you tapped on Save and the account setup was done; here, you tap Next and move on to the more complicated parts.

The first choice you have to make is between IMAP and POP, and many people have no idea what IMAP and POP are. I wasn't sure what the difference was when I first encountered these settings.

Here's what you need to know: IMAP stands for Internet Message Access Protocol; it allows an e-mail client (like the Mail app on the iPad)

Figure 3-6
The IMAP and POP choices are at the top of the screen. You need to pick the right one for the e-mail service to work.

to access e-mail messages on a remote server. What this means is that the e-mail you're seeing is not actually on the device you're using; instead, the device is looking at the e-mail on an external computer. The main advantage to this is the automated syncing if you have multiple devices that can access your e-mail account. If you read an e-mail on one of them, the message gets marked as Read on the server, so every other device that accesses the account shows the accurate status of your messages and activity. On the downside, if you delete a message on any device, then it is gone from all of them. Poof! Once you delete a message on the server, it is deleted on the devices as well.

The other e-mail choice is POP, which stands for Post Office Protocol. It's used by e-mail clients to get messages from the e-mail server.

What happens is that the e-mail client (such as the Mail app on the iPad) goes out on the Internet to your e-mail server and downloads the new messages directly to the device. Once you read the e-mail on the device and delete it, the message is deleted from the e-mail client (like the Mail app on the iPad). But ... an important distinction here ... the e-mail survives on the server. This means that when you instruct another device (your iPhone for example) to go out to the server to get e-mails, that message you deleted from the other device (your iPad) is still sitting there on the server waiting to be read. So if you have an e-mail account on an iPad and a laptop ... and an iPhone and a desktop computer ... you'll get the same message four times with a POP-type e-mail account, and you'll have to delete, file, or mark it as read on all four separate devices.

To set up the e-mail program on the iPad successfully, you need to know which of these two services you use. Different e-mail hosting companies choose the service format they prefer. Some offer IMAP service and some offer POP service. The best bet is to contact the company and ask which type of service you're receiving.

Once you know which of the two types of account services you have, you can move onto the questions related to your incoming mail server. You'll gather information about this from the e-mail hosting company, too. Typically, it will look something like: mail.*yourdomain.com*, where *yourdomain.com* is replaced with the name of your domain. For example, since the domain for the e-mail address I am adding is www.ipadfullyloaded.com, the incoming mail server will be: mail.ipadfullyloaded.com.

The next thing is to enter the user name for your account, which is usually the full e-mail address. If necessary, enter your password, but it should auto-fill based on your entry on the previous page. The final step is to configure an outgoing e-mail server, because we not only want to get e-mail but to send it as well. Again, all the information in this menu area is available from the company you use for your e-mail. Once you have entered your outgoing mail server and the username and password, it's time to tap Save. That's when the iPad goes out to see if the e-mail account information you entered is correct.

General E-mail Settings

There are some general e-mail settings that are accessible in the Settings panel. To access them, tap on the Settings app and then on Mail, Contacts, Calendars. You can set the following here:

- **Show:** Here you can choose the number of recent e-mails to show. You can pick 50, 100, 200, 500, or 1,000 messages. If you have more than 1,000 e-mails in an account, it will show only the most recent 1,000. This used to be capped at 200 e-mails, which always seemed a little small so the new limit of 1,000 is a great change.

- **Preview:** You can set the number of preview lines you see, from none to 5. I like 2, since that usually gives me enough information about the e-mail to decide if I need to open it or delete it.

- **Minimum Font Size:** You can pick the size of the font, from Small to Giant. I like Medium, but choose the one that looks best to you.

- **Show To/CC Label:** This shows or hides the To and CC fields when you're viewing e-mail.

Figure 3-7
The e-mail settings available on your iPad.

- **Ask Before Deleting:** This asks you to confirm every deletion. I know that it is important to understand that deleting e-mails means they will go away but this just drives me crazy, so I turn it off.
- **Load Remote Images:** This allows images that are being sent in the e-mail to be loaded on your iPad.
- **Organize By Thread:** This is very cool because it allows the e-mail messages to be organized by the subject line.
- **Always Bcc Myself:** You can blind copy yourself on every message you send if you need to keep track of the messages sent from your iPad.
- **Increase Quote Level:** When you turn this on, it adds a level of indentation to the original e-mail text when you Reply or

Forward. I find this makes it easier to follow the e-mail message thread so I keep it turned on.

- **Signature:** This designates the signature that appears at the bottom of your sent e-mails. The default is "Sent from my iPad."
- **Default Account:** This is the account that the iPad will use to send e-mails from other apps.

Set these as you want to—it *is* your iPad, after all.

Push vs. Fetch

After choosing your e-mail settings, you need to choose how the e-mail client will go out and get the e-mails from the e-mail server.

The two methods that the iPad uses to get e-mail are Push and Fetch. If you tap on Settings, and then Mail, Contacts, and Calendars, you see a button called Fetch New Data in the middle right side of the screen. Tap on that button to bring up the Push and Fetch menus.

The first method is Push. This means that e-mails are pushed from the server to the iPad whenever new e-mails are present. E-mails are on the iPad as soon as the e-mail server receives them, as long as the iPad isn't turned completely off and is connected to the Internet. And this is great, but the real-time service comes with a price ... in the form of battery life. Constantly monitoring your account to keep your mailbox current requires power. To help users preserve battery life when enjoying Push delivery, Apple provides an off switch. When you're running low on battery power or want to conserve your remaining power, turn off the Push service.

The other option for receiving e-mails on

Select Schedule	
Push	✓
Fetch	
Manual	

If Push is not available, the Fetch schedule will be used.

Figure 3-8
The Advanced setting showing where you can select between the Push, Fetch, and Manual delivery of your e-mail.

your iPad is to Fetch it. This is usually set up to happen in regular intervals—every 15 minutes, every 30 minutes, or hourly—or you can Fetch your messages manually. The less often you go check to see if you have new messages, the longer your iPad battery will last. So this really is a matter of priority. I usually have my iPad go Fetch new mail every 30 minutes.

The Advanced button in the Fetch New Data menu is where you can change the way each e-mail account checks for mail. Those who use the Push method can use this area to switch over to Fetch or Manual delivery. Those who use the Fetch method can change delivery to Push or Manual. To change your settings, just tap on the account you want to change and pick the new method of e-mail retrieval.

There is one final way to get your e-mail and that is manually. If you change your setting from, say, a 30-minute Fetch interval to Manual retrieval, the E-mail app won't go get new messages until you tell it to go out and Fetch your e-mail. This setting is really useful when you're running on a low battery.

To get your e-mail when the Fetch is set to manual, you have to open the mail program, which then goes out to check if you have mail. If the Mail app is open, then you need to tap on the Update button on the bottom of the Accounts panel. It looks like a three quarter circle made up of an arrow.

Reading Your Mail

To read your e-mail, just tap on the Mail app and tap to select the inbox if you have one e-mail account. If you have multiple e-mail accounts then you have some other options. When you have multiple e-mail accounts on your iPad, you can look at the unified inbox, which shows all the e-mails from all the accounts without actually having to go into each individual account. There are also individual inboxes so that you don't have to go into each account just to get your mail.

The iPad is pretty smart and changes what it displays depending on the orientation of the device. If you hold the iPad in portrait orientation, all you see is the currently selected message. But when you turn the iPad sideways to landscape orientation, you see not only the currently selected message but also the inbox showing the message list with a two-line preview. This is one of the reasons I like to read my e-mail in landscape orientation on my iPad—the more info on the screen, the better.

If you have multiple e-mail accounts on your iPad, it is pretty easy to change which one you're accessing at any given time. On the top of the inbox is a button that shows the currently selected account. It also shows you how many unread e-mails are in the account and offers an Edit button when an inbox is selected. The Edit button allows you to delete or move multiple e-mails at a time. With an

Figure 3-10
The landscape view not only gives you a view of the e-mail, it also gives you a view of the currently selected inbox.

Figure 3-9
E-mail looks really great on the iPad in portrait mode, but as you can see in Figure 3-10, the landscape mode gives you more information.

inbox selected, tap on Edit, and then select the e-mails you want to delete or move by tapping the messages in the list. You will know if you have selected an e-mail because a red circle with a white check mark appears in the circle to the left of selected messages. You can then Delete, Move, or Mark the selected e-mails by using the buttons on the bottom of the screen. There is no way to select multiple e-mails with a single tap; you have to select each e-mail individually. The Mark button allows you to flag the e-mail or Marked as Unread.

To change e-mail accounts, tap on the account name. This takes you out of the inbox and shows you a list of accounts. Tap on one of the e-mail accounts and you can

then look at the folders in that account or you can go back further to a list of accounts by tapping on the Accounts button on the top of the screen.

When you are reading an e-mail, there are some helpful tools available to help you manage your mail. The most obvious is the trash can. By tapping the trash can, you send the e-mail to the trash. Tapping the folder icon allows you to save the e-mail to any of the folders. Not all e-mail accounts have folders to which you can save e-mail. The last two options are to forward/reply to the e-mail you are reading. When you tap on the reply button you are presented with the following options: Reply, Reply All, Forward, and Print. You can print only to an AirPrint-enabled printer. You can also tap on the New Message button, which opens a blank e-mail in which you can type a new message.

Sending Photos
One of the easiest things to do is e-mail photos from your iPad. All you have to do is open the Photos program, tap on a folder, and then tap on the image to open it. Tap on the Share

Figure 3-11
The bar across the top of your e-mail message. You can see the Inbox, the Previous and Next buttons, a Folder button, and a trash can. There is also a reply icon and a new message icon.

icon, which opens a drop-down menu with the share options and Email Photo is the top choice. Tap Email Photo and the Mail app opens with the image embedded in the body of the message. But what do you do if you have already written the e-mail and want to add a photo? Here is how you can do that:

1. Tap on the Mail app.

2. Start writing a new message; when you get to the place where you want to add a photo, press the Home button. (It's the actual physical button on the bottom front of the iPad.)

3. Tap on the Photos app.

4. Navigate to the photo you want to add to the message.

5. Tap on the photo and then tap on the Share button at the top right corner of the screen.

6. Tap Copy Photo from the list of choices (it is at the bottom of the list).

7. Press the Home button.

8. Open Mail. Your half-written message should be on the screen.

9. Press and hold your finger where you want to insert the photo until the magnifier opens.

10. Remove your finger from the screen. The Select | Select All | Paste menu will appear.

11. Tap Paste and the image that you copied appears in your e-mail.

Many apps allow you to send content as an e-mail directly from the app. These apps take the content and insert it into an e-mail, allowing you to add messages and a recipient.

CALENDARS

With the release of iOS5 and iCloud, the Calendar app finally works the way you think it should. At last, the calendars on my iPad, iPhone, and computer all work the same way and all show the same information seamlessly.

I still have a calendar on my wall, but it hangs there because I like the photos—I no longer use it to keep track of important dates and events. I keep my calendar on my computer ... and on my iPad ... and on my iPhone ... and it is accessible at iCloud.com as well. You would think with the way the calendars all sync that I would never be late for a meeting, but here is one thing that you have to always remember: You need to actually *look* at the calendar once in a while!

There are five views for your calendar: Day, Week, Month, Year, and List. Each of the views offers the same information but in a different format. This versatility makes it easy to get an overview or detailed information about what's on your calendar.

- The **Day** view shows you the whole day by hour at a glance.

Figure 3-12
The Calendar Year view shows you the whole year at a glance.

Figure 3-13
The Add Calendar option allows you to add new calendars to the iPad.

- The **Week** view shows your events scheduled for the week.
- The **Month** view offers information for the whole month on a single page.
- The **Year** view shows the entire year at a glance.
- The **List** view is a line-by-line display of events on the left side and a detailed day view of events on the right.

Create a Calendar

You can have multiple calendars on your iPad and for the first time you can create calendars right on the iPad. On the top right of the Calendar app you can tap the Calendar button, which brings up a list of the calendars on your iPad. There is an Edit button on the top right of the Show Calendar list and when you tap

it you see the option to Add Calendar ... Just tap that and you can enter the new calendar name and pick a color from the list. Each of the calendars needs a different color. You must have Calendars turned on in iCloud for Add Calendar to function correctly.

If you have the iCloud service on multiple devices, the new Calendar will be on all the devices automatically.

Create an Event

Calendars are helpful only if you can enter information into them. Here's how to enter an event into your iPad calendar.

1. Tap on the Calendar app.

2. Tap the + button on the bottom right corner of the screen to open the Add Event window.

3. Enter a Title for the event.

4. If you want, add a location in the Location field or use this space as a secondary field for Event info.

5. Tap the Starts/Ends area to open the date controls.

6. Adjust the day, hour, minute, and AM/PM wheels to set the start time of the event.

7. Adjust the day, hour, minute, and AM/PM wheels to set the end time of the event.

8. Or, if the event lasts all day, like a birthday, turn on the All Day switch.

9. You can also set the Time Zone of the event. This is really useful if the event takes place at different location, like when you're on vacation.

10. Tap Done at the top right to finish entering in the Starts and Ends times.

11. You can now set the Repeat options for recurring events. First, pick the frequency of the event. (Leave it as "None" if the event doesn't repeat.)

12. Choose "Every Day," "Every Week," "Every 2 Weeks," "Every Month," or "Every Year."

13. You can now add Invitees (people you want to add to the event.) When you tap this, a new window opens and you can either type in the name of people that you want to attend or tap the + button to open your contacts list, from which you can add people easily.

14. Now you can set an Alert so you have a better chance of remembering your event. Alerts can be set for five minutes before the event's start time to two days before.

Figure 3-14

The Add Event window where you can enter all of the information about an event.

15. If you set an Alert, you can set a Second Alert. (Never miss an anniversary again!)

16. Next, you can pick which of the calendars the event should be scheduled under. For example, I make sure that all my work events are in my work calendar, while personal events are in my personal calendar.

17. Next, you can set your availability for the event—either Busy or Free.

18. You can now add a website URL and any notes for the event if you'd like.

19. Tap Done to complete the entry.

If you add attendees, the Calendar app will automatically send those folks an e-mail inviting them to the event. Once you have entered an event, it shows up in your calendar and you can edit or delete it as needed.

If you are invited to an event, then there is an invitation in the invitation box on the top of the screen. It is right next to the Calendars button. It looks like an arrow going into an open box and has a number next to the icon. The number corresponds to the number of invitations for future events that you have received.

If you have a Microsoft Exchange calendar set up at work, you can sync it with your iPad and the calendar will show up in the iPad Calendar app. You do this the same way you would set up the iPad to access a Microsoft Exchange server for your e-mail:

1. Turn on your iPad.

2. Tap on the Settings app.

3. Tap Mail, Contacts, Calendars.

4. Tap Add Account and choose Microsoft Exchange.

5. Enter your Exchange Server account information.

6. Tap Next.

7. Enter the server information.

8. Tap Next.

9. Turn on Mail, Contacts, Calendars.

Your Exchange Server accounts are now being synced wirelessly and automatically to your iPad, including the contacts and calendars.

CONTACTS

When I was younger (a lot younger) I used to be able to remember the phone numbers and addresses of my friends and family, but that was before smartphones made it easy to carry all that info with me everywhere I go.

Figure 3-15
The Contacts address book in portrait mode.

Combine that with the fact that now that people have multiple e-mail addresses, and home, work, and cell phone numbers, there is an easier way—the electronic contact list.

The Contacts app on the iPad looks much better when the device is used in landscape mode than it does in portrait mode. Check it out in Figures 3-15 and 3-16 and you'll see what I mean.

The Contact app shows all your contacts in a neat and organized way. It looks just like an old-style paper address book, with a list of contacts on the left and the individual contact information on the right.

Add a Contact

Adding a contact to your iPad address book is pretty easy. Just turn on the iPad, tap on the built-in Contacts app, and follow these steps:

Figure 3-16
The same Contacts address book in landscape mode looks a whole lot better.

Figure 3-17
Entering the information in the address book is straightforward. Just enter the information and then tap Done.

1. Tap on the + located at the bottom of the screen.

2. Enter the contact's first name, last name, and company info.

3. To add a photo, tap the add photo button in the Contacts app. This enables you to pick a photo for this contact. Choose from the images that are loaded on your iPad, or if the person is there with you, you can use the built-in camera to take her photo.

4. Tap on mobile and pick the type of phone from the pop-up menu. Enter the contact's phone number.

5. Enter as many different phone numbers for a contact as necessary. As you start to type a new number, a new number box appears below the existing one(s).

6. Next is e-mail. Tap on the type of e-mail (e.g., home or work) to select it and then enter the e-mail address.

7. After you enter the first e-mail, you will be able to enter a second, third, fourth, and so on in the same manner you did with the phone numbers.

NOTE

Be careful; if you inadvertently delete a contact in one place (let's say your iPad), then the contact is gone from all the other places you access this address book (your iPhone, for example).

8. You can also enter a contact's website (or two, three, four, etc. of them) in the home page box.

9. Next, tap in the add new address button to enter a mailing address.

10. You can then add a second address, or even a third, fourth, or fifth address, if needed.

49

11. Add any notes you want associated with this contact.

12. If needed, tap the add field button to add custom fields, including a prefix, the phonetic spelling of the first and/or last name, middle name, suffix, nickname, job title, department, instant message information, birthday, and/or an important date.

13. After you've entered all of the contact's information, tap Done at the top right corner.

Sharing Contacts

The default file format used for address book data is called a vCard. This format is an electronic business card and can contain not only name, phone number, e-mail, and address information; but you can actually keep the profile photo in the vCard format. The cool thing is that vCards can also be exchanged over the Internet, or even on a CD or jump drive, and can be sent in e-mails. Since the iPad doesn't have a USB port, the only good way to get a vCard into the iPad Contacts is by e-mail. The good news is that vCards are sent as e-mail attachments or using the Message app and can be loaded instantly into the iPad's Contacts.

Here is something that Apple did right when it comes to the address book on the iPad. They made it really easy for you to share your contacts with others. You can share any of the contacts in your address book with a simple tap.

1. Tap on the Contacts app.

2. Tap on the contact you want to share.

3. On the bottom of the screen, tap Share.

4. Choose whether you want to send the contact information by e-mail or using the Message app.

5. Tap e-mail and this opens an e-mail with the contact's .vcf file attached and you can tap Send to mail the contact info.

6. Tap message and the Message app opens with the contact information embedded. Add a recipient and a message, and then tap Send to send the message.

The .vcf file extension is a version of the vCard, so it is compatible with all address book/contact programs that can use vCards.

iCLOUD OVERVIEW

The idea behind the iCloud service is a good one and it seems that Apple has taken what it started with MobileMe and made it really useful. During the Apple announcement of the new iPad, a lot was made of the iPad being part of the post-pc era. It is clear to me that for the iPad to rule in this post-pc world, there needs to be a way to keep your information synced between your devices and maybe more importantly a way to keep your media purchases available at all times without needing to have a computer.

The iCloud service is doing this and is a huge step forward from the lackluster MobileMe accounts of the past. The best part for the consumer is that the service is free. The only downside in my mind is that you are being locked into the Apple purchasing ecosystem, which means you are reliant on Apple not to change the way the service works, and Apple does not have a great track record of that. Just ask the people who relied on iDisk, iWeb, or iWork beta—all services that Apple has discontinued with the adoption of iCloud.

Internet Browsing

The Skim

Safari • Alternative Browsers • Flash and HTML5

The iPad brings Internet browsing to a portable device that is easier to use than a laptop or a smart phone and comes preloaded with Apple's Safari Internet browser. Browsing the Internet on the iPad puts most of the Internet at your fingertips in a size that is easy to read and more convenient than using a computer. Now I said *most* of the Internet and not *all* because the iPad does not support Adobe Flash, which means that any website that uses Flash or Flash components will not render correctly on the iPad.

I use the Safari browser on my Apple laptop and desktop, so using it on my iPad is just plain easy. The same bookmarks are available on all my devices and when I update a bookmark on one device it is automatically updated on the rest because I have the iCloud service turned on.

When the original iPad was released, the included version of Safari didn't have tabbed browsing or a bookmarks bar, while other browsers did. But Apple has not been resting—they keep improving and updating Safari and it has become better with each version. But Safari isn't your only option—there are actually a great many browsers available for the iPad; some are free while others cost, and they all have plusses and minuses.

SAFARI

The iPad comes preloaded with Apple's web browser Safari (just as the iPhone does). As the iPad and its iOS have matured and improved, the Safari web browser has drastically improved along with them. The current version of Safari supports tabbed browsing, allows you to pick which search engine to use, has a Bookmarks bar, and allows for private browsing (that is, enables the user to browse the Internet without leaving a trail). Let's start with how to access the Safari settings and what you can and can't do.

Safari Settings

You might think to look for the Safari settings in the Safari app, but you must access them in the Settings app. Turn on the iPad, tap on the Settings app, and then tap on Safari on the left side of the screen. This brings up the Safari option menu on the right side of the screen. You can adjust the following settings:

- **Search Engine:** Choose your search engine for the search bar. You choices are Google, Yahoo!, or Bing. My preference is Google, but you can choose whichever one you want. The real power here is that you can change your mind and switch to a different service at any time.

- **AutoFill:** The AutoFill feature allows you to save the basic information used to fill out forms on websites so that you don't have to fill it out the next time you go to the same website. This feature is set to "off" by default. When you tap AutoFill to turn it on you are presented with a menu that allows you to Use Contact Info and then pick which contact information to use. You can also turn the Names and Passwords option on or off separately, and

you can clear all old Names and Passwords. It is my preference to turn on AutoFill and turn off Names and Passwords.

- **Open New Tabs in Background:** This on/off switch controls how you view new tabs when you open them. When this option is turned on, new tabs are opened but the browser stays on the current tab. When this option is turned off, the browser goes to the new tab as soon as it is opened.

- **Always Show Bookmarks Bar:** One of the biggest changes over the years has been the inclusion of a Bookmarks bar that mimics the desktop version of the browser. I keep this option turned on so that I can access my Bookmarks bar, which holds the websites I go to the most. Later on in this chapter you'll find out how to edit the Bookmarks bar.

- **Private Browsing:** When you browse the web you leave a trail, or cache, in your browser history, enabling anyone who uses your iPad access to your web browsing history. This is where you can stop that. When you turn on Private Browsing, you can search the web without leaving a trail.

- **Accept Cookies:** With this setting you can increase the security and privacy of your browsing by not allowing the browser to store any cookies. This does mean that the browser will not store any usernames and passwords, so you must enter them every time they are required. This feature is really useful when more than one person is using the same iPad.

- **Clear History:** You can clear your browsing history here. Just tap the Clear History button and a dialog box opens asking if you really want to clear your history. Tap Clear if you do or tap Cancel to return to the main menu.

- **Clear Cookies and Data:** If you have been allowing cookies to be stored on your iPad, you can remove that info at any time—just tap here.
- **Fraud Warning:** This is a simple on/off switch that should be left turned on. This setting allows Safari to try to warn you about websites that may be fraudulent.
- **JavaScript:** You can turn JavaScript on or off using this switch. Turning JavaScript off means that any site that uses JavaScript to display content will not look right on Safari.
- **Block Pop-ups:** This is where you can block pop-up ads; I keep this turned on.
- **Advanced:** This tab offers you access to the data that is stored on your iPad from the websites you have visited, and this is also where you can turn the Debug Console on or off. If you have Accept Cookies set to Never then there might not be any information here.
    - **Website Data:** This is a great feature, allowing you to see which websites have left data on your iPad. The list might look rather small when you first open this menu, but tap on the Show All Sites button at the bottom of the list to see exactly what is being stored.

        To delete any of the data, swipe your finger from right to left over the site name and a Delete button appears on the right; tap it to delete the info or you can tap Remove All Website Data, which removes the same data as when you tap on the Clear Cookies and Data in the main Safari menu.
    - **Debug Console:** This option in the Advanced tab is useful for programmers and web designers to find out what went wrong when there are web page errors

Figure 4-1
The Settings panel in the Settings app for the Safari Web Browser app.

There is one more setting that impacts the Safari browser and it is located in the iCloud settings menu. Tap on the Settings app, then on iCloud in the left column. If you have signed up for the iCloud service you will see that you can turn Bookmarks on or off here. Having them turned on allows the iPad and your computer to have the same set of Bookmarks, and when you update your Bookmarks on one device they get updated across all your devices that have this turned on.

Using the Safari App

Now that you know where and how to change the settings for Safari, let's look at how to use the app in closer detail. To launch Safari on the iPad, just tap on the Safari app icon. Across the top of the screen are the Back, Forward, Bookmarks, and Export

Figure 4-2
The top section of the Safari app.

buttons, and then the Address entry bar with Reload and Cancel buttons followed by the search bar as shown in Figure 4-2.

The Back and Forward buttons take you to the previous web page, and if you have gone to a previous page, then the Forward button allows you to go forward. If you haven't gone back, the button is grayed out. The Bookmarks button opens the Bookmarks folder, which includes the new Reading List. When tapped, the Export, or Share, button opens a drop-down list that allows you to:

- **Add Bookmark:** Tap on this to add the current page to your Bookmarks. A dialog box opens and allows you to edit the name of the bookmark and decide exactly which Bookmarks folder you want to save it in.

- **Add to Reading List:** The Reading List is a place to save web pages that you want to read later. This is really useful for saving websites and articles you want to read but don't want to add as separate bookmarks. The Reading List is not meant for permanent storage but just a quick holding place, and once the content is read, the user usually deletes the link.

- **Add to Home Screen:** This is still one of the coolest things that you can do with a

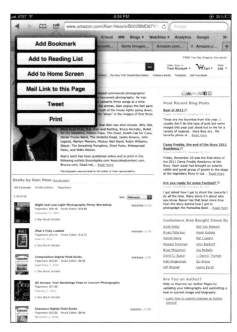

Figure 4-3
The Export menu of the Safari app.

webpage on your iPad. By tapping on this button, you can add a link to the current page that shows up outside of Safari on the home screen or any other screen of the iPad. The link looks just like an app icon and behaves the same way. Tap it and Safari opens and takes you to that page. I use this to create links to sites I frequent, and then I put these links in a folder and can access them from my home screen easily. Tapping the Add a Home Screen button opens a dialog box where you can name the link, then tap Add and it's done.

- **Mail Link to this Page:** A great way to share a link is to e-mail it, and this function enables you to e-mail it directly from the Safari app, instead of having to go into the e-mail app.

- **Tweet:** This allows you to tweet out the current page link to your followers on

Twitter. Twitter is covered in more detail in Chapter 12, but this is part of the integration between the iOS and Twitter that was introduced in iOS5.

- **Print:** If you have an AirPrint-enabled printer, you can send the webpage directly to the printer. You can adjust the number of copies but not much else.

Below the control bar is the Bookmarks bar. This contains the Bookmarks that you have saved in the Bookmarks Bar folder. Remember you can turn this bar on or off in the Settings app. One of the really nice features is if this bar is turned off in the Settings app it still exists and comes into view when you tap in the address entry bar. Then you can tap on a bookmark in the Bookmarks bar and it automatically goes away. Next is the Tabs bar where the currently open web sites are, making it easy to switch between open sites.

The Safari app looks really familiar to anyone who has ever used a web browser and it works exactly the way you expect it to. Just tap in the address bar, enter the website URL on the keyboard, and tap Go. The browser then opens the website—as long as the iPad is connected to the Internet either over Wi-Fi or via the cellular network. You can also access the Google Search (or Yahoo! or Bing) via the search bar on the top right part of the screen. Just tap the search bar, type in your search terms, and then tap Go. Tapping the search bar brings up a list of recent searches. And there is another search bar that pops up on top of the keyboard when you are typing anything. You can use this to search for a word or phrase on the current web page—a very nice touch.

The Safari browser has some other built-in features, including the ability to select and copy text and look up definitions of single

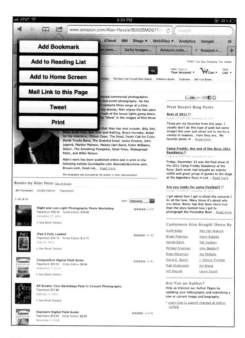

Figure 4-4
Holding your finger on a word allows you to look up the definition in the built-in dictionary.

words. Just hold your finger on a word and a magnifier appears. Make sure you have the correct word selected and then take your finger off the screen. The Copy | Define button appears, then just tap on Define and the built-in dictionary appears, giving a definition of the selected word. If there is a link on a page, you can tap on it to open the link in the current page or hold your finger on the link and a menu appears allowing you to Open the link, Open in New Tab, Add Reading list, or Copy the link.

ALTERNATIVE BROWSERS

The built-in Safari browser has an advantage over other browsers on the iPad for the simple fact that Apple can integrate functions into

Figure 4-5
Browser+ HD showing the Bookmarks panel. The large thumbnails make it easy to find what you are looking for.

Figure 4-6
The menu options for opening a web page in Browser+ HD.

the browser that other app developers don't have access to, but there are some good alternatives. The real question to ask yourself is, "Do I need to buy a web browser when I already have Safari loaded for free?" For many people the answer is no, the built-in Safari app is just fine, but there are folks out there who want something more or just different. Here are some of the best options available to you.

Browser+ HD ($2.99)

When you launch Browser+ HD for the first time you are given the opportunity to watch a video on how to use the app. Now usually I resist apps that take something I know how to do (browse the Internet) and make it complicated, but this app takes a different approach

to web browsing and I recommend that you watch the video.

Browser+ HD uses the whole screen for your web browsing by hiding the menus on the bottom and on the right sides. To get to the address and search bar you need to swipe from the bottom of the screen—here is where it can be a little tricky, as you have to start outside of the screen on the bezel or the page just scrolls. To access the Bookmarks, History, and Settings menus you need to swipe from right to left, remembering to start outside of the viewing area. This is where the browser shines: It keeps the bookmarks as really nice thumbnails, allowing you to see your choices.

Reading websites on the browser is nice since you see only the website, not address bars, menus, or anything else. It is clean and slick

Figure 4-7
A page opened in Overlay mode in Browser+ HD.

Figure 4-8
The Dropbox link page.

looking, and adds a cool feature that opens links as an overlay instead of opening a new tab or window. Just hold your finger on the link and wait until the pop-up menu appears that gives you a choice to Open the link in that window, Open in Overlay mode, or Copy the link. If you press Open in Overlay, the new window opens over the current window and doesn't close the original window. You can close the overlay window by tapping on the X on the top right corner. This is great for visiting websites like Facebook, where there are lots of embedded links that you might want to check out without leaving the site.

iCab Mobile ($1.99)

I covered the iCab Mobile app in the original *iPad Fully Loaded* book and I still use it all the time, mainly due to the great integration with

Dropbox and the look and feel of the browser. The developer behind the app has not stopped updating and improving iCab Mobile, including adding support for Dropbox. iCab Mobile allows you to import and export your iCab bookmarks, and transfer downloads, files, web pages, and images to your Dropbox account. There is more on Dropbox, including how to set up a Dropbox account, in Chapter 8. To link your iCab Mobile browser to a Dropbox account, just follow these easy steps:

1. Tap on the iCab Mobile app.

2. Tap on the Settings/Tools icon on the top right corner of the screen. It looks like a little gear under the search bar.

3. Tap on Dropbox in the list on the left.

4. Tap on the Link Dropbox button and the Link Account dialog box appears.

Figure 4-9
The Settings panel in the Settings app for the iCab Mobile app.

5. Enter the e-mail address and password for your Dropbox account and tap on the Link button.

6. You can now edit the name of the folder on Dropbox and export or import your bookmarks.

If you are a user who likes a lot of lot of options, then iCab Mobile is definitely the browser for you. There are two different places on the iPad with options for you to tweak; the first is in the Settings app. Tap the Settings app and then tap on iCab Mobile. The list of apps appears on the left side of the screen. If the iCab Mobile app is not visible, you might have to scroll down—it all depends on the number of apps you have loaded on your iPad.

The settings for iCab Mobile in the Settings app are as follows:

- **URL Completion via…:** This setting allows you to control how URLs are completed when you start to enter them in the address bar of the app.
  - History URLs ON/OFF
  - Bookmark URLs ON/OFF
  - History Titles ON/OFF
  - Bookmark Titles ON/OFF
  - Sort Order URL/Title
- **History:** These settings allow you to control the web browsing history.
  - Max Number Items 50 (The default is 50, but you can enter any number here you want.)
  - Delete when quitting ON/OFF
- Bookmarks: These settings allow you to control how bookmarks are added.
  - Add Homepage ON/OFF
  - Add Address Book ON/OFF
  - Add History ON/OFF
- **Cookies:** These settings allow you to control the cookies that are saved on your computer.
  - Accept Cookies Always/Never/Only from visited document
  - Delete when quitting ON/OFF
- **Downloads:** These settings allow you to control the amount of data that is allowed to be downloaded depending on the connection to the Internet. This is great when you need to control the amount of data being used.
  - Max size (WLAN) 10MB/25MB/50MB/ 100MB/200MB/400MB/No Limit
  - Max size (Edge/3G) 5MB/10MB/25MB/ 50MB/100MB/200MB/No Limit

- Connections (WLAN) 1-6
- Connections (Edge/3G) 1-3
- Download Attachments ON/OFF
- Delete when quitting ON/OFF

- **Kiosk Mode:** This mode can be turned on and off, and when on shows you the current available updates to the app and all the information about iCab Mobile that you could want.
  - Activate Kiosk Mode ON/OFF
  - Navigation Controls ON/OFF
  - Kiosk Homepage
  - Go to Kiosk Home after (min)
  - Allowed sites: 10 URL Filter entries

- **Fullscreen Mode:** The Fullscreen mode settings configure how the whole screen will be used in the Fullscreen mode.
  - Fullscreen Icons: Visible/Transparent/Nearly invisible/Invisible
  - Show Status bar: ON/OFF
  - Show Progress bar: ON/OFF

- **User Interface.** You can tweak the user interface to your heart's content.
  - Auto clear URL: ON/OFF
  - Quick Starter: ON/OFF
  - Pull down to Reload: ON/OFF
  - Pull to create Tab: ON/OFF
  - Pull l/r to switch Tabs: ON/OFF
  - Orientation: Autorotation/Portrait/Landscape

- **Private Browsing.** There are times that you don't want to leave a trail when you browse the Internet and you can control those options here.
  - Private Browsing: ON/OFF
  - Time Until Deleting: 0min/1min/2min/3min/4min/5min/7min/10min/15min/20min/30min

- Deactivate History: ON/OFF
- Delete Cookies: ON/OFF
- Clear Session: ON/OFF
- Clear Page Storages: ON/OFF

- **Other:** Here are the rest of the settings that you can adjust as needed. They don't really fit into any single category so they are listed as Other.
  - Homepage: Open at Launch: Last Session/Last Page (active Tab)/Homepage/Quick Starter/Empty Page
  - Display IDN: Never/Always/Only 'safe' ones
  - Browser ID: The list here is too long to print, but this browser can mimic everything from IE 9 to the PlayStation 3 browser
  - Text Encoding: The list includes everything from Standard to Hebrew
  - Do Not Track: Off/Opt-Out/Opt-In
  - HTTP Timeout: Standard/30 Sec/60sec/90sec/120sec/180sec
  - History of Closed Tabs: Off/3/5/10/15
  - Save Screenshots as: JPEG/PNG
  - Always Allow Zooming: ON/OFF
  - Javascript 'print': ON/OFF
  - Auto Fill Out Forms: ON/OFF
  - Apps open URL i.Tabs: ON/OFF
  - VGA Output: Web Page/Screen/Screen+Touches/Off

- **Low Memory Conditions**
  - Show Warnings: ON/OFF
  - Release Tabs: No/Critical Conditions Only/Always

That may be an impressive list of settings that you can control, but it's just the tip of the iceberg when it comes to iCab Mobile. There is a whole other set of settings that you can access

Figure 4-10
The Settings panel inside the iCab
Mobile app.

Figure 4-11
The Gestures Settings panel.

from inside the app. You have already seen the list when you set up the Dropbox link. Start the iCab Mobile browser and tap on the Settings/Tools menu located on the top right corner (remember that it looks like a little gear). This is one really complete control panel, with the different menus on the left and the choices on the right, as you can see in Figure 4-10. We have already configured the Dropbox link, so there are just two other menus to cover in detail—adjusting gestures and accessing modules. The rest you can explore at your leisure.

Let's find out how to adjust the gestures used in the iCab Mobile app. To edit what your fingers do, tap on General Settings in the left column, then in the right column located in the second panel tap on Gestures. This menu

is shown in Figure 4-11 and as you can see allows you to adjust 1-finger, 2-finger, 3-finger, and 4-finger gestures. It's a very cool bit of customization.

To access the Modules menu, tap on Modules in the left column and a list of plug-ins or modules is shown on the right. These include things such as: AirPlay Enabler for Video, Facebook, Translation by Google, and much more. You can install the defaults, enable all, or disable all by tapping on the buttons across the bottom or you can just tap the check marks by the individual modules to enable or disable them. You can also tap on the Module name to see the options available for that module.

To access any of the modules when you are browsing the web, tap on the Module button, which looks like a puzzle piece and is located on the right side of the Bookmarks bar under

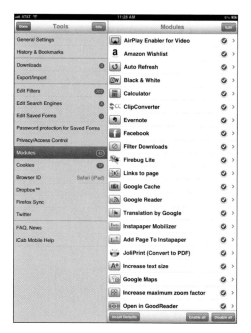

Figure 4-12
The Modules menu options.

Figure 4-13
The Modules menu in use.

the search entry area. This brings up the list of modules and allows you to access them, or you can just tap two fingers on the screen to bring up the icon view of the Modules.

FLASH AND HTML5

Spend a couple of minutes on the Internet on your computer and chances are that you have seen a Flash movie or a Flash element. Flash is used everywhere and the iPad does not support it—never has, never will. There are two reasons for that: the first is that Apple will never support Flash and the second is that Adobe has shifted its attention from developing Flash for mobile devices to focus on PC browsing and other mobile apps. Adobe is also working on developing HTML5 to replace Flash on mobile devices. You can read the full press release at blogs.adobe.com/conversations/2011/11/flash-focus.html.

There is another reason that Apple might not want Flash to run on their devices and that is that with Flash, developers can bypass the App Store and get Flash applications on to the iPad through the web browser. This is something that Apple definitely does not want. Regardless of the reason, waiting for Flash on the iPad is a waste of time.

There is an alternative to Flash called HTML5 and it is gaining more traction all the time. Safari on the iPad supports HTML5, as do all the Apple web products. HTML5 does not play Flash movies but can be used to build websites that act like Flash without actually using Flash.

HTML stands for Hyper Text Markup Language and is the language of the Internet. HTML5 is the fifth revision of the HTML standard, which is always under development. The problem with HTML5 is that older web

Figure 4-14
This is the website for
www.wechoosethemoon.org
as viewed on a computer. This
website was built using Flash.

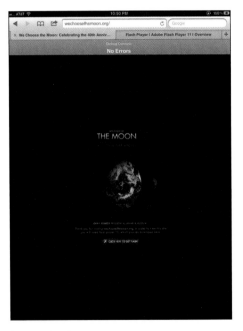

Figure 4-15
This the same website as viewed on
the iPad. If you click on the moon it just
takes you to the Adobe website so that
you can download Flash. Since the iPad
doesn't support Flash, there is no way
to access the site.

browsers don't support it, so while the Safari browser on the iPad does, some others don't. You can test to see if your browser supports HTML5 by going to html5test.com using the browser in question.

The idea behind HTML5 was to provide support for the new breed of multimedia devices while still keeping the language simple and easily readable by humans and understood on a wide range of devices. The HTML5 language would be able to handle a lot of the functions for which the browser previously needed browser plug-ins, such as Flash, to deal with.

There are some Internet browsers that are available on the iPad that can access Flash-based movies, but what they do is translate those movies to HTML5 before delivering the content to your iPad. The one browser that I use for this is Skyfire for iPad, but as HTML5 becomes more commonplace I find the need for this browser diminishing. The main thing to remember is that some websites still use Flash for their content, and these websites are not fully functional on the iPad. More and more, website developers are creating websites using HTML5 instead of Flash and these are fully compatible with the iPad.

I used to believe that the lack of Flash on the iPad was a real detriment to the user experience but now I no longer think that is true. Widespread adaptation of the HTML5 standards means that the lack of Flash support will not be noticeable in the future.

PART 2

Media Consumption

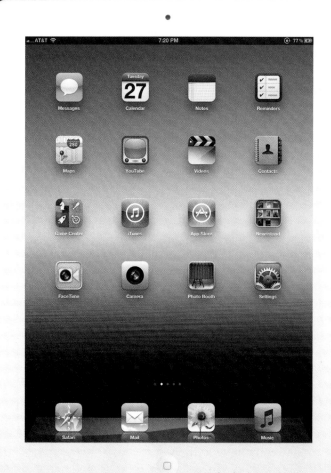

iTunes and iTunes Match

The Skim

Everything changed when Apple released the first iPod along with the iTunes software. Back then, iTunes was all about music, but now it's about so much more. Today you can use your iPad to play all sorts of media content, including music, movies, TV shows, and eBooks—and Apple would love for you to buy all your content through iTunes.

As you will see in Chapter 6, you can access the content that you purchase from Apple at any time using the iCloud service. This includes music, TV shows, movies, and eBooks. The content that you add yourself (that is, content that you do not buy in the iTunes Store), however, can only be transferred over to your iPad using iTunes and cannot be downloaded from the iCloud service. The one exception to this is music. With the iTunes Match service, Apple uploads the music in your iTunes library to the iCloud service so that it is always accessible, no matter where that music came from.

First, let's get your music into iTunes.

Figure 5-1
I have a lot of CDs that I want to be able to listen to on all of my devices, including my iPad. That means ripping them all into iTunes.

GETTING YOUR MUSIC INTO iTUNES

I have a lot of CDs and still buy them from time to time since I like the physical packaging and CD booklets. Actually, I love the old vinyl albums with the large album cover artwork, but I digress. I purchase most of my new music right through the iTunes Store, but I still want to get the music from my CDs into iTunes and then onto my iPad.

Ripping the Music into iTunes

Transferring the music you have on CDs onto the computer is easy and takes place right in iTunes, as long as the computer has a CD drive. Basically, you're going to take, or rip, the music off the CD and make it part of your iTunes library.

The basic process is pretty simple and boring. Just insert a CD into the computer's CD drive. Answer Yes when the iTunes asks if you want to import the CD. The music is then imported into iTunes. Eject the CD. Repeat with a new CD as many times as you want … or can stand. As I said, it's a pretty boring process.

Now let's do a through walk-through and look at the things that can make this go smoothly. The first and most important thing to do is set your Preferences in iTunes. Here's how you do that:

1. Open iTunes on your computer.

2. If you're working on a Mac: Open the iTunes Preferences, and then click on iTunes > Preferences.

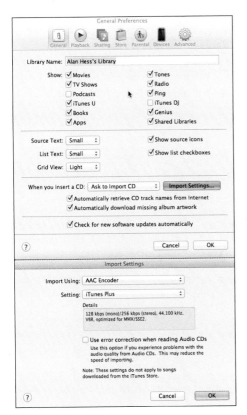

Figure 5-2
The Preferences for CD ripping in
iTunes 10.6.

If you're working on a PC: Choose Edit >
Preferences from the drop-down menus.

3. In the General tab, there are some choices
   in the drop-down menus to the right of
   where it says, "When you insert a CD":

   - Checking **Show CD** includes your CD
     in the Devices list on the left side of the
     screen.

   - Select **Begin Playing** if you use your
     computer as a stereo and just want the
     CD to play when inserted.

   - **Ask to Import CD** is the default setting
     and prompts the program (when you

insert a new CD) to ask if you want to
import the music to your iTunes library.

- **Import CD** triggers an automatic
  import of the music from an inserted
  CD into the computer without a separate directive from you.

- **Import CD and Eject** is the setting to
  use if you are going to rip a bunch of
  CDs. It will automatically import the
  music from an inserted CD, eject it
  when done, and wait for the next.

4. The next box is very important: the
   Import Settings menu. Settings include
   what encoder to use and how it should
   function. The menu also offers an error
   correction feature when reading CDs that
   are giving you problems. The settings
   attempt to balance out file size vs. quality.
   Available encoders include:

   - **AAC Encoder:** Advanced Audio Cod-
     ing is the latest and greatest audio
     conversion process that gives up a little
     quality for a big savings in space. This
     format does a great job of getting the
     best quality with the least space used
     and is the encoder I use on a regular
     basis. But if you want the best possible
     audio quality in the music files you're
     ripping, then look closely at the next
     two options.

   - **AIFF Encoder:** Both the AIFF and the
     Apple Lossless Encoder copy the CD as
     a perfect duplicate. This gives you the
     best quality available, but these files also
     take up the most space.

   - **Apple Lossless Encoder:** For all intents
     and purposes, this option is the same as
     the AIFF Encoder. It produces a perfect
     copy, but you pay for that in its large
     file size.

- **MP3 Encoder:** This encoder imports a music file as an MP3. Don't use this encoder—MP3 is old and tired. There are better options, like the AAC Encoder described previously.

- **Wave Encoder:** These files are huge, and I recommend skipping this one as well.

5. After you pick an encoder, you can select the quality setting for your audio files from the list. If you pick the AAC Encoder, you can choose between iTunes Plus (the highest quality), High Quality (the medium choice), and Spoken Podcast (best for non-music recordings). If you choose the AIFF Encoder, Apple Lossless Encoder, or Wave Encoder, you can only set the quality to Automatic. If you do pick the MP3 Encoder, you can also choose between Good Quality, High Quality, and Higher Quality.

6. Use error correction when reading CDs that are scratched or damaged. This slows down the import process, but it's better to spend a little extra time to make sure your audio is imported correctly.

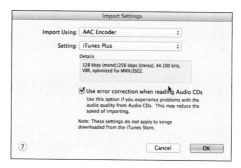

Figure 5-3
My Settings in the Import Settings.

Now you are ready to insert a disc and import some music into iTunes.

1. Open iTunes.

2. Insert a CD into your computer's CD drive.

3. Depending on the settings you created, the CD will wait to import or import automatically.

4. If you are asked, go ahead and import the CD.

5. When the CD is done importing, it automatically ejects or you can eject it manually … again, depending on the settings you entered earlier.

If everything went well, you should now have a new album in your iTunes library with the right track listings and the album cover art automatically inserted. Life isn't always perfect though, so here is the best way to get that new music looking and acting the way you want.

Since I usually import one CD at a time, it's easiest for me to find the new content I just downloaded by sorting the music in my iTunes library by Albums. Just click on the Music tab on the left, and then click on the Albums tab across the top. Over to the left are the four view options that control how the data is dis-

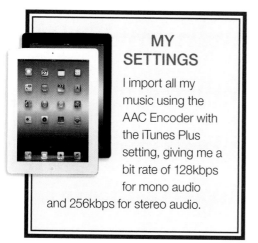

MY SETTINGS

I import all my music using the AAC Encoder with the iTunes Plus setting, giving me a bit rate of 128kbps for mono audio and 256kbps for stereo audio.

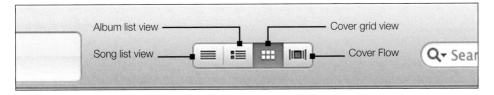

Figure 5-4
The four view options in iTunes change the way the album covers are shown.

played. The first is a song list, the second is an album list, the third is a grid of the album covers, and the fourth is called Cover Flow, which shows the album cover on the top half of the screen with the data on the bottom half. In all the view modes other than the list mode, the album artwork is shown. The albums that don't have any artwork are just generic squares with big music notes in them.

Finding Album Cover Artwork

To get the album artwork if it's not inserted automatically, set the view to grid mode, right-click on the album, and click "Get Album Artwork." This works … sometimes. When it doesn't, there are other options.

The most useful of these options is the CoverHunt website, located at www.coverhunt.com. Once you are there, type the album name in the SEARCH box. There's a good chance you will find the artwork you need. If that fails, use any of the music sites on the Internet or try the band's official website. What you're looking for is an album cover image of the music that you just imported into iTunes.

Once you have the artwork on the screen, you need to:

1. Copy the image file to your computer's clipboard. To do this, right click on the artwork and select Copy.

2. Back in iTunes, with the albums being shown in the grid mode, right click on the album and select Get info.

3. After Apple warns you that you are about to edit multiple tracks, click Yes and then click on the Info tab.

4. You'll see a box on the right called Artwork. Highlight the box and press ctrl-z on a PC or command-z on a Mac to paste the image into the box.

5. Click OK.

If all went well, the album now has the right artwork when it appears in your iTunes library.

Figure 5-5
The art work for the Album is now entered.

73

Adding Album Titles and Track Names

The other problem with music files that can occur is that the album and tracks don't have the right names ... or *any* names, for that matter. Usually, iTunes knows the name of every album you import as well as every track on that album. It does this by looking up the information in a big Internet database called Gracenote. If the computer you are using isn't connected to the Internet or the album is one of the really rare ones that isn't in the Gracenote database, then you have a little work to do to get the information into iTunes. Here's what you're facing:

1. Select the first track on the album.

2. Choose File > Get info.

3. Click the Info tab.

4. Enter all the information for the track and for the CD.

5. For live albums, click on the Options tab and check the box for a gapless album. (This option removes any break between songs, giving you seamless playback.)

GRACENOTE

If you have to enter track information for a CD, please do everyone else a favor and submit the info to Gracenote. Do this by selecting all the tracks and clicking Advanced > Submit CD track names. You're done. THANK YOU!

6. Click the Next button to get to the next track and enter that track's information, and so on.

Now you should have an album with artwork and title information showing in iTunes. When you sync your iPad and computer, all this info will be in both places.

iTUNES MATCH

iTunes Match is a new service offered by Apple that stores all of your music on the Internet and gives you access to it anyplace and anytime as long as you have an Internet connection.

The way this works is that Apple looks at your iTunes music library and determines which of the songs are available in the iTunes Store. Any songs that match are automatically added to your iCloud. For example, if you ripped your Beatles *Abbey Road* CD into iTunes, Apple looks at that and sees that the *Abbey Road* album is available in iTunes and automatically adds those songs to your iCloud even though you didn't actually buy the album in iTunes.

Apple is betting that since it has more than 20 million songs in the iTunes library that most of your music is going to be there already, but what if you have music that is not available in the iTunes Store? For example, I have a quite a few live recordings that were never released commercially and are therefore not in the iTunes Store. Apple actually uploads these songs to the iCloud to make them available on all your devices. This allows me to access my Grateful Dead live concert recordings on my iPhone and iPad everywhere.

Now for the downsides—there is a limit to the number of songs that you can have in iTunes Match and the service is not free.

11	✔ Blackbird	⊕	2:18	The Beatles (White...	Rock
12	✔ Piggies	⊕	2:04	The Beatles (White...	Rock
13	✔ Rocky Racoon	▶	3:41	The Beatles (White...	Rock
14	✔ Don't Pass Me By	Download from iCloud	les (White...	Rock
15	✔ Why Don't We Do It In The Road?	⊕	1:42	The Beatles (White...	Rock
16	✔ I Will	⊕	1:46	The Beatles (White...	Rock
17	✔ Julia	⊕	2:54	The Beatles (White...	Rock
1	✔ Birthday	⊕	2:43	The Beatles (White...	Rock

items, 7.5 hours, 680.9 MB

Figure 5-6
The little clouds next to the track names show that they are part of my iCloud.

The maximum number of songs that you can upload is 25,000, which does not include any music purchased from the iTunes Store. The iTunes Match service costs $24.99 a year, and I think it is a great deal. I no longer have to worry about syncing songs to my iPad before traveling since I can access all of my music all of the time, as long as I am connected to the Internet.

Before we get started you need to make sure that you have iTunes 10.6 or later on your Mac or PC, along with an Apple ID. The music must be in a format that iTunes can play, which includes AAC, MP3, WAV, AIFF, and Apple Lossless. You can use the same iTunes Match account on up to 10 devices, including iPhones, iPod Touches (third generation or later), iPads, and Apple TVs.

To turn on iTunes Match, follow these directions:

1. Open iTunes on your computer.

2. Click iTunes Match on the left side of the screen.

3. Enter your Apple ID and password.

4. Click on the Subscribe button, and then iTunes will start scanning and matching your music and uploading it to your iCloud account.

Figure 5-7
I can listen to the *Abbey Road* album in the Music app on my iPad.

5. When the scanning, matching, and uploading are complete a cloud icon appears next to the songs stored in the cloud.

Now you need to turn on the service on your iPad:

1. Turn on your iPad.

2. Tap on the Settings app.

3. Tap on Music in the list on the left.

4. Turn on iTunes Match.

5. Turn on Show All Music to see the music stored in the iTunes Match.

PLAYING MUSIC ON YOUR iPAD

Now that all of your music is available on your iPad, let's walk through accessing and playing your music.

To play your music on the iPad, all you need to do is tap on the Music app to open a menu bar at the bottom of the app:

- **Store:** This takes you right into the iTunes Store.

- **Playlists:** This lets you access playlists you have created on your computer, and it also lets you create playlists right on the iPad. Tap on New, give the playlist a name, add songs from the list, and then tap Done when you're finished. You can then

download the songs from the iCloud and start to play your newly created playlist.

- **Songs:** This shows the music on your iPad or in the iTunes Match service sorted by song title.

- **Artists:** This shows the songs available on your iPad or in the iTunes Match service sorted by Artist name.

- **Albums:** This shows the songs available on your iPad or in the iTunes Match service sorted by album name.

- **More:** Tap this to access music on a Home Share network, or sort by Genres or Composers.

- **Search bar:** Start to type in this area and the results begin to appear on the screen.

Now that you have the song or album you want to play, it is time to look at the top of the screen. This is where the controls are for the music player. From the left to the right are the Back button, Play/Pause button, Next button, Playback Viewer, Volume control, and AirPlay button. The AirPlay button is present only when an AirPlay-enabled device is on the same network.

Figure 5-8
The Menu bar at the bottom of the Music app screen.

Figure 5-9
The Menu bar at the top of the Music app screen showing the play controls.

The rest of the controls are simple—tap Play to play, slide to control the volume, tap Next to go to the next track, tap Back to go to the previous track. You can also use your finger to control the playback by swiping left and right in the Playback Viewer.

The Music Player app is different from the other apps as it doesn't stop when you tap the Home button. This allows you to play music while you do other things on the iPad. For example, you can play music while reading an iBook or while browsing the Internet.

STREAMING OR DOWNLOADING?

The question of whether the songs are streaming or being downloaded always seems to crop up when talking about the iTunes Match service. The answer changes depending on the device being used. When a song is downloaded, the actual track is saved to the device and takes up memory; when a song is streamed, it just plays on the device and the track is never actually stored on the device.

On the iPad (and the iPhone or iPod Touch), the song starts to play as it is being downloaded to the device. That means that once it has played, the song is actually on the device and can be played again without needing to go back out on the Internet. The Apple TV only streams the songs and does not download anything to the device.

What this means for iPad users is that although you can access all of your music that is saved in the iCloud, you still need to leave some space on the iPad to be able to download music. And although you can freely delete songs from the iTunes library and download them again when needed you must be connected to the Internet to do so, and if you use the 3G or 4G cellular network to do so you can blow through your data plan pretty fast.

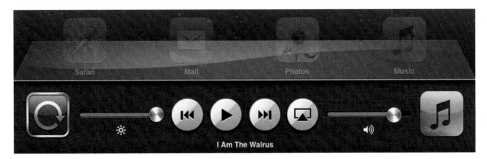

Figure 5-10
Access the music controls by double tapping the Home button and swiping left to right on the multi-tasking bar at the bottom of the screen.

To access the music controls, tap the Home button twice in quick succession to open the multi-tasking bar, then swipe from left to right to bring up the music controls. This gives you access to your music player at all the times.

GETTING YOUR MOVIES INTO iTUNES

Buying movies is one thing, but what about the DVDs that you already own? To get your movies onto your iPad, you need to get them into iTunes first. There is no way to directly get your movies from a DVD onto the iPad without a computer.

With music, it's easy—just insert the CD into the computer's CD drive and the iTunes application rips the music right off the CD and imports it into iTunes, allowing you to transfer it to your iPad easily. This basic process does not work when it comes to DVDs. You have to rely on an external, third-party program to do it.

Just to be clear: I am not telling you to rent a movie and rip it to the computer nor am I telling you to go to a friend's house and help yourself to his movie collection. What I am telling you is that there is a way to transfer the DVDs you have bought to a computer, and then to your iPad.

I am not a lawyer and I am not offering legal advice, but all that I have read about copy-protected content states that it is legal to copy your DVDs in "fair use" scenarios such as this. If you own a legal copy of a CD or DVD, then you have the right to make a version of that content to play on your iPad. That's according to U.S. copyright law, so you should be good to go.

The confusion comes with another section of the law that states that if there is some type of copy protection on the media, you are not allowed to break it. This means that part of the law says you are permitted to copy the material to a different device, but other parts of the law state that you cannot do it if you break a special encryption on the CD or DVD. If you have concerns, then please don't copy any of your movies—Apple will gladly sell you new copies in the iTunes Store.

I believe that you should be allowed to make a copy of your legally purchased material as long as you don't turn around and sell the copies or even lend them out. Just think of the copies as being part of the original. And just as it is impossible to read the same physical copy of a book in two places at the same time, it's not a good idea to have the same movie playing in two places at the same time.

Getting your movies onto your iPad is a three-step process:

1. Get the movie off the DVD and onto your computer.

2. Get the movie into iTunes in a form that the iPad can use.

3. Transfer the movie to the iPad.

To get the movie off the DVD you need a specialized software application. The best program for this is HandBrake, which describes itself as "an open source, GPL-licensed, multiplatform, multithreaded video transcoder, available for Mac OS X, Linux and Windows." Let's look at what that means and how this program, which seems to do something that the movie studios frown upon, manages to stay around.

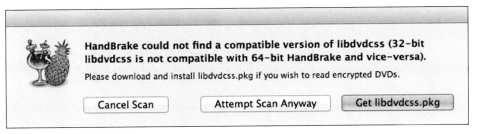

HandBrake could not find a compatible version of libdvdcss (32-bit libdvdcss is not compatible with 64-bit HandBrake and vice-versa).

Please download and install libdvdcss.pkg if you wish to read encrypted DVDs.

[Cancel Scan] [Attempt Scan Anyway] [Get libdvdcss.pkg]

Figure 5-11
HandBrake will let you know if you need to download the program it needs to rip a copy-protected DVD.

HandBrake is open source and thus free, meaning that no one actually owns it and no one profits from it. It's updated and maintained by a worldwide group of developers that gives the movie industry no real target for a lawsuit.

Although HandBrake can rip DVDs, it cannot rip copy-protected DVDs all by itself. For that, it looks for a separate helper program, and—here is the cool part—the HandBrake application points you to that program on the Internet. This allows you to download the second application and with the two programs working together you can rip a movie file from the DVD, load the content onto your computer, move it into iTunes, and sync it onto your iPad.

DVD Ripping on a Mac

When working on a Mac, the key to making a copy of media from a copy-protected disc is a program called libdvdcss, which HandBrake looks for on the computer and if it doesn't find it will help you download it.

DVD Ripping on a PC

When you want to copy a protected DVD on a PC that's running Microsoft Windows, you'll need a little extra help. The process is nearly as easy for PC users as it is for those on

a Mac, but it's a little more expensive.

While Mac users get DVD-ripping tools for free, PC users must pay about $52. This is because the best program for the PC to get around copy protection is the AnyDVD application from www.slysoft.com.

The AnyDVD program runs automatically in the background. It makes a copy-protected DVD look like a regular disc that can be copied to your computer. When AnyDVD is running, HandBrake can rip any DVD that you put into your computer.

Using HandBrake

At this point, let's assume that your Mac is equipped with libdvdcss in the Applications folder or your PC is running AnyDVD. It's time to run HandBrake and rip your DVD.

1. Start HandBrake.

2. Insert the movie you want to rip into the computer's DVD player. If the DVD starts to play, click Stop and quit the DVD player application.

3. In HandBrake, set the source by clicking the Source button and selecting the DVD.

4. Click on the Toggle presets button and then click on the little arrow next to the Device menu choice.

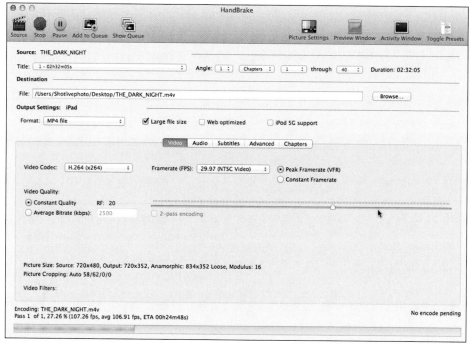

Figure 5-12

The HandBrake screen showing that I have about 25 minutes left in the ripping process. I use an older computer to rip my movies, which takes longer but I set it to work overnight so it doesn't tie up my working machine.

5. Tell HandBrake what type of Movie Settings to use to create a copy from your DVD by choosing the iPad preset. This sets the optimal settings for movies that will be played on an iPad.

6. You can now adjust what you want HandBrake to rip. The Video Settings are selected for you but you can adjust the audio track, the subtitles, and the advanced settings (I leave these alone), and even add chapter names to movies if you want them.

7. Choose a destination for your movie files. I usually pick the desktop—because the movie will end up inside of iTunes, this is just a temporary holding spot.

8. Click on Start and be prepared to wait … for a long time.

The speed and power of your computer system determines how long it takes to rip a movie from the DVD to the computer. For example, my older Macbook Pro takes a few hours to rip a movie, but a newer machine with a faster chip and a lot of memory cuts that time down to about 15 minutes. Regardless of the computer, the best plan is to think ahead and set up the computer to rip the movie at night so that it's all done in the morning and you didn't waste any time waiting for it to complete.

Here are some things to know about Hand-Brake to help you get the best results:

- **Pick the right audio track.** Many movies have multiple audio tracks, and few things are as disappointing as spending hours waiting for a movie to be ripped and then finding out you have the director's comments instead of the movie's soundtrack.

- **Get the entire movie.** If you're converting a DVD that contains separate episodes or multiple versions of a movie, you can copy them all by adding chapters to the queue instead of just running the program. This way, when you run the HandBrake queue, all the chapters or episodes will be ripped.

The other types of movies that you might want to transfer over to the iPad are those that you have made yourself. It is so easy to create videos these days. From little Flip video cameras and cell phone video cameras, to regular cameras with video capability, and even the built-in video camera on the iPad … anyone can be a moviemaker. If you have home movies that you've made, it is easy to watch those on the iPad as well. Wouldn't it be great to have the movie from your last vacation with you … or maybe your wedding video, so you can show family and friends?

The obstacle to loading home videos on an iPad is that some movies are not in the proper format to be recognized by the iPad or iTunes. As a result, when you try to sync the movie to your iPad, you get an error message that tells you the movie is in the wrong format.

No worries! HandBrake can help by converting a movie from one format to another. Just follow the directions from the previous section. But instead of picking a DVD as the source, navigate instead to your movie file.

Now that the movie is in the iTunes application on your computer, you can transfer it over to the iPad by syncing with a USB cable. It is important to know that the movies that you rip will not be available on the iCloud service. These movies cannot be uploaded to or downloaded from the iCloud.

FREE eBOOKS

The iBooks app turns your iPad into a great digital book reader and because it supports both PDF and the popular ePub file format, you can get a lot of free content for your iPad—and all you need is a web browser on your computer.

First let's look at where to find these books; then we will cover getting the books onto the iPad; and finally we will talk about getting covers on the books, since a good-looking bookshelf is just better than a plain-looking one.

There are a great may places on the web were free electronic books are readily available. Two of the best places to get free books are Project Gutenberg and ePub Books.

Project Gutenberg (www.gutenberg.org) is home to more than 38,000 books, all of which you can download and read on your iPad for free. The thing to remember with Project Gutenberg is that it stores the book files in many different formats—just make sure you download the ePub file format.

ePubBooks (www.epubbooks.com) is a great resource for free electronic books that are published in the ePub format. Because the iPad and iBooks use the ePub format, the books from this site work great. Many of the books here are also available from Project Gutenberg, but if you download them from ePubBooks you don't have to worry about

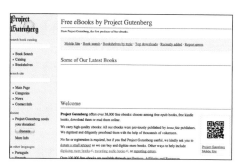

Figure 5-13
The Project Gutenberg website.

Figure 5-14
The ePubBooks website.

NOTE

While it seems like it should be possible, if you go to the ePub websites from your iPad you cannot download the books to be used in iBooks. You must use a computer to download them and then sync across to the iPad.

making sure you have the right format since they are all in the ePub format.

After you have downloaded the electronic book to your computer, you need to add the book to iTunes. Open iTunes, click on File, and then click on Add to Library. Navigate to where the electronic books are stored on the computer and click Continue.

The book will automatically be added to your Books section in your iTunes. The problem is that they won't look really nice—just a gray box with image of a book. Click on the book, click on File, and then select Get Info to bring up the information for the book file. You can then add the artwork for the book cover—all you need to do is to find an image file of the cover that you want and copy it into the artwork section of the File info window. This is the same basic process as getting album cover artwork, which we covered earlier in this chapter

All that's left to do is to sync the iPad with the iTunes and your free ePub books will be available in the iBooks app. Because you didn't purchase these eBooks from Apple, they will not be available from the iCloud. If you delete the book from your iPad, the only way to get it back is to re-sync from the computer.

Movies, Television, and Music

The Skim

When Apple released the iPad, many people commented that the device just looked like an oversized iPod Touch ... and they weren't wrong. The iPad was built so that users could consume content—preferably content purchased though the variety of Apple Stores. Want to watch a movie? You could buy or rent it at the iTunes Store. Want to listen to new music? You could buy it at the iTunes Store. Since then the iPad has become a much more versatile device with the inclusion of built-in still and video cameras and a slew of business applications, making the device equal parts content consumption and content creation.

CONTENT CONSUMPTION

I hope that this doesn't come as a surprise to anyone, but Apple is in the business of making a profit. One of the ways Apple does that is to sell content for its computing devices—and no device has been as successful as the iPad. The original iPad and the iPad 2 had really nice screens that enabled people to watch TV shows and movies with great clarity, but the new iPad takes that to a whole different level with the Retina

Figure 6-1

Currently I have more than a few albums on my iPad, but that's because I like to listen to a variety of music.

display. Movies and TV shows look even better, and now that you can re-download any Apple Store purchase, including movies, at any time from your iCloud account the iPad truly is a beautiful device for your content consumption.

RULES FOR DIFFERENT TYPES OF CONTENT

It used to be that content that you bought from Apple was not treated equally. Movies that you purchased through the iTunes Store, either on the iPad or on the computer, used to be treated differently than TV shows, music, apps, and eBooks. When you purchased a movie there was no way to download it a second time, so if you deleted it by mistake you had to purchase it again.

This purchase model was more like the way physical media is treated than digital media. For example, if you go in to a store and purchase a DVD and then lose or destroy it, you can't go back to the store and get another copy for free. All of that has changed with the release of the new version of the iPad operating system (iOS 5.1) and iCloud. Thanks to iCloud, your Apple Store–purchased content is available to you everywhere, and that includes movies for the first time.

Movies

You can buy and rent movies on the iPad and on the computer through the iTunes Store. Movies that you buy on the iPad can be transferred to the computer and vice versa. In the past, if you deleted a movie from your iPad and computer, that movie was gone forever. With the release of the new iPad operating system in March 2012, that all changed. With iOS 5.1 and later, movies are now stored in the iCloud as well. Since this is part of the software that runs the iPad, it applies to all models of the iPad (and the iPhone and iPod Touch).

If you have ever purchased movies through the iTunes Store, you can see them by doing the following:

1. Turn on the iPad.

2. Launch iTunes.

3. Tap on Purchased at the bottom of the screen.

4. On the top left corner, tap the View button and pick Movies.

5. You now see a list of movies that you have purchased in the iTunes Store.

6. Choose a movie and tap on the cloud icon next to it to download the movie directly to the iPad.

TV Shows

There was a time that you could rent TV shows from the iTunes Store, but no more. Currently you can buy TV shows by the episode or as a complete season. Apple now makes it possible to complete a season, which means that you can buy the remaining episodes of a TV season after purchasing single episodes. The cool thing is that all your previously purchased TV shows are available on the iPad and can be downloaded anytime you are connected to the Internet via Wi-Fi. The files are too big to download over a cellular connection.

To look at the available TV shows on your iPad, just do the following:

1. Turn on the iPad.

2. Launch iTunes.

3. Tap on Purchased at the bottom of the screen.

4. On the top left corner, tap the View button and pick TV Shows.

5. You can now view either by Season or Episodes. Search the shows and then just tap on the show or episode you want to load on the iPad.

6. Tap on the cloud icon to download that episode, or tap on the season to bring up all the shows in that season and download either the single episode or the whole season.

Music

One of the nicest advances in the iPad ecosystem is that the music you buy on the iPad is automatically downloaded to your computer account (as long as you turn that feature on—I'll tell you how in a moment) and music you buy on your computer is automatically downloaded to your iPad.

Figure 6-2
You can set up iTunes to automatically download music, apps, and books you purchase on your iPad to your computer, and vice versa.

You can download the music you have purchased through the Apple iTunes Store anytime through your iCloud account, and if you add the iTunes Match service you can download any of your music, even the albums and tracks that you have ripped from your CD collection or music purchased at other online stores that is in your iTunes library. This means that you can delete music from your iPad and download it again anytime you are connected to the Internet.

In the past, the music you bought in the Apple iTunes Store was DRM (Digital Rights Managed) protected, a form of copy protection, and could be played only through the iTunes software or on an iPod. That all changed years ago and now you can play the music you buy on any device or computer, and you can even burn it to CD.

Here's how to turn on the automatic download feature for music on the computer:

1. Turn on the computer.

2. Launch iTunes.

3. On a Mac, click iTunes and then click on Preferences. On a Windows PC, click on Edit and then Preferences.

4. Click on Store.

5. Check the automatic downloads that you want to be downloaded to your computer; your choices are Music, Apps, and Books.

Apps

When Apple first introduced apps for the iPhone, it changed the world. There are now apps available for just about everything on the iPhone and iPad, with new ones being released every day. Apple recently announced that more than 25 billion apps have been downloaded—that's a lot of apps! As with other iTunes products, once you buy an app you can re-download it from the iTunes Store at any time. You can see which apps are on your iPad and which can be downloaded again without a fee. On the iPad, just follow these directions:

1. Turn on the iPad.

2. Tap on the App Store app.

3. At the bottom of the screen, tap on Purchased.

4. You can see which apps are already installed and which you can download from the cloud to your iPad.

eBooks

When you purchase electronic books (eBooks) from the iBookstore they are available forever—or as long as the book exists in the iBookstore. That is why it is always a good idea to back all the purchases up to a computer is possible. Once the eBooks are on your computer, just back then up like you would any data. When in the iBookstore you can look at your previous purchases and download them again at will. You can also set the iPad to automatically download any newly purchased eBooks. That is covered a little later in this chapter.

Figure 6-3
You can view your previously purchased books in the iBookstore and download any of them again at any time.

USING YOUR COMPUTER TO BUY CONTENT

It's easy to use your computer to buy content for your iPad. The iTunes software has a built-in iTunes Store that allows you to buy all the content in one place. When you launch iTunes, you see a link to the iTunes Store in the left column. This opens the iTunes Store right inside the iTunes program. The first thing that you need to do is to sign in to the iTunes Store using your Apple ID. If you are already signed in you will see your Apple ID in the upper right corner of the window; if you are not signed in, enter your Apple ID and password to do so.

Across the top of the iTunes Store are the following buttons: Home, Music, Movies, TV

Figure 6-4
The iTunes Store Sign In screen.

Figure 6-5
Here are albums that I could complete—
and I am not proud that I own Aly & Aj
or the Jonas Brothers.

Shows, App Store, Books, Podcasts, iTunes U, Ping, and your account name (which you can click to get into your Account Settings).

- **Home:** The Home button takes you to the iTunes home, where you can see the currently featured music, movies, and TV shows all in the same place. I don't spend much time here, preferring to shop in the individual stores.

- **Music:** The Music Store is where you can buy whole albums or individual songs. The store's home page shows the current releases and hot music, but has some really cool features that are not immediately apparent. The first is that you can click on the little arrow next to the Music Store button to bring up a list of music genres, allowing you instant access to a specific music type.

  If you have bought individual songs in the past, Apple has created an easy way for you to buy the rest of the album without having to pay for the individual songs again. Since Apple has hidden the link for this so well I created a short url that, if entered into a web browser on the computer with the iTunes library, opens the Complete My Album feature right in iTunes: http://goo.gl/vQfXg.

- **Movies:** The Movie Store allows you to buy or rent movies in both SD and HD formats. All the movies available here can be viewed on the iPad. Click on any movie and you see the Buy or Rent information over on the left, a Plot summary on the right, and Reviews on the bottom of the page. You also get to see what other movies customers purchased after purchasing that one, along with the movie credits.

  Click on the View Trailer button to open a window and watch the movie trailer. If you rent a movie, you have 30 days to start watching it and 24 hours to finish viewing the movie once you have started. You can transfer movies that you buy in the iTunes Store on your computer to your iPad either using a USB cable or wirelessly.

- **TV Shows:** You can buy individual episodes or whole seasons here. If you buy a whole season before all episodes have aired, you will get the new episodes automatically as they become available.

If you buy TV shows on your computer, you can always download them on your iPad when you are connected to the Internet via Wi-Fi. You do not have to transfer the files from the computer to the iPad. If you purchase a TV show season, you can always check to see if there are episodes available by clicking on the Store Menu at the top of the screen, then choosing Check for Available Downloads... If there is any content available for your account, it is automatically downloaded.

- **App Store:** This is where you can buy apps for your iPad, iPhone, or iPod Touch. You can buy the apps here and download them onto the iPad automatically or you can transfer the apps when you sync the device.

  The one thing that is really different about apps is that they are always being updated and it is easy to keep the apps current on your iTunes. On the left side of the app you can see the library of content, and if there are apps that have updates available a number appears next to the word Apps (showing the number of apps that need updates). Click on Apps, and then click on the Check for Updates link at the bottom of the page. This checks the App Store for updates and gives you the option to Download All Free Updates.

- **Books:** You can access the iBookstore in iTunes but you can't read any of the books on your computer. You can click on the Get Sample button, but instead of downloading the book sample to your computer it automatically downloads it to any device(s) that have automatic downloads turned on.

- **Podcasts:** You can download podcasts here. There are both audio and video podcasts that play just as well on the

computer as they do on the iPad. The best part is that they don't cost anything.

- **iTunes U:** This is the portal to the free iTunes U information—either individual lectures or full courses. The courses work better on the iPad than they do on the computer since some of the content is available only in iBooks, which means it can run only on an iPad, iPhone, or iPod touch. Some of the courses also link to apps, which don't run on the computer either. There is a ton of content here and the best part is that it is all free.

- **Ping:** This is the Apple social network and a way for you can find out what other people are listening to or watching. Ping is a very interesting service but it doesn't seem to be getting much of a push from Apple. It's rare that I visit the page. To me the most interesting part of the home page is on the right side, where you can see what concerts are coming to a venue near you and where you can open a Live Nation or Ticketmaster ticket window with just one click.

- **Account Settings:** While you can't actually buy anything here, this is where you can do the following:

  - **Control your Apple ID:** You can change the Apple ID and the billing information right here. You can also see how many computers are authorized to play content purchased with your Apple ID and you can Deauthorize All the computers with a single click. Since the content you buy from the Apple Store, other than music, is still copy protected and can be played on only five computers total, being able to deauthorize all the machines is useful if you have hit your limit and need to start over.

- **iTunes in the cloud:** This where you can find out which devices are using this Apple ID and are authorized to download your purchases from iTunes in the iCloud service. You can view any purchases that have been marked as hidden and turn on or off the iTunes Match auto-renew if using that service.

- **Check your purchase history:** This allows you to see all the purchases made with this Apple ID.

- **Ping:** You can turn Ping on or off here.

- **Nickname:** You can edit your nickname here.

- **Manage your reviews and ratings:** This shows how many reviews you have made and allows you to see them. You can actually go and remove any of your ratings or reviews.

- **Manage the Alert Me settings:** I have set alerts for some of my favorite authors and this is where I can see those alerts and remove any that I no longer want.

- **Manage the recommendations and Ping postings:** If you want to send messages and see recommendations when using Ping, you can check that option here.

- **Manage your passes:** This is where you can manage your Season Passes—that is, the TV shows that you have bought an entire season of at the same time. Since you can buy a TV season before all the episodes have aired you will receive e-mail notifications when a new episode is available. You can turn on or off the e-mail notifications here. You can also see the Season Passes that are complete—that is, you have received all the episodes for.

Figure 6-6

It's easy to check if there are any downloads available for your iTunes account.

- **Manage your subscriptions:** Even though subscriptions are done only through the apps on the iPad, you can see the details here and turn the auto-renew option on or off. It's very useful to see all your subscriptions in one place.

All the content that you buy on the computer needs an Apple ID associated with it. If you want the content purchased here to be available on the iPad, you need to make sure that you use the same Apple ID on your iPad.

In the past, it was easier to buy content on the computer and sync it over to the iPad. You would have to plug the iPad into the computer using the included USB cable, open iTunes, and check what content you want to transfer. Now I find myself buying the content on the iPad instead, and here is the cool part:

After I purchase the content on the iPad I can download the new content to the computer. If you purchase anything on the iPad, then just go to the iTunes program on your computer and click on Store from the menu across the top of the screen, and then click on Check for Available Downloads... and the content you purchased on the iPad starts to download. This works for all content purchased through the iTunes Store, including movies.

USING YOUR iPAD TO BUY CONTENT

Buying content on the iPad is easy, but the Stores are spread out into different apps. There are five different places to buy content on your iPad:

- iTunes app
- App Store app
- iBooks app
- iTunes U app
- Newsstand app

This can lead to some confusion and frustration, and for some unknown reason Apple calls the iTunes Store on the iPad simply "iTunes" instead of something more descriptive, like "iTunes Store."

iTunes App

The iTunes app looks a lot like the iTunes Store on the computer. The layout of the app is easy to navigate, with the different types of content located across the bottom. You can pick between the following types of content:

- **Music:** This is where you can buy songs and albums. The music is automatically added to the download list for the iPad and starts to download immediately. Click on something that you like and tap the price for either the album or a single tune to download it.

Figure 6-7
Click on an album that you want to buy and you will see the details and price.

Some tracks can be purchased only as part of the album. Some albums have extra content that is computer only, and this seemed to get more attention from Apple before the iPad was released because although you can buy albums with this extra content on your iPad, you can't actually see it on the iPad. For example, Pink Floyd's *The Wall (Deluxe Experience Edition) [Remastered]* is available on the iPad for $29.99 and includes 62 items, but the Bonus item LP will not download to the iPad and instead downloads the next time you launch iTunes on your computer. If you are using only an iPad and not a computer at all, then you will never have access to the computer-only content.

Figure 6-8
Many songs are available only if you by the whole album.

Figure 6-9
The movie page for *Real Steel* on the iPad ...

- **Movies:** Buying or renting movies on your iPad is a snap. Just find a movie you want and tap on it. You can then see the options available for both SD and HD versions. The store opens the movie page to the more expensive, larger HD version first, but a quick tap on the SD button brings up the standard definition version of the movie and is usually $5 cheaper to buy and $1 cheaper to rent.

Tap on the price to buy or rent the movie and it is automatically added to the download list. When you rent a movie on the iPad, the movie can be watched only on the iPad—there is no way to transfer rented movies to the computer. You have 30 days to start watching the movie and once you start watching it you have 24

Figure 6-10
... and the same *Real Steel* movie page on the computer.

hours until it is automatically removed from your iPad. You can watch the movie as many times as you want in that 24-hour period.

- **TV Shows:** Browse and tap to buy TV shows here. Apple used to allow you to rent TV shows, but that is no longer the case. You can buy individual TV show episodes or you can buy complete seasons, even if all if the episodes have not been released yet. When a new episode is released you get an e-mail allowing you to download the new episode, usually within a few hours of the show airing.

- **Ping:** You must be running iTunes on a computer to use the Apple social network Ping. You can turn on Ping on the computer in iTunes, but it is my opinion that until Apple does something to make Ping more useful, there is very little point to bothering with it.

- **Podcasts:** This tab gives you access to the podcasts available for download.

- **Audiobooks:** This is where you can purchase audiobooks. Remember that they are large and you need a Wi-Fi connection to download them. They are also expensive; for example, the audio book for *The Hunger Games* is $23.95 and *The Girl With the Dragon Tattoo* is $26.95. You won't find an audiobooks tab in the iTunes Store on your computer; instead you can find audiobooks under the Books tab in iTunes on the computer.

- **iTunes U:** This tab acts a link to open the new iTunes U app, which is covered later in this chapter. I expect to see this tab disappear soon since the iTunes U content is now available through the iTunes U app.

- **Purchased:** This is where you can see all the music, TV shows, and movies that have been purchased under the currently used Apple ID, and more than that, you can download any of these items again anytime you have an Internet connection.

Figure 6-11
The Downloads page showing the download queue.

At the top left corner of the screen you can pick to either View: Music, View: TV Shows, or View: Movies. Then, just tap on the show or the artist, depending on the view, and download any of the previously purchased content by tapping on the cloud icon. I love this capability on my iPad since it means that I don't have to load up the device with a bunch of stuff but instead can just download content when I want it.

- **Downloads:** This is where the current list of downloading content is.

What you won't find in the iTunes app is any way to buy apps, eBooks, iTunes U classes, or magazines subscriptions. That content is handled in the following stores.

App Store App

To buy apps for the iPad you need to use the App Store app. There are a lot of apps available for the iPad. At the Apple announcement for the new iPad, it was revealed that there are more than 200,000 apps that are just for the iPad, and you can buy them all at the App Store.

Now, not all apps are compatible with the original iPad. For example, you cannot load the new iPhoto app or the Adobe Photoshop Touch on the original iPad; you get an error message stating that the app requires a front-facing camera if you try to install one of them. The App Store has six different buttons across the bottom, which give you instant access to the following:

- **Featured:** This is where Apple shows you what is new and exciting. If you're an app developer, you really want to have your apps mentioned here. This is the main apps page and usually the spot where I start my app shopping.

- **Genius:** If you have the Genius service turned on, the App Store looks at your previous purchases and recommends new apps.

- **Top charts:** This is where you can find the top paid and free apps. There is a Categories button on the top left where you pick a category and see the top free and paid apps for that specific category.

- **Categories:** There are 22 categories of apps available here. Tap on one of the categories and it lists the apps either by Release Date, Most Popular, or Name. Just tap the Sort By button to choose the sorting method that works best for you. For some categories, like Games for example, a Featured page opens first. Tap on the Release

Figure 6-12
The update notification on the App Store icon.

Date button right next to the Featured button at the top and then you can sort by Name, Most Popular, or Release Date.

- **Purchased:** This is a very important button. This is where you can see the apps that you have already purchased and you can download them again.

- **Updates:** This is where you see which apps have updates available.

You can keep your apps up-to-date in this app as well, and since having to check all the time to see what is and isn't current is tedious, Apple lets you know when an app needs to be updated with a small number notification on the Apps Store app icon. The small number on the top right lets you know how many of your apps need to be updated. For example, the small 1 in the red circle in Figure 6-12 means that at least one app needs to be updated. To update your apps:

1. Turn on the iPad.

2. Tap on the App Store app.

3. Tap on Updates, located on the bottom right corner of the screen.

Figure 6-13
The download Updates page.

Figure 6-14
You can choose what to download automatically to the iPad on the Automatic Downloads Settings page.

4. A list of apps that need updating is shown.

5. Tap on the individual app to learn more about the update.

6. Tap on Update All or update each individual app.

iBooks App

Buying eBooks on the iPad takes place in the iBookstore. The iBookstore, which I cover in detail in Chapter 7, is hidden within the iBooks app. What you need to know right off the bat is that the eBooks purchased on the iPad can be read only on the iPad, iPhone, and iPod Touch.

iTunes U App

iTunes U used to be a part of the iTunes Store until Apple spun it off as its own app. It is covered in detail in Chapter 9.

Newsstand App

The Newsstand App Store is a specialized App Store that allows you to get magazines and newspaper subscriptions easily. The Newsstand is covered in detail in Chapter 7.

Automatic Downloads

You can set up your iPad so that any music, apps, and books you purchase on your computer or on another iPad automatically download to your iPad. Here's how:

1. Turn on the iPad.

2. Tap on the Settings app.

3. Tap on Store in the list on the left.

4. Turn on the Automatic Downloads for Music, Apps, and Books.

You can also set up to Use Cellular Data for downloads, but a word of warning—this can inadvertently use up a lot your data plan, especially if you share the same Apple ID on multiple device for purchases, so be careful. To be clear, if you buy a lot of music while sitting at your computer and have this setting turned on, the music can start to download automatically to your iPad.

GETTING YOUR CONTENT ONTO AND OFF THE iPAD VIA SYNC

Prior to the iOS5 operating system on the iPad, you had to sync the iPad to a computer that was running iTunes to make it work. There was no other option. Now that has changed and you can buy an iPad and use it without going anywhere near a computer. The content you purchase is stored in the iCloud, and other than movies, you can download the content again at any time. It's all very cool and easy to use, but that doesn't mean you can't sync the iPad to a computer. In fact, there are some real advantages to syncing your iPad to a computer:

- **No Wi-Fi needed:** One of the real advantages of USB syncing is that you don't need a Wi-Fi network. For example, when I travel with both my laptop and my iPad I can transfer movies from my laptop to my iPad without having to connect to a Wi-Fi network. The laptop can hold a lot more movies than the iPad, so I can carry a ton of content.

- **Speed of data transfer:** Transferring information via the USB cable is much faster than transferring the information over a Wi-Fi connection.

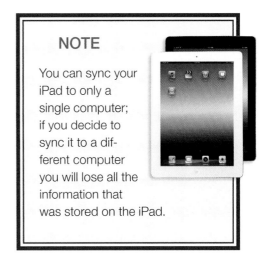

NOTE

You can sync your iPad to only a single computer; if you decide to sync it to a different computer you will lose all the information that was stored on the iPad.

When you plug your iPad into your computer and launch iTunes (if it didn't start automatically) you will see that your iPad is now listed under Devices on the left side of the iTunes window. Go ahead and select it by clicking on it. This is where you set up how iTunes and the iPad play with each other, and you want to have them play nice because it will make your life a lot easier.

The first screen that comes up is the Summary page that gives basic information for your iPad. From here you can use the tabs across the top of the window to control the media that you put on the iPad, but the first thing to do is set up the Options on the front page to your liking.

The front page is divided into four sections:

1. The first section shows the info for the attached iPad, including the Capacity, Software Version, and Serial Number.

2. In this area you can find out if you are running the latest version of iPad software, and it's here that you can restore the iPad to its original settings if it starts acting up.

3. The third area deals with where the back-ups of the iPad are kept. You can either back up your iPad to the iCloud or to the computer, and you can encrypt the computer backup if you want.

4. The fourth section is the main Options menu, which is important. The following are the options, and what I have picked and why:

   • **Open iTunes when this iPad is connected**: Usually the only time I connect my iPad to the computer is to charge it, so I leave this unchecked.

   • **Sync with this iPad over Wi-Fi:** I have this checked so that I can sync over Wi-Fi.

   • **Sync only checked songs and videos:** I have this unchecked since it is grayed out if you have the Manually manage music and videos checked, and I do.

   • **Prefer standard definition videos:** This was more important when you couldn't download movies, TV shows, and music directly from the iCloud. With the incredible resolution on the new iPad I no longer have this checked. Movies just look too good at the highest resolution on the new iPad.

   • **Convert higher bit rate songs to ___ AAC:** You can pick the bit rate of the songs that are loaded on the iPad. Your choices are 128kbps, 192kbps, or 256kbps. Again, this is a great way to save space, but with the ability to delete music and then grab it off the iCloud there is less reason to reduce the quality of the music.

   • **Manually manage music and videos:** I keep this checked because I like to be in control of what goes on my iPad.

Figure 6-15
The Apps page, where I can add apps to my iPad and sort them on the screens on the right.

With this checked, the iTunes program cannot change the content of my iPad.

   • You can also configure the Universal Access for the iPad if needed here.

When it comes to loading content onto the iPad I like to be in control, so I go to each of the tabs that the iPad shows when attached to the computer and set them up manually:

   • **Info:** This is where you can sync the Address book contacts, iCal Calendars, Mail accounts, and Notes. This is also the place where you can replace the content on the iPad on a one-time basis—that is, it doesn't update the information every time you sync, just the first time. Since most of this information is actually synced wirelessly I have none of these checked, and I suggest that you don't check these. They tend to cause conflicts and multiple entries in the Calendar and your Address Book.

   • **Apps:** This is the window where you add all those cool apps and where you can add data files for specific applications on the iPad. It also allows you to organize where the apps are located on the iPad. You can sort the apps by Name, Category, Date, or Size. Once you've selected an app to be synced onto the iPad, you can then move it around and place it wherever you want it. It's much easier to do that here than on the actual iPad.

- **Tones:** This is where you can sync any ringtones (now called notes) that you have purchased though iTunes.

- **Music:** If you don't have the iCloud service and want music on your iPad this is the place to add it. Instead of trying to sync the entire music library, I select specific playlists, artists, and genres to sync. The important part of this is that here is where you can choose the playlists and smart playlists to sync to your iPad.

- **Movies:** Here is where you can add the movies you want to the iPad. What's really nice is that you can see the size of each movie right next to its icon. This is important because the movie files are BIG and can take up a lot of the space on your iPad. With files this size you can see how easy it would be to fill the whole iPad with movies pretty easily.

- **TV Shows:** Apple sells a lot of TV shows and I have a season or two of my favorites. Here is where you can add those shows to the iPad, and there is something pretty nice built right in. You can automatically sync a selection of shows based on rules that are a lot like a simplified smart playlist. I have mine set to automatically transfer all unwatched episodes of all shows, which automatically adds those episodes I download with my Season Pass.

  You can also add any episode or season using the Show menu and if you keep

scrolling down you will see a place to include episodes from playlists, so you can make a smart playlist for your TV shows.

- **Podcasts:** Do you listen to or watch podcasts? Well then, here is where you add those to your iPad. It's a shame that there is not a way to have smart playlists for podcasts, but at least you can input a single sync rule. I usually have mine set to automatically include all unplayed episodes of selected podcasts, which keeps those that I listen to all the time updated.

- **iTunes U:** This is where you sync all the iTunes U material, and it has the same layout and rules as the podcasts section, which seems right since it really is just a different type of podcast.

- **Books:** I use the iPad to read books so I have the Sync Books checkbox selected, but I don't want all my books on the iPad so I also have the Selected Books radio button checked. I have my books sorted by author since that is usually the way I buy books, but you do have the option for sorting by title. This is also the area where you can select to sync any audiobooks and, again, I have checked the Selected Audiobooks since I don't want all my audiobooks on the iPad.

- **Photos:** On the PC side of things you can select images from any folder that has images in it. On the Mac side of things, there are many more choices, especially if you use iPhoto. You can add photos from your computer to your iPad here.

Backing Up

Apple might not consider your iPad a personal computer, but in some ways it is very similar to one. One way that the iPad is like a computer is that you can lose the information stored on it, and so you need to back it up once in a while.

Apple makes backing up very easy because it backs up your iPad automatically when it syncs with iTunes, or you can back up anytime by right clicking on the iPad in the devices list and choose Back Up. The backup contains the settings and some data, but it doesn't actually make new copies of the media that you have on the iPad. The media (music, movies, apps, and photo content) are already on the computer and can be reloaded if you restore the iPad.

Restoring

Sometimes things go wrong. It happens, and when it does the best course of action is to restore your iPad so that it goes back to the factory settings and then restore from a backup. You can also restore from a backup by right clicking on the iPad in the device menu and choose Restore from backup.

When you use the restore function for your iPad, all the data is deleted from the device including the music, movies, contacts, photos, and calendars. All the settings are set to the factory defaults. You can then reload your data from a backup. To restore your iPad, just do the following:

1. Open iTunes and plug in the iPad.

2. Select the iPad from the devices list.

3. Tap on the Summary tab and then tap on the Restore button.

You will be prompted to back up your Settings before restoring the device to the factory defaults. Backing up all depends on whether you have recently backed up and whether there is any information on the iPad worth saving.

You will be prompted to restore the iPad: "Are you sure you want to restore the iPad to its factory settings? All of your media and other data will be erased." It sounds ominous but if you need to do it and you have a backup, then go for it.

Once the Restore is completed, you are asked if you want to use the backup to reload your info onto the iPad. Go ahead and use one of the backups, or if you want a clean slate, just say no.

There you have it, a backup and restore for the iPad. My advice is to make sure you back up your iPad often, since it can be a real pain to get everything back after something goes wrong.

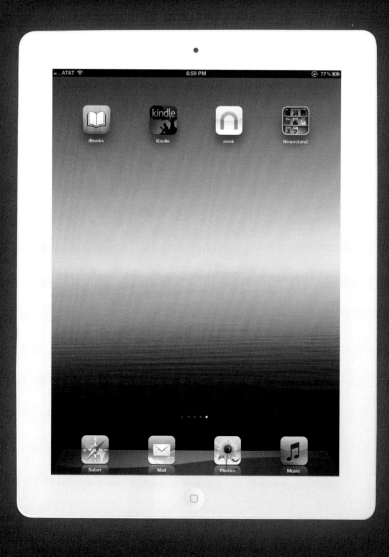

Books and Magazines

The Skim

The iPad makes for a great eBook reader. Since the release of the original iPad, I have read more books on it than I have paper versions. I love being able to carry 10 or 20 books with me without the weight or bulk of the paper versions. There is no doubt that the other eBook readers have looked at the success of the Apple tablet and have tried to compete with it by releasing devices that do more than just enable you to read eBooks. The Amazon Kindle Fire and the Nook Tablet are two good examples of this.

Apple refers to electronic books or eBooks as "iBooks," and the app you use to read eBooks is named "iBooks" as well. This can get a little confusing. For the sake of clarity in this book, "iBooks" refers to the app that allows you to read the electronic books, and the actual electronic books are referred to as "eBooks."

iBOOKS

The iBooks app is free, but it doesn't come pre-installed on the iPad. So, if you want to read eBooks on your iPad, you must visit the iTunes App Store and install it. You can install it directly to your iPad or via your computer.

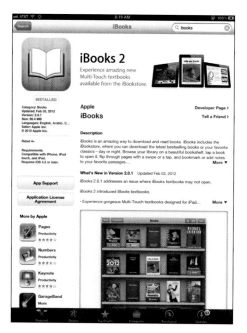

Figure 7-1
The iBooks app in the App Store.

Installing iBooks on the iPad

Getting the iBooks app on your iPad is really easy. Just follow these steps:

1. Turn on the iPad.

2. Tap on the App Store icon.

3. You should see an offer to download a free copy of iBooks. Tap Download.

4. You will be prompted to enter your Apple ID password but you will not be charged anything since the iBooks app is free.

5. If you don't get the invitation to Download iBooks:

   A. Tap in the search bar on the top right and enter iBooks, and then tap on Search.

   B. The iBooks app is the first choice.

   C. Tap the Free button (and, if prompted,

enter your Apple ID and password) to download the app.

That's all there is to it. Now you have the iBooks app on your iPad.

Installing iBooks on a Computer

If you would rather use your computer to get a copy of iBooks then just do the following:

1. Turn on the computer.

2. Start iTunes and click iTunes Store on the left side of the window.

3. Enter *iBooks* into the search bar on the top right corner.

4. Select the iBooks app that is in the iPad apps search results.

5. Once you have downloaded the iBooks app to your computer, you'll need to sync your iPad to install it.

With the iBooks app on your iPad, you can start using your iPad as an eBook reader. The next thing you have to do is get actual eBooks onto your iPad.

Launching iBooks

To start using iBooks, tap the iBooks app, because this is not only where you read eBooks but where you can organize and purchase them as well. The first time you run the iBooks app you are asked if you want to Sync Bookmarks. Doing this allows you to keep the same bookmarks and notes on multiple devices as long as they are all using the same Apple ID.

This means that if you have an iPhone, iPod Touch, or another iPad, the books will all be on the same page no matter which device you are using. If you start reading a book on your iPad at home and want to continue reading on the train but only have your iPhone, then the books will be in sync. Just tap Sync or

Figure 7-2
The iBooks library mode showing what eBooks I currently have on my iPad.

Don't Sync—and don't worry, since you can always change this setting later in the Settings app on your iPad.

THE iBOOKS INTERFACE

The iBooks interface has three distinct looks:

- Library mode
- iBookstore
- Reading mode

The following sections describe these modes in detail.

LIBRARY MODE

The library mode shows you the books that you have on the iPad and in the default mode looks like a bookshelf. Across the top of the screen are four buttons: Store, Collections, View modes, and Edit. Just tap on the buttons to see the following:

- **Store:** This takes you to the iBookstore, where you can browse and purchase eBooks to read on your iPad.

- **Collections:** Tapping this button opens a drop-down menu that allows you to switch between collections, create a new collection, and edit the collections. The default is to have two collections—Books and PDFs— which you cannot delete, move, or edit.

  You can create new collections for any anything you like. For example, you can create collections by author, subject, genre, or anything you want. Each eBook can be in only one collection at a time.

  To create a new collection, just tap New, type in the new collection name, and tap Done. To delete, change the order of the collections, or change the name of the collection, tap on Edit to bring up the edit mode. Tap on the white dash in the red circle and the word Delete appears on the right side of the collection—tap Delete to delete the collection. Tap and hold on the three horizontal dashes on the right side of the collection and you can change the order just by dragging the collection up or down. Tap on the name of the collection and you can edit it.

- **View:** The View buttons allow you to switch between the Bookshelf view and a List view. The Bookshelf view is represented by the four squares and the List view is three horizontal lines. When in the Bookshelf view you can move books around by holding your finger on the book you want to move until it enlarges, and then (without moving your finger off the screen) you can drag the book anywhere on the bookshelf. When the book is in the desired position, just lift your finger. When you are in the List view, there are four ways to sort eBooks:

- **Bookshelf:** This keeps the books in the same order as the Bookshelf view.

- **Titles:** This sorts the books alphabetically by title.

- **Authors:** This sorts the books alphabetically by author last name.

- **Categories:** This sorts the books into the type of book.

- **Edit:** The final button on the top of the screen allows you to move books into different collections or remove them from your iPad. Tap the Edit button and you will see that the Menu buttons across the top of the screen have changed. Now there are four buttons: Move, Delete, Select All, and Done. Tap on a book to select it and the Move and Delete buttons become active. If you want to move books to different collections, do the following:

1. Tap on the Edit button.

2. Tap on the books you want to move.

3. Tap on Move.

4. Tap on a collection to move the books into it. You can also make a new collection by tapping on New, typing the name of the collection, and tapping Done. Then you can tap on the new collection and the selected books will move into that collection, and then the edit window closes and the new collection opens.

To delete books from your iPad, tap on Edit, then select the books you want to delete by tapping on them and then tap on Delete. You will be asked if you are sure you want to delete the selected books; tap Delete to remove them from the iPad or Cancel to keep them. One great thing about iBooks is that if you delete a book

from the iPad that you bought on iTunes or in the iBookstore, you can always re-download the same book for free later on.

There is one more function on this page and it's usually hidden away. There is a way for you to search your iBooks library. To get the search bar you must pull the whole bookcase toward the bottom of the screen using your finger. The search bar will appear on the top of the screen right above the top of your books.

iBOOKSTORE

The iBookstore is where you can buy eBooks on the iPad. It looks just like the other Apple stores and works in the same way, but it is accessible only through the iBooks app.

Figure 7-3
The main screen of the iBookstore looks a lot like all the other online Apple stores but instead of movies or music, it's all about books.

At the top left corner of the iBookstore is the Library button, which allows you view the books stored on the iPad. Next are the Featured and Release Date options, which show the latest books, either in the Apple Featured view or in a simplistic Release Date view. Finally, there is a search bar that allows you to search the iBookstore.

Across the bottom of the page are the view options:

- **Featured:** This is where Apple shows what's new or what they are

recommending. Think of it as the display window in a store, where the products that they think will garner the most sales are displayed.

- **NYTimes:** Tap this to show the current *New York Times* best seller list in both fiction and nonfiction.

- **Top Charts:** These are the top-selling paid and free books in the iBookstore. Tap on any book to bring up that book's page.

- **Categories:** There are 25 different categories to pick from here, ranging from Arts &

BUYING BOOKS ON THE COMPUTER USING ITUNES

You can buy eBooks on your computer using iTunes 10.3 or later, but you can't read them on your computer. That's right—although you can buy eBooks on your computer, you cannot read them unless you have an iPad, iPhone, or iPod Touch.

To buy an eBook on your computer, just do the following:

1. Turn on the computer.

2. Launch iTunes.

3. Click on iTunes Store on the right side of the screen.

4. Click on Books on the top navigation bar.

5. Browse the iBookstore until you find something that looks good. You will notice that the iBookstore looks the same as the Music, Movie, and other iTunes Stores.

6. Once you click on a book, you have the option to buy the book or download a sample. I always download a sample first, and if I like it I can buy the whole book from the iBooks app.

Once you have purchased a book or downloaded a sample of a book on your computer, you must sync the iPad to transfer the book to the device.

Once you have tapped on the Buy Book or Get Sample button, the store automatically closes and the library opens and the new book is automatically downloaded.

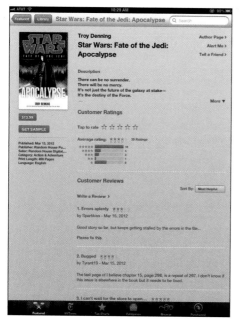

Figure 7-4

Tap on any book to go to that book's page, where you can buy it or download a sample.

Entertainment to Travel & Adventure. Tap on the category to open a page that looks just like the Featured page, but is just for those books that fit into that category.

- **Browse:** The Browse window is an advanced search for the store. You can pick the category, list the authors, and sort between free and paid books. Not as much fun as actually walking around a bookstore, but a lot faster.

- **Purchased:** This is where you can go to see all the eBooks purchased under your Apple ID, and you can download any of them that are not on your iPad at any time.

Tap on any book to open that book's page, where you can buy the book by tapping on the price (you can also buy the book by tap-

ping on the price next to the book cover image); download a free preview by tapping on the GET SAMPLE button; go to the author's page, where you can see other books by the same author; set an alert so that you are notified when that author releases a new book; Tell A Friend about the book, which takes the information and puts it in an e-mail for you; and see reviews of the book.

READING iBOOKS

There is more than one reading mode in iBooks, and it depends on the type of book being read. The most common type of book in the iBookstore right now is the regular eBook, which is the electronic equivalent of the printed book.

Since the iPad is an electronic device, though, a new breed of eBooks is starting to arrive. These new eBooks have extras that are not available in the printed versions, including embedded video and audio clips, hyperlinks to web services, and other extras. The third type of eBook that can be read in iBooks is a PDF file. This allows you to access any PDF in iBooks without any extra apps. (More on PDFs in Chapter 8.)

Normal Books

To read an eBook, just tap on it to open it. When the eBook first opens, the screen shows a menu bar across the top and a slider (with a page number and current location identifier) across the bottom. Both of these tools fade from view after a few minutes, but you can bring them back by tapping on the top of the page.

The menu on the top of the page consists of the following:

- **Library:** Tap this to go back to the Library view showing your book.

- **Contents/Bookmarks/Notes:** Tap this and the view changes to the Contents/Book-marks/Notes page. This allows you to jump to any chapter or bookmark you have set. You can also see any notes or highlighted sections that you have in the book. That's right—you can make notes or highlight text in any book easily, but it's not obvious how to do this. To leave a note or highlight text, do the following:

1. Open a book.

2. Hold your finger on the word where you want to leave a note or highlight.

3. Wait until the Define | Highlight | Note | Search menu appears. You can now use the blue handles to select the text.

4. Tap on Define and a definition appears along with buttons that allow you to Search Web or Search Wikipedia.

5. Tap Highlight and you get a choice of five colors and the ability to add a note.

6. Tap on Note and the note form appears.

7. Tap on Search and the iBooks app will search the whole book for the term.

- **Appearance:** This button allows you change the brightness of the screen, change the font size and type, and change the theme. As I write this, there are three themes that you can use: Normal, Sepia, and Night. The Normal Theme is black text on a white background, the Sepia Theme is black text on a light brown background, and the Night Theme is white text on a black background. The Theme menu also allows you to turn on or off the Full Screen mode. With the full screen turned on, you get more text on the page, but in all honesty, it doesn't make much difference.

NOTE

To remove a note, tap on the Note tab in Contents/Bookmarks/Notes to see the notes, then swipe from right to left on the note you want to remove and tap Delete when it appears.

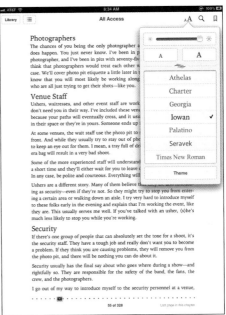

Figure 7-5
In the Reading mode of the iBooks app, you can change the brightness, size of the text, font, and theme of the current book by tapping on the Appearance button on the top right corner.

Figure 7-6

When you turn a page in an eBook, it looks as if you are actually turning the page.

Figure 7-7

The Beatles Yellow Submarine enhanced book has embedded video clips right in the page. You just tap on the Play buttons to watch them.

- **Search:** The Search menu allows you to search for any term in the book.

- **Bookmark:** Tap on the bookmark icon and it places a bookmark on the current page. To get back to the bookmark, tap on the Contents/Bookmarks/Notes menu icon and pick Bookmarks.

The reading experience on the iPad is really cool and very intuitive. Want to turn the page? Just use your finger to swipe from right to left and the page turns. Swipe from left to right and the page turns back the other way. The animation that actually shows the page turning adds to the whole experience. One last thing is the slider across the bottom of the screen. This slider allows you to speedily get to any page in the book just by sliding from one side to the other. It also lets you know how many pages are left in the current chapter. Just a quick word of warning: I have inadvertently skipped back hundreds of pages instead of turning just one page when I swiped across the slider from right to left. Just make sure you swipe in the middle and not the bottom edge to turn a page.

Enhanced Books

Many of the newer eBooks are now embedding audio and video as part of the books. This means that there are some new controls showing up in the books themselves. One of the best examples of this is the free eBook based on *The Beatles Yellow Submarine*. You can get it for free in the iBookstore by searching for "Yellow Submarine" and then choosing the free iBook version. This children's book includes animated aspects on each page along with a series of video clips. This book also has a narration feature that you can turn on by tapping on the speaker icon at the top of the screen.

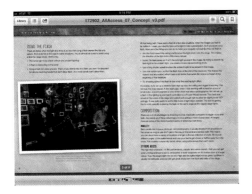

Figure 7-8
Reading a PDF proof of one of my books on the iPad gives me an idea of how the book will look when it's printed. There are no fancy page curls when you turn pages in PDF view.

PDFs
The PDF view is the simplest view of all. There are no fancy page graphics or text options. You turn the page by swiping from left to right or right to left, and you can jump to any page by using the thumbnails located across the bottom of the screen. Each page can be made bigger or smaller in the same way as you would an image—by placing two fingers on the screen and moving them together to make the page smaller or by moving them further apart to make the page bigger.

iBOOKS ALTERNATIVES
iBooks is not the only app for reading eBooks available on the iPad. There are also apps by the other big eBook reader companies including the Kindle app from Amazon and the Nook app from Barnes & Noble. There was a lot of talk in 2011 about what Amazon and Barnes & Noble were going to do regarding the terms of service for apps that allow in-

app purchases, and specifically about buying content for the Kindle app or the Nook app on the iPad.

To recap the problem, Amazon and Barnes & Noble would have to pay Apple if there was to be eBook purchasing from within the apps. Both Amazon and Barnes & Noble realized that they still wanted their readers (apps) on the iPad, but without having to pay Apple a piece of each book sold, and the solution was to just remove any method of purchasing content from inside the app. So if you want to buy Kindle books or Nook eBooks you have to do it through a web browser and not through the app—there isn't any mention of purchasing books or links to do so from the app. Lets start with the Amazon Kindle app and website, and then move to the Nook and the Barnes & Noble website.

Kindle App
The Kindle app allows you to turn your iPad into a Kindle book reader and gives you the ability to read Kindle-formatted eBooks on your iPad. This is a really good thing since Kindle is the most popular eBook reader and the Amazon Kindle store is the biggest eBook marketplace.

As I mentioned earlier, what this app allows you to do is read all those books on your iPad, but what it doesn't have is a direct way to buy any of those Kindle books. It used to, but due to a change in the Apple terms of service for apps it was removed. It doesn't matter because I will tell you how to buy Kindle books and install them on your iPad without much work.

The first thing that you need to do is download the Kindle app and then sign in to your Kindle account or sign up for one—you will see a window that asks for your Amazon

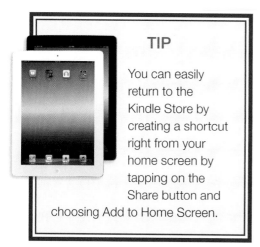

TIP

You can easily return to the Kindle Store by creating a shortcut right from your home screen by tapping on the Share button and choosing Add to Home Screen.

Figure 7-10
The Kindle Store on the iPad in the Safari web browser. Amazon has done a great job with this—it is easy to get around and use.

Figure 7-9
You must enter e-mail and password to access your Kindle books.

account e-mail address and the Amazon account password. After you enter your e-mail and password, tap Register this Kindle. If you don't have a Kindle account, you need to set one up. Here's how:

1. Turn on the iPad.

2. Tap the Safari app.

3. Navigate to www.amazon.com/manageyourkindle.

4. A sign in screen opens, asking you to enter the e-mail you want to use at amazon.com.

5. Check the No, I am a new customer button.

6. Enter your name, e-mail, and password info. Tap on Create account and you're done!

You can also use your Kindle app to read documents, including PDFs and Word docs. When you register the Kindle app as a Kindle device, it gives you an e-mail address that you can send documents to. This e-mail will be in the format of *xxxxxxx*@kindle.com and although you can't answer these e-mails or

Figure 7-11
The individual pages for the books allow you to buy right now and read in either the app or in a web browser.

use it for correspondence, it is very cool that you can e-mail documents to your Kindle app. You do need an Internet connection to access these documents.

To buy Kindle books in the iPad, just do the following:

1. Turn on the iPad.

2. Tap on the Safari app.

3. Navigate to www.amazon.com/ipadkindlestore.

4. Browse the titles available. Choose one and tap on the Buy button.

5. Choose "Read in App" to read the book on your iPad Kindle app. You can also "Read in Browser" to read the book in the Kindle Cloud Reader.

6. When you tap Read in App, the Kindle app opens automatically and the book you just purchased starts downloading.

Reading your book using the Kindle app on the iPad is really easy and the controls work exactly the way you think they would. You can turn the pages by swiping right to left or left to right. Tap on the bottom of the page to bring up a menu that allows you to change the text font or point size, jump to any of the chapters, search the book, or sync the book to the furthest location across all your devices.

If you have a Kindle and want to be able to access your Kindle purchases on the iPad or would just rather shop at Amazon than the iBookstore, then this app is a must.

NOOK App

The NOOK app enables you to read books purchased for the NOOK eBook reader from Barnes & Noble on your iPad. The NOOK app requires a Barnes & Noble account, but with that you get access to free eBook samples; more than 500,000 free eBooks; and over 2 million NOOK books, magazines, and newspapers. When you first launch the app, it asks you to sign in to your account. If you have an account, then tap the sign in button and enter your information. If you don't have an account, you need to set one up before going any further:

1. Turn on the iPad.

2. Tap on the Safari app.

3. Navigate to www.nook.com.

4. On the top of the browser page there is a My Account tab. Tap on it, and then tap on Account Settings.

5. Tap on the Create an Account button and follow the directions.

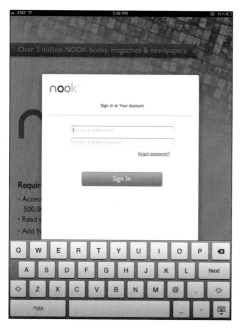

Figure 7-12
The NOOK app needs your Barnes & Noble account information so that your purchases in the NOOK store website will show up in the app.

Figure 7-13
The individual book page in the NOOK store.

Now when you launch the iPad app, you enter that same B&N account information. To purchase NOOK books on the iPad, you need to use the Safari Internet browser because purchasing from inside the app is not supported:

1. Turn on the iPad.

2. Open the Safari app.

3. Navigate to www.nook.com.

4. Tap Sign In on the top of the page and enter your account information.

5. Tap on NOOK book.

6. Search for a book you want to buy and tap on the Buy Now button.

Now the NOOK website looks good, but in terms of use it seems to crash a lot. The NOOK app works great, but its website on the iPad can drive you crazy, since it seems to hang up during the purchasing processes, leaving you wondering what to do. I recommend using this app only if you own a NOOK and want to read your previous NOOK purchase on the iPad.

NEWSSTAND

When the original iPad was released, many people thought that it would be the savior of the floundering magazine and newspaper market—and with the release of the Newsstand app in iOS 5 that might just end up being the case. The app isn't really anything special or revolutionary, but instead it just makes it much easier to keep all your maga-

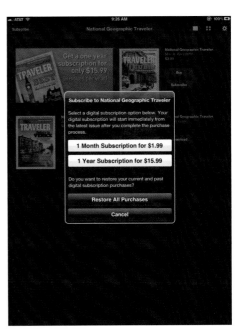

Figure 7-14
The Newsstand showing seven magazines that I currently have on my iPad.
The Store button on the top right allows
me to go to a special store with Newsstand content.

Figure 7-15
The *National Geographic Traveler*
magazine is a free app and offers a free
sample issue, but if you want the magazine you have to pay.

zines and newspapers in one place. It also has
a direct link to the magazine and newspaper
apps that can be used in the app.

While many iPad users might not know what
the Newsstand app does or what it is used for,
others are starting to use it and publishers are
seeing an increase in digital subscriptions. For
example, Conde Nast reported a 268 percent
jump in digital subscriptions since the Newsstand app was released in October 2011.

Using the Newsstand is really easy, since it is
basically just a bookshelf accessed by a single
tap. The Newsstand app comes preloaded
on your iPad and when you first tap on it,
it is just an empty shelf. On the top right of

the book shelf is the Store button. Tap it and
you are taken to the Newsstand section of
the App Store where you can get a variety of
publications, ranging from *Good Housekeeping*
magazine to *U.S. News Weekly* for the iPad.

As you will see, most of the publications
listed are free—that's right, free. But that's
actually a little misleading since the app is
only a gateway to the actual publication and
most of those are not free. So for example,
tap on the "free" *National Geographic Traveler*
magazine app and the store closes and the
Newsstand app opens with the new magazine
on the top left part of the shelf. Tap on your
new magazine and what you get is an option
to buy the latest issue for $3.99, or you can

subscribe to the magazine for $15.99. You can also download a free sample issue to see if you like the publication. So while the app is free, the magazine isn't.

The advantage to the Newsstand app is that all your publications are in the same place and the apps are updated automatically, showing you when you have new issues of publications you subscribe to. This makes it easy to see what you have read and what's new.

SUBSCRIPTIONS

When the iPad 2 was released, Apple announced its plans for a subscription model for content on the iPad and ignited a fire-storm of controversy. To offer subscriptions on the iPad, Apple takes a 30% cut and the publisher cannot offer a link to a website that bypasses this or offer a cheaper alternative through the app. Many people believed that the subscription model would fail, but with the release of the new iPad the subscription model is still standing and growing.

I currently subscribe to two magazines on the iPad. One is *Wired*, a traditional paper magazine that was one of the first magazines to come out with an iPad version, the other is *Light It*, a magazine designed for the iPad only. Both magazines allow me to archive older issues and download newer content. One of the big differences is that although *Wired* still puts out a paper version of the magazine and needs to appeal to a wider audience, the *Light It* magazine doesn't and can appeal to a smaller targeted audience.

Figure 7-16
One of the main sticking points for publishers when Apple announced the subscription model was that the publishers wanted the subscriber information. Now that decision is in the hands of the consumer, who can decide whether to share that info with the publisher.

PART 3

Work and School

Your Portable Office

The Skim

I'll let you in on a little secret: I do all my writing on an Apple MacBook Pro using the Pages application. One of my favorite features is that the Pages program on my computer works a lot like the Pages app on my iPad. I never have to think about saving my files because it is done all the time automatically. I can't tell you how much comfort that brings me when I'm working.

I have also started to do a lot more work directly on the iPad now, and the best part is that I didn't even realize that I was doing it. Instead of going to my office and turning on the laptop, I just tapped the Home key on my iPad, tapped on Dropbox, picked the file I was working on, and tapped it to open it. When I was working on the last book, I did all the PDF markups in iAnnotate on my iPad. It was easy and convenient. Then there are the iWork applications (Pages, Numbers, and Keynote) that Apple adapted into iPad apps.

iWORK

Apple created three apps that together to make up the iWork suite:

- **Pages:** a word processor app
- **Numbers:** a spreadsheet app
- **Keynote:** a presentation app

121

Figure 8-1
The iCloud Settings showing that
Documents & Data is turned on.

---

iWORK BETA

In the past, documents created with the iWork apps on the iPad could be shared using the iWork.com public beta. However, Apple is shutting down that service on July 31, 2012. The reason that I am mentioning this is that the iWork.com beta service is still mentioned in the version of the software that is available as I write this book, and the images in this book show that. According to Apple, as of March 2012 there were already over 40 million documents stored on iCloud by millions of iWork customers.

Each of the iWork apps runs on the iPad and retails for $9.99. That's just under $30 for three apps that turn your iPad into a viable business tool. Now there is no reason to buy all three apps if you don't need them. Not everyone needs presentation software, so buying Keynote might not be worth it to some. You don't need to have all three apps at the same time for them to work, and you can always start with one app and buy the others as you need them.

All three of the iWork apps use the iCloud service to keep your documents available to all your devices and your computer. When the files created with the iWork apps are saved to the iCloud, it allows you to access the files using any web browser and any other iPad or iPhone as long as the device is signed into the same iCloud account. For example,

I can create a letter on my iPad and access it on my iPhone. For this to work, you have to make sure that the Documents & Data settings are turned on in the iCloud settings.

To turn on the iCloud Documents & Data settings, just do the following:

1. Turn on the iPad.

2. Tap on the Settings app.

3. Tap on iCloud in the list on the left.

4. Make sure that the Documents & Data setting is turned on.

This now allows the iWork apps to access the iCloud and save the documents you create on the iPad. It also gives the apps access to your other files stored on the iCloud.

With the iCloud service enabled, the first time you run any of the iWork apps you get a pop-up window that lets you know that the

Figure 8-2
When opening Keynote for the first time, you are asked if you want to use iCloud.

iCloud service is available and asks if you want to use it to "Automatically store your documents in the cloud to keep them up-to-date across all your devices and the web." You can either tap on Later or Use iCloud.

If you tap Use iCloud, every document you create from then on will be saved in the iCloud. Now what this doesn't say is that it will automatically sync with the iWork programs on your computer, but I believe that Apple is working on that functionality and by the time this book is out I hope that the desktop versions will automatically sync with the iCloud and the iPad apps. Ok, that might just be a dream but I envision a future where I will be able to access a document and edit it without having to worry where the document

is or what I am using to edit it. Seriously, how great would it be to work on a paper at work on your computer, and then access it from your iPad later at home without having to create multiple copies across all the devices? I can wish, can't I?!

Since the basic file handling and iCloud access for all three iWork apps work the same, let's look at the basics for all three, and then we will get into the details for each app.

After you open an iWork app for the first time and are asked if you want to use iCloud, you then get the option of viewing a basic tutorial. The good news is that these tutorials include some good basic information and they are available for viewing and reviewing anytime.

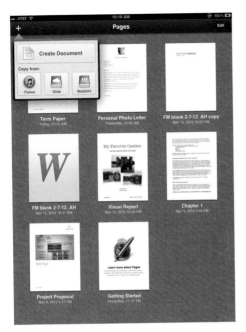

Figure 8-3
Tapping on the + in Pages brings up the new document menu where you can either import a document from iTunes, iDisk, or WebDAV, or Create Document in Pages (as shown).

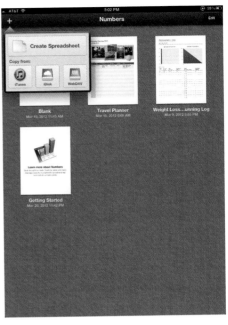

Figure 8-4
Tapping on the + in Numbers opens the Create Spreadsheet menu.

• Classic Letter	• Poster
• Formal Letter	• Syllabus
• Personal Photo Letter	• Party Invite
• Modern Photo Letter	• Thank You Card
• Classic Resume	• Recipe
• Project Proposal	• Flyer

Each of the apps has a great set of templates that are available when you create a new document. First, open a new document, and then you can pick from the templates. In the Documents view, tap the + on the top left corner and pick Create Document (in Pages, see Figure 8-3), Spreadsheet (in Numbers, see Figure 8-4), or Presentation (in Keynote, see Figure 8-5).

After you tap on the new document in the individual apps, the templates open. In the Pages app you can choose from the following templates:

• Blank	• Term Paper
• Modern Photo Letter	• Visual Report

In the Numbers app you can choose from the following templates:

• Blank	• Travel Planner
• Checklist	• Expense Report
• Loan Comparison	• Invoice
• Budget	• Employee Schedule
• Mortgage Calculator	• Team Organization
• Personal Savings	• GPA
• Auto Log	• Stats Lab
• Weight Loss & Running Log	• Attendance

Figure 8-5
Tapping on the + in Keynote opens the
Create Presentation menu.

In the Keynote app, you can pick themes
instead of templates:

- White
- Black
- Gradient
- Photo Portfolio
- Renaissance
- Cerulean
- Showroom
- Chalkboard
- Modern Portfolio
- Harmony
- Parchment
- Craft

In the Document view of the apps, you will
see an Edit button on the top right corner
of the page. Tap the Edit button and the
documents start to wiggle and you see three
options on the top left corner—a share icon,
a duplicate icon, and a trash can icon. When
you tap on one or more of the wiggling documents you can then tap on the duplicate icon
to make copies of the selected documents,
or you can tap on the trash can to delete the
selected documents. If you select a single document, you can tap the Share button, which
brings up the Share options. Currently there
are five Share options, but the iWork.com
and iDisk options are no longer viable since
Apple has discontinued those services and
I expect that a future update to the app will
not include these options. The other three
Share options are:

- **E-mail:** This attaches the selected document to an e-mail and allows you to send it
  to someone. When you tap E-mail, you get
  to pick the file format to use. You can send
  the file as either an iWork version (Pages,
  Numbers, or Keynote), a Microsoft Office
  equivalent (Word, Excel, or PowerPoint), or
  as a PDF.

- **iTunes:** This allows you to transfer the file
  to the computer through iTunes. When
  you tap iTunes, you then get to pick the file
  format to use. You can send the file out as
  either an iWork version (Pages, Numbers,
  or Keynote), a Microsoft Office equivalent
  (Word, Excel, or PowerPoint), or as a PDF.

- **WebDAV:** This allows you to sign into a
  WebDAV server. You will need the Server
  address, User Name, and Password. If this
  is something you need, you will have the
  information from your workplace. You will
  then be able to upload the documents to
  the WebDAV server

Before taking a closer look at the individual
iWork apps there is something really important that you need to know. The apps save
constantly, so any change you make to a file
is immediately saved when you make it, not
later when you go to save the file. There is
no Save command in these apps at all. This is
really important since it can impact the way
you work on your files.

Now for those of us (the few, the proud) who
use the iWork applications on the Mac, we
are already used to this cool feature and no
longer worry about constantly saving files
since the programs do it for us. However, if
you are a person who sometimes creates new
documents based on already-created documents and then uses the Save As feature
to create a new document at the end of the

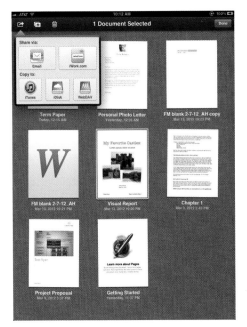

Figure 8-6
Tap Edit, and then select the document you want to export and tap the Share button to bring up the Share options.

editing process, this can be a real change in thinking. There is a way around this, and that is to duplicate the document before you start to edit. For example, if you want to make changes to a letter but you also want to keep the original, you need to first duplicate the file, and then edit it.

All three of the iWork apps work in the same way, so this process works for Numbers and Keynote as well, but I am using Pages for this example.

1. Tap on the Pages app.

2. Make sure you are in the Documents view, which shows thumbnails of all the documents available to edit. If you are in the document editing window, tap on the

Documents button on the top left corner.

3. Tap on the Edit button on the top right corner and the apps will start to wiggle.

4. Tap on the document you want to duplicate to select it (it will be outlined in yellow).

5. Tap on the Duplicate button, it is the second from the left on the top of the screen and looks like two squares over each other with a + in the middle.

6. You now have a duplicate document that you can rename by tapping on the name under the document and entering a new name.

7. Tap on Done after entering the new name, then tap on the document to edit it.

Now let's look at the apps in a little more detail:

The Pages App
The Pages app is a word processor, but you can also use it to make some pretty cool page layouts and reports. As listed earlier, the app comes with a cool list of templates that cover everything from letters to resumes, and term papers to recipes. When you first create a new document in Pages, you get to choose one of the templates, or just use a blank template.

Once you open the document you can start editing it.

The screen layout of the Pages app adapts to what you are doing to take advantage of the iPad screen. The app tries to show only the tools needed for what you are doing at the moment, keeping open as much of the screen real estate as possible for viewing your document. For example, tap on Text and the Text menu appears on the top of the screen giving you access to the fonts, text size, and

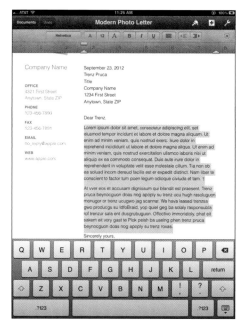

Figure 8-7
The Pages layout changes depending on what is selected on the screen. Here the text is highlighted, so the Text menu is shown at the top of the screen.

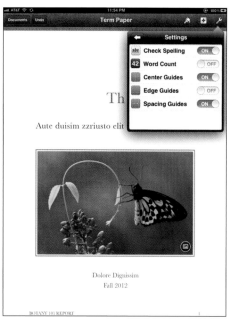

Figure 8-8
The Settings menu in Pages.

other text editing options. If there is an image in your document and you tap on it, then the Text menu disappears, the keyboard goes away, and the Image Editing menu appears. This keeps the interface clutter free.

Across the top of the screen there are five buttons that are always there. The five buttons are the following:

- **Documents:** This button takes you out of the editing mode and back into the Documents view. Here you can see the files that are on your iPad or in the iCloud service, if you are signed in.

- **Undo/Redo:** This button allows you to undo or redo the last commands. Tap it

to undo, hold your finger on it to bring up redo.

- **Formatting:** This button looks like a little paintbrush. Tap this button to change the style of the text, change the fonts, and adjust the layout.

- **Media:** Next to the paintbrush is the Media button; it is a + on a square background that when tapped allows you to insert media, tables, charts, and shapes.

- **Tools Menu:** The final icon looks like a small wrench. Tap this button to share or print your document; search inside the document; set up a document; access the Pages setup; access the help menu; and access the Settings menu, where you can turn the spell check on and off, get a word count, and turn on or off the guides.

Typing on the iPad can be a little awkward—especially if you are holding the device in two hands—but there is a neat trick that splits the keyboard in two. You can tap and hold on the Hide Keyboard button until the Split Keyboard menu pops up. (The Hide Keyboard button is in the bottom right corner and looks like a keyboard with an arrow under it.) Tap on Split Keyboard, and the keyboard comes apart with half on one side of the screen and the half on the other side, making it easier to type with your thumbs when you hold the device in two hands.

But there is a much cooler way to do the same thing, or at least I think it is. When the keyboard is together, just place a finger on each side of the keyboard and swipe out to the edges—and the keyboard comes apart! When the keyboard is apart, just place a finger on each edge and push the two halves together to make the keyboard whole again.

The Numbers App

I have said it before and will say it again—I am not a number-crunching type of guy and never did use a lot of spreadsheets. But while this Spreadsheet app can do a lot of the calculations of a standard spreadsheet, it is really designed for the rest of us.

When you're in the app and you tap on the + and then Create Spreadsheet, the templates that appear for you to pick from include options such as Budget, Mortgage Calculator, Personal Savings, and Weight Loss/Running Log. It has an Attendance Sheet, a GPA Calculator, and even a Travel Planner. Of course, there is also a Blank spreadsheet that allows you to enter anything yourself.

The Numbers app screen layout is very similar to the Pages app, where most of the screen is taken up with the actual spreadsheet instead

Figure 8-9
The Blank spreadsheet showing the table formatting available.

Figure 8-10
Need to edit a cell? Just tap on the cell, tap on the Formatting button, and then tap on Cells to choose the type of formatting.

of unneeded menus and palettes. Across the top of the screen are the Formatting, Media, and Tools Menu buttons. If you want to select a cell to edit, just tap on it. If you want to change the formatting of a cell or table, tap the Formatting menu button (it looks like a little paintbrush) and you can change how each cell is formatted.

For a spreadsheet to be useful to me, I need to be able to access it whenever I need it. That's why the Numbers app and iCloud service are so useful together. I can create a spreadsheet on my iPad and, since it is kept in the iCloud, I can access it on my iPhone. For example, if I create a Travel Planner spreadsheet with a packing list, I can access and update the spreadsheet from my iPhone, and then when I'm back on my iPad the new info is automatically there.

The Keynote App

The first thing that you will notice when you launch Keynote is that the app runs only in landscape mode. This is because Keynote is a presentation software that is meant to be shown on a monitor or television, or using a projector and screen setup. Since the orientation of all of those displays is landscape, there is no reason for Keynote to work in portrait mode.

The Keynote app offers 12 different templates that range from simple single colors like Black and White to more complex views like

Figure 8-11
Adding a slide to your presentation is easy. Tap on the + at the bottom of the thumbnail view and then pick the type of slide you want to add.

Figure 8-12
Tap on the Tools button to bring up the Tools menu.

Showroom and Modern Portfolio. Tap on the template to open a new Presentation, and the first slide is shown. Tap on the + at the bottom of the thumbnail view to add a new slide from the available template. Building a presentation here is really easy. Tap on any element to change it by either using the menus that appear or tapping on the Formatting tool (the paintbrush icon).

Where Keynote really shines is when connected to an external display and used to give presentations. The output on the big screen is controlled by swiping on the iPad and there is even a built-in pointer. When on any slide, hold your finger on the screen and a bright red dot appears on the screen. Without picking your finger up, you can now slide it around just like you would if you were using a laser pointer.

If you have an Apple TV, then you can take the Keynote app to the next level by wirelessly using the iPad to give presentations. You need to have an Apple TV that is second generation or later, and it needs to be running iOS 5.1 or later. Both the Apple TV and the iPad need to be on the same Wi-Fi network. To make this work, double-click the iPad's Home button to open the multi-task bar, and then swipe from right to left where the volume and play controls are located. An AirPlay button will appear. This will give you the presenter screen on your iPad so you can see your notes and the full presentation that is playing on the television connected to the Apple TV.

OFFICE ON THE iPAD

Start talking about doing work on the iPad and the first question that often comes up is, "What about Microsoft Office?" I am surprised that Microsoft hasn't created a version of its best-selling business applications for the iPad yet. In February 2012, a rumor surfaced along with photos showing a Microsoft Office iPad app. As I write this, there is no sign of the app in the App Store but I believe that sooner or later Microsoft will realize that there are a huge number of people with iPads and most of them would love an Office app. Until that happens, there are other options.

You can export all of the iWork apps files into their Microsoft equivalents. You can also use the iWork applications to edit Office documents on the iPad using the iCloud. Just follow along:

1. Open a web browser on your computer.

2. Navigate to iCloud.com.

3. Sign in to your iCloud account.

4. Click on the iWork logo.

5. Click on the gear symbol in the top right corner.

6. Click Upload Document and a pop-up window opens allowing you to navigate your computer.

7. Find the file you want to upload and click on it, and then click Choose and the file will be uploaded.

The next part is to open the file on the iPad:

1. Turn on the iPad.

2. Open the iWork app for the file you want to open (Pages for Word docs, Numbers for Excel spreadsheets, or Keynote for Power-Point presentations).

3. In the Documents view, tap on the new Office document to open it.

4. The app will now convert the file but gives you the option to open as a copy, preserving the original.

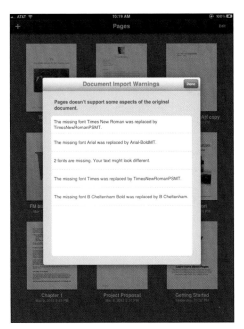

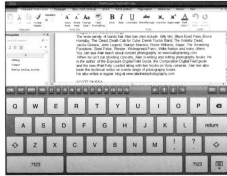

Figure 8-14
Using the CloudOn app you can access the Office apps and open and edit your files in Microsoft Office on the iPad, as long as you are connected to the Internet.

Figure 8-13
When you open a Word document in Pages on the iPad, a message shows what had to be changed or converted in the file.

5. Any changes that are made to the document are then shown. These changes are mostly formatting changes, since the iPad has a limited number of fonts and so substitutions often have to be made. Also, because Pages doesn't run the same exact way that Microsoft Word does, there might be problems with any custom templates or specialized formatting.

6. The document opens in the app.

The Office file is now transferred to and editable on the iPad, and the copy is automatically saved on the iCloud service. That means you can download the edited copy onto your computer from iCloud anytime, and because you can pick the file type when you download

files from the iCloud.com site you can open the edited file in Office on your computer.

CloudOn

There is a new free service available for the iPad that promises to bring together a web-based version of Microsoft Office and your Dropbox account, which allows you to get Office files on your iPad and updates them automatically. The only downside is that you have to be connected to the Internet. This service is the real deal and I suggest that anyone looking for Microsoft Office on the iPad give this a serious look.

Download the CloudOn app from the App Store and launch it. You can sign up for an account right on the iPad. Transferring files in and out of the app is done by Dropbox, so you will want to sign up for a Dropbox account. (Dropbox is covered in the next section.)

One very cool feature of the CloudOn service is that it automatically saves your documents when you exit the program, in the same way

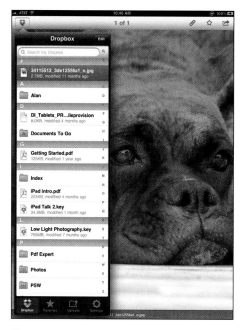

Figure 8-15
Dropbox allows you to access your files from anywhere you have Internet connectivity. It supports multiple file types and you can view all of them right in the app.

that the iWork apps do. This means that the edited version is in Dropbox automatically.

Dropbox

If there is one app or service that makes the iPad really useful as a portable office solution, it is Dropbox. Dropbox is basically a cloud-based folder that holds your files and automatically syncs between the computer, iPad, Internet, and any other app that accesses it so that the files are always up-to-date on all of your devices.

The beauty of Dropbox is that it is easy to set up, easy to use, and free. That's right, the basic service is free. There are four steps to using Dropbox on your iPad and your computer:

1. Download the Dropbox app to your iPad.

2. Sign up for a Dropbox account.

3. Download the Dropbox program to your computer.

4. Sign in to link the iPad to the Internet and to any computers you have Dropbox installed on. The Dropbox shared folder is now available for use

Getting the Dropbox app is easy, just go to the App Store and search for Dropbox, and then install it. Tap on the app to launch it and sign up for an account right on the front page of the app. All you need to do is enter your first name, last name, e-mail, and a password, and then tap on Create Free Account.

Once you are signed into Dropbox, any file you put in the Dropbox folder is accessible from the computer, the Dropbox website, and the iPad. In Dropbox you can share folders with others so that multiple people can access the same folder. You can also upload photos stored on your iPad into Dropbox, which enables you to send images to others automatically. To upload your images directly into the Dropbox folder, just do the following:

1. Tap on the Dropbox app on your iPad.

2. Log into your account.

3. Tap on the Dropbox menu on the top right corner.

4. Tap on the Uploads button on the bottom of the menu.

5. Tap on the + on the top right corner of the menu.

6. Tap on the photos you want to upload.

7. Tap on the Dropbox button on the bottom of the list to pick a location to save the image.

8. Tap on Choose to pick the folder or tap on Create Folder to make a new folder. If you make a new folder, type in the name and tap create, and then click on Choose with the new folder highlighted.

9. When the view showing the selected images is back on the screen. Tap on the Upload button located on the top of the menu to transfer the files to Dropbox.

Hopefully this is a sign of things to come, and soon we will have the ability to upload any type of file from the iPad to Dropbox. Right now the only files that can be added from the iPad to Dropbox are photo files. That is, you can't create documents in the iWork apps and then load them into Dropbox.

ALL ABOUT PDFs

PDF files are everywhere and the iPad is no different; even the iBooks app will read PDF files. There are some great PDF apps for the iPad, but to me two stand above the rest. The first is iAnnotate, which is great for marking up documents, and the second is PDF Export, which enables you to fill out PDF forms among other things.

One of the most common ways I get a PDF onto my iPad is by e-mail. When you get an e-mail with an embedded PDF and you want to open it on your iPad, hold your finger on the PDF icon in the e-mail. A menu opens with options; tap on Open In ... and then tap the PDF app you want to use. This opens the file right in the chosen app.

To e-mail a PDF out of the app, just tap on the Export button at the top of the app when the document you want to export is shown. This will give you the option to Mail Document, Print, or Open In .... Tapping on Mail Document will save the file and embed it into an e-mail.

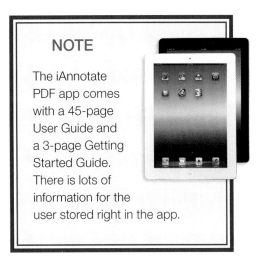

NOTE

The iAnnotate PDF app comes with a 45-page User Guide and a 3-page Getting Started Guide. There is lots of information for the user stored right in the app.

iAnnotate PDF ($9.99)

The iAnnotate PDF app is one of the most powerful PDF editor apps that I have come across. It allows you to fully annotate PDF files so that they can be read in standard PDF readers like Adobe Acrobat and Preview. This allows you to receive PDFs by e-mail, Dropbox, or through iTunes sync, and then mark them up and return them from the iPad. You can also customize the tool bars so that you see only the tools you use.

iAnnotate has a lot of annotating tools on the right side of the screen that you can hide at any time just by sliding the tab closed:

- **Note:** Just tap on the location where you want to leave a note.

- **Pencil:** You can use this to draw freehand on your document.

- **Highlight:** This tool enables you to highlight any text. Start by moving your finger over the text you want to select, and then remove your finger. You will see trim handles that allow you to adjust the selection. (This is great for those of us with fat fingers.)

Figure 8-16
I used iAnnotate to edit the PDF files from my last book right on the iPad. I loaded the files into Dropbox, and then accessed and marked them up on my iPad.

Figure 8-17
The full set of tools available in the app.

- **Freehand Highlight:** You can highlight anything in any color using this tool.

- **Underline:** You can underline the text on the page. The controls are the same as the highlight tool.

- **Typewriter:** This tool allows you to type notes directly onto the PDF. Tap the location where you want to type a note and the built-in keyboard appears.

- **Toolbox:** This is where the rest of the tools are hiding, and there are a lot of them. Fifty-six different tools to be exact, as you can see in figure 8-17 (which shows 35 of the possible 56 choices), and you can show any of them in the toolbar.

To access and edit the different toolbars, do the following:

1. Tap on a toolbar to select it.

2. Tap on the gear icon at the top of the toolbar to edit it or delete it.

3. In the Edit window, tap and drag a tool to the toolbar you want.

4. Tap on the + on the bottom of the menu to add more toolbars.

5. To access the toolbars, swipe over them to open.

You can set the toolbar to your liking and this can save a ton of time if you are a big PDF annotator. I know of no other PDF app that has this many tools and gives you this much control over where they are.

PDF Expert ($9.99)

The PDF Expert app allows you to not only read and annotate PDF documents, it also lets you actually fill out PDF forms. If filling out forms is important then this is the app for you, and since you can use it to annotate as well, it might just be the only PDF app you need on your iPad.

When you open the PDF Expert app you have four choices on the left:

- Documents
- Recents
- Network
- Settings

Tap on Documents and you will see two pre-loaded PDF files—a PDF Expert Guide and a What's New file. The Recents tab shows you the files you opened recently, which is very useful when you have a ton of files loaded. The Network tab allows you to transfer files over to the app without having to connect it by USB cable or by sending yourself an e-mail. When you tap on the Navigate button, you are presented with two options—the first is the address of the iPad on the network, the second is a button that tells the app to look for nearby servers including WebDAV servers. On the top left of the Network menu is the Add button. Tap this button to access your cloud-based storage, including MobileMe and Google Docs, but the solution that I use is Dropbox.

To set up the PDF Expert app to use Dropbox, just tap on the Dropbox button. Now enter your name and password for the Dropbox account. The Dropbox account will now be listed under the favorite servers in the Network list.

Tap on the Settings tab on the left and you get the following options:

- **Passkey Lock:** You can passcode lock the app so it requires a passkey to open it. This is great if you use the iPad for business and also let the kids play with it. It means they can't get into and delete the important stuff, but be careful you don't lose the passkey because there is no way to recover it.

- **Wi-Fi Drive:** This app allows you to share its data with computers on the network using WebDav protocol. There are detailed instructions to set this up right here.

- **PDF Viewer:** The Settings here allow you to turn Highlight lnks on and off and Highlight Form Fields. It is also where you can scroll pages either horizontally or vertically, and you can adjust the lowest page zoom to either page width or the whole page.

- **Auto-open:** Turn this option on and the documents will automatically open after being downloaded.

- **Support:** You can send feedback to the PDF Expert app team right here.

- **Legal Notes:** This includes all the legal stuff that no one ever reads.

To show the power of the app, here is a quick walk-through with a real-life example of getting, filling out, and retuning a PDF. I downloaded the 1040 form onto my computer since as I write this it is tax time here, but you can do this with any PDF form.

1. Open Dropbox on your computer.

2. Create a new folder in Dropbox called PDF Expert.

3. Put the 1040 PDF file into the PDF Expert folder in my Dropbox.

4. Open PDF Expert.

5. Tap on Network.

6. If you haven't added your Dropbox account, do so now (you can find instructions for this earlier in the chapter).

7. Open your Dropbox and tap on the PDF Expert Folder.

8. Tap Sync, which enables two-way synchronization. The folder is added to the Documents list and the Sync button will appear on the bottom left corner.

9. Tap Sync This Folder.

10. Tap on the file you want to edit (in this case it's the 1040 tax file).

11. All the fields that can be entered are highlighted.

12. Start entering the information into the form.

13. When you are done tap the Back button on the top left corner of the screen.

14. You will see a list of your documents.

15. Tap the Sync button on the bottom left corner.

16. Tap either Push Changes or Full Sync.

17. This syncs the PDF Expert folder with Dropbox so that the same file is now updated back on the computer.

If you are filling out PDF forms, then this app is the one to use. You can even add a signature. This really appealed to the geek in me, since you get to sign on the screen with your finger.

If you need to sign a PDF, just hold your finger on the screen until the Note | Text | Signature button appears, and then tap on Signature. This opens the Signature panel. You can change the color and size of the "pen" by tapping on the controls on the top

of the page. Then just sign your name on the dotted line. It might take a try or two. To start over tap on the New button on the top of the page—it looks like a blank page. Once you have the signature done, tap Save. Your signature will now appear in the PDF and you can position it and resize it as needed. If you need to change the signature or just want to experiment with using your finger to sign stuff, tap on the Pen tool on the top of the screen to open the Signature panel.

AIRPRINT AND ALTERNATIVES

We have covered getting the files on and off the iPad using iCloud and Dropbox, but what if you actually need to get a hard copy of your documents (or e-mails or anything else)? Apple has got you covered here with the AirPrint capability built right into the iPad. The only downside is that the printer needs to support the AirPrint protocol and the list of compatible printers, while growing, is not that long.

To see the complete and current list of AirPrint-compatible printers, visit support.apple.com/kb/HT4356.

There is no need to set up any drivers or special software. All you do is tap the Print command and pick an available printer and you are good to go. But if you don't have an AirPrint-enabled printer, there is a nifty computer application called Printopia that allows you to print to any printer connected to your computer as long as you are using a Mac. Sorry Windows users, this one isn't for you.

What you do is run the Printopia application on your Mac, which allows you to share the printer connected to your computer with the iPad. You can also print to virtual

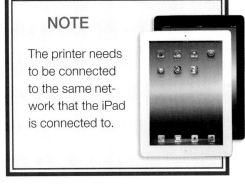

NOTE

The printer needs to be connected to the same network that the iPad is connected to.

Figure 8-18
The Printopia service allows me to print my e-mails (or anything else) to any printer attached to my Mac, even if the printer doesn't have AirPrint functionality.

printers to save any printouts to your Mac as PDFs. On the downside, Printopia costs $19.95, but there is a free demo. Go to www.ecamm.com/mac/printopia to check out this cool program.

There is no need to install anything on the iPad because it "sees" the Printopia printers as AirPrint printers. I'm sure that when I buy my next printer, it will have AirPrint built in, but for $19.99 I can use my current printer with the iPad and it works great.

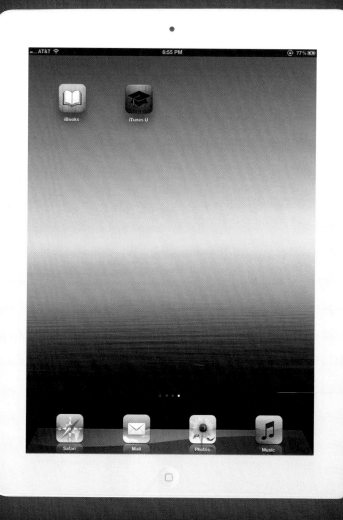

Education

The Skim

Textbooks • iBooks Author • iTunes U
Creating iTunes U Courses • iPads and Special Education

The year 2012 started with a push by Apple to make the iPad a part of every child's education, and while the push is aimed at high school to start with, it's pretty easy to see where this use of the technology can go. Apple made an announcement in early 2012 of a plan it hopes will change the way the iPad is used in education. The main features of Apple's plan include:

- An upgrade to the iBooks app
- The release of a new kind of electronic textbook and the free software needed to create these new textbooks
- Spinning off iTunes U as a separate app
- The introduction of entire courses available for free in iTunes U

TEXTBOOKS

There has been a lot of talk about Steve Jobs' vision for the future, and part of that vision was to "reinvent the textbook." Because traditional textbooks are expensive to make and expensive for schools to buy, a school needs to use the same textbook for years so that the initial investment pays off. This also means that textbooks are not updated very often and can become out-of-date soon after being published. There is also the physical wear and tear—including highlighting, dog-eared pages,

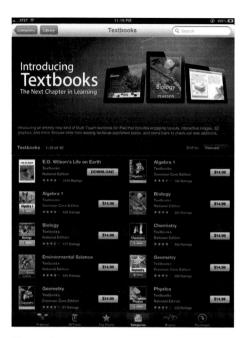

Figure 9-1
The current available textbooks.

- *Life on Earth;* Wilson Digital; free (first two chapters)

- *Algebra 1;* McGraw-Hill; $14.99; 1.11GB

- *Biology;* McGraw-Hill; $14.99; 1.5GB

- *Environmental Science;* Pearson; $14.99; 793MB

- *Geometry;* Pearson; $14.99; 2.31GB

- *Algebra 1;* Pearson; $14.99; 2.35GB

- *Biology;* Pearson; $14.99; 2.77GB

- *Chemistry;* McGraw-Hill; $14.99; 959MB

- *Geometry;* McGraw-Hill; $14.99; 1.22GB

- *Physics;* McGraw-Hill; $14.99; 1.25GB

The textbooks are available in their own section of the iBookstore. For more on accessing the iBookstore, just check out Chapter 7, which covers iBooks and the iBookstore in more detail.

It has been a long time since I was in high school, but I still remember those days quite clearly and I would have loved to use a textbook like this. So what is it exactly that makes these new textbooks better than their paper counterparts? The new electronic textbooks are interactive, with embedded video; photos and photo galleries; 3D objects; audio files; and the ability for students to highlight sections, bookmark important stuff, search the book and glossary, and take notes.

As you can see from the following figures, the textbooks can have embedded interactive images, quizzes with the ability to see if the answers are correct, and videos—and you can even manipulate objects in 3D with your fingers. In the past, it was difficult to create electronic textbooks with embedded content because the formatting tended to be very rigid. This new format allows a much greater flexibility in how the books look and function.

and basic abuse—that the books take. Think of it from a student's point of view: You get a book in which a student has already made notes in the margins or highlighted blocks of text, making the book difficult to use. What about taking your own notes or highlighting parts you want to review or study later? The answer is use an electronic textbook on your iPad. At least, that is the answer that Apple is going with.

According to Apple, the publishers who are responsible for 90% of the textbooks used in kindergarten to the twelfth grade are on board with the project. At the launch of the new textbooks and iBooks 2, there were eight full textbooks available, along with the first two chapters of a ninth textbook. There are now ten textbooks—let's look at the ten that are available.

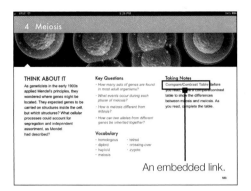

An embedded link.

Figure 9-2
The textbook can have questions, links (like the one to the Compare/Contrast Table), and even a vocabulary list that links to the word definitions.

There are some downsides to the textbook offerings and concept. The first is that the textbooks are large files, and just as large books are heavy and can easily fill up a student's backpack, the textbooks can fill up an iPad very easily as well. For example, the largest book currently available is the *Biology* textbook from Pearson, which comes in at 2.77GB, and the smallest is *Environmental Science*, from Pearson, at 793GB. If you take an average of 1.5GB per book, that 16GB iPad will fill up pretty fast. That also means that the textbooks cannot be downloaded over 3G networks, since they far exceed the 2MG data cap.

The second problem is a much bigger one: How are iPads to be purchased and distributed to the students? At the least expensive, iPads are $499 each—that's not cheap, especially with the way the textbook system works now. Under the current system, the school buys textbooks and loans them out to students for the year. The same textbook is usually used for five years. Will the school buy

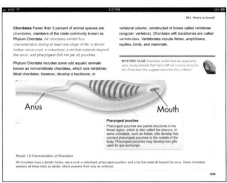

Figure 9-3
The photos and graphics are interactive, allowing the student to zoom in and out.

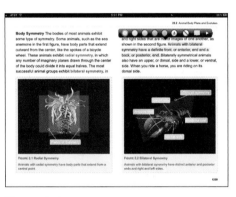

Figure 9-4
You can highlight sections, take notes, and rotate diagrams in 3D.

each kid an iPad and allow her or him to use the device for a year, and then give it back? And, how long will the iPad be usable? The original iPad that I still use once in a while is only two years old; while it works great now, I am not sure how it will be working in three years. And not all students are going to take the same care of their iPads as the school would like. I have seen how some of them treat their current textbooks and can only imagine what an iPad would look like after a few years. There are obviously a lot of things that still need to be worked out with the implementation of these textbooks and how iPads will be used in the classroom.

iBOOKS AUTHOR

Part of the Apple textbook announcement was the availability of the free application for the creation of iBooks textbooks. Technically, the application can be used to create any kind of iBooks, but the push is for the creation of textbooks.

The good news is that the application is free to anyone with an Apple computer running OS X 10.7.2 or later. That means that if you are running a Windows machine, you are out of luck right now—there is no way to easily create the same type of interactive textbooks for the iPad on a PC. The idea behind the iBooks Author software is that anyone can create a textbook quickly and easily, and the software allows just that. The hope is that there will be an explosion of iBooks content created easily and quickly.

iBooks Author is available only through the Apple App Store on the Mac. Just search for iBooks Author and you will see the app is available for free.

When you first open iBooks Author you are presented with six templates and, again, although you can write any type of iBook, these templates are all geared toward textbooks. The six templates are:

- Basic
- Contemporary
- Modern Type
- Classic
- Editorial
- Craft

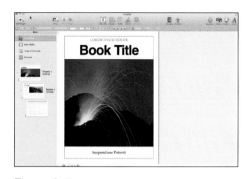

Figure 9-5
The iBooks Author layout showing the Editorial Template.

To get started, simply click on the template that you want to use. The application then opens to the main page where you can create your own book. The layout and controls are very similar to the Apple iWork applications (the Apple versions of a word processor called Pages, a spreadsheet application called Numbers, and a presentation software called Keynote), and if you have used the Pages Word Processor before, this will look really familiar.

The screen is divided into three parts, with controls across the top, book layout on the left, and the working area ring in the middle as shown in Figure 9-5.

Now it's just a matter of adding content and creating your book. You can add pages, and adjust the text and orientation. You really can do just about anything that you can think of, and even better, you can save the design as a template, allowing you to use it multiple times so all of your books to have the same look and feel.

A neat feature of iBooks Author includes the addition of widgets, which allows you to add Galleries, Media, Reviews, Keynote

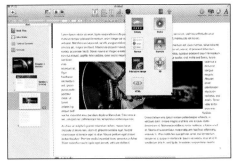

Figure 9-6
The iBooks Author application makes it easy to add content of various types.

files, Interactive elements, 3D elements, and HTML directly into the book.

Once you have created the book in the app, it's time to see how it actually looks on an iPad. Here's how:

1. Connect your iPad to the computer with the supplied USB cable.

2. Turn on the iPad.

3. Tap on the iBooks app.

4. Click on the Preview button in iBooks Author.

5. Select the iPad from the list that opens.

6. Click on Preview at the bottom of the list.

7. Click OK on the warning that iBooks needs to be open. (iBooks does need to be open for this to work.)

8. The book will be transferred over to the iPad. Now you can see what the book looks like right on the iPad.

This application really puts the power of publishing into the hands of just about everyone.

iTUNES U

iTunes U is a collection of classes and courses from schools available through iTunes, and it is growing every day. You can download the classes and courses directly onto your iPad or computer, and although iTunes U has been available for years, the new focus is on full courses instead of just individual lectures.

Part of Apple's push into education includes revamping the iTunes U section of the iTunes Store. The biggest change is that iTunes U is now a separate app, allowing you to access the iTunes U library directly, instead of having to go through the iTunes app. There are other changes, too. There are now full courses available—including the reading material, videos, and audio—all in self-contained packages. You can even see a list of assignments and check them off when you complete them. Note that although iTunes U has been updated and includes new content and a new look, it remains free.

Accessing and Using iTunes U

To access iTunes U on the iPad, you need to download the iTunes U app from the App Store. Tap on the App Store, tap on the search bar on the top right, enter *iTunes U* and tap Search on the keyboard. Tap on the iTunes U app under the iPad listing. Now you can install the iTunes U app.

To use the iTunes U app just click on it and you will see the bookshelf look that is used in the iBooks app and the Newsstand app, only a little darker. Apple seems to really like the bookshelf graphic and it works well here. Each course is shown on the bookshelf just like a book.

Across the top of the app are three buttons, the first is the Catalog button, which opens up the iTunes U store allowing you to get the courses into the app. Next up is the button that controls how the courses are shown in the app, either in bookshelf view or list view.

Figure 9-7
The iTunes U interface showing four full
courses that I have downloaded.

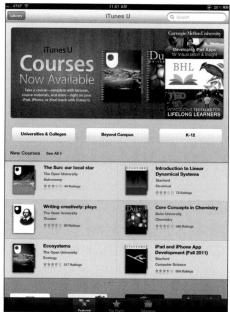

Figure 9-8
The iTunes U Catalog is growing all the
time. The look of the app is the same
as the iTunes Music Store, the Movie
Store, and the rest of the iTunes stores.

If you use iBooks, then this is all going to look
really familiar. Next is the Edit button, which
allows you to delete classes. Tap Edit, then
select a course and tap Delete on the top left.

The iTunes U Catalog

To access the iTunes U Catalog, tap the
Catalog button on the top of the screen in the
iTunes U app. The iTunes U Catalog looks a
lot like the rest of the iTunes stores, making
it very comfortable to navigate. The screen is
divided into three sections—the top, where
Apple features classes and courses; the middle,
where courses are listed; and the bottom,
where you can select between the Featured,
Top Charts, and Categories. All you have to do
is tap on a course that looks interesting.

Each course has a Description, Subscribe
button, and Materials List. Now while the

course is free, not all the materials are. For
example, the Duke University Core Concepts
in Chemistry course has a materials list with
471 items, including a few that are not free
and one that is available for iPhone only.
When you tap on the Subscribe Free button
you will get a warning telling you that iTunes
U courses may use supplemental materials
that need to be purchased. You must tap OK
to agree to this warning, shown in it's entirety
in Figure 9-9, before the course will begin to
download.

On the Catalog screen there are three
important buttons in the middle of the screen
that allow you to easily find courses by type
of school. The buttons are: Universities &

Figure 9-9
The Yale University Autism and Related Disorders iTunes U course warning. Tap on OK to download the core material.

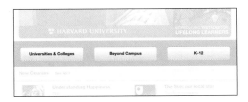

Figure 9-10
The iTunes U page showing the school Categories button.

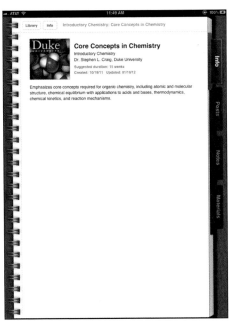

Figure 9-11
Duke University's Core Concepts in Chemistry class Info page.

Colleges, Beyond Campus, and K-12, as shown in figure 9-10

Tap on these buttons to see a list of schools that have content on iTunes U. For example, tap on the Beyond Campus button to find listings for organizations ranging from American Theatre Wing to the Washington National Opera. Tap on any of these and to open a page listing the available classes or courses from that institution. Is your school on the list?

Once you have downloaded a course in the iTunes U app, you access it by tapping on the course. When the course opens, you see the

Description of the class, and on the right, tabs that allow you to see the Info, Posts, Notes, and Materials for the course.

Info: To view the Info page you can tap on the Info button on the top of the screen or on the right tab The Info page can include some or all of the following:

- **Overview:** Gives you an overview of the class and is the first screen that you see when you open the course for the first time.

- **Instructor:** This is the information about the instructor.

- **Outline:** A full outline of the course. This is especially worth looking over, as it gives you an idea of what to expect and a road map of the class.

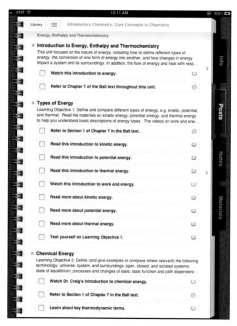

Figure 9-12
Duke University's Core Concepts in Chemistry class Posts page.

Figure 9-13
Duke University's Core Concepts in Chemistry class Notes page.

- **Credits:** If there are credits for the course they are listed here.
- **Requirements:** If the course has a prerequisite or requirements, they are listed here.
- **Optional Apps for the Course:** This is where any optional apps are listed.

Posts: The Posts are the class. This is where the learning happens; just start at the top and work your way through the course. For example, in the Introductory Chemistry class you start with Introduction to Energy, Enthalpy, and Thermochemisty by watching a video. Just tap on the link and the video starts, and the next element is a web link to an online textbook. There are also checkboxes next to each element so that you can keep track of where you are in the course.

Notes: Taking a class usually means taking a few notes and since we are talking iPad here, there is no reason not to take your notes right on the device. You can do that right here. The Notes tab is where your notes and highlighted stuff lives. The really cool part is that if you add a bookmark or highlight in an iBooks textbook or any book associated with the course, the information shows up here. Want to add a new note? Just tap on the + on the top right of the screen.

Materials: This tab takes you to the full material list, allowing you to go directly to the individual materials. Tap on the i and you can get info on each of the materials.

I have always believed that iTunes U was one of the best things about the Apple iTunes Store. There is a stunning amount of

Figure 9-14
Duke University's Core Concepts in
Chemistry class Materials page.

knowledge just waiting for people to download
it and now that it is a separate app, I believe
more people will take advantage of it. The best
part is that most of it is totally free.

For the Educators

If you want to build your own course for
iTunes U it is pretty straightforward; all
you have to do is follow the step-by-step
instructions in the iTunes U Course Manager.
But there is a catch—your institution needs
to have an iTunes U site, because only
instructors affiliated with an institution that
has an existing iTunes U site can access
iTunes U Course Manager.

You will need to contact the person on your
campus who is in charge of the iTunes U
program and request access and a sign-in
URL. You can then sign in and start building

courses for your educational institution. You
can include audio and video, presentations,
documents, PDFs, iBooks textbooks for the
iPad, any ePub books, any iOS apps, and web
links. While anyone with access to iTunes U
can access your material, you can use it for
instruction in your actual classroom.

Here are the basic steps to creating your
own class:

1. Create an Instructor Profile: This is where
   you enter the information about yourself,
   including a photo if you want, that will
   be seen on the instructor page of all your
   courses.

2. Create New Course: Here you have two
   options for the type of course—In-Session
   or Self-Paced. In-Session courses take place
   in real time, with calendar-based posts and
   assignments, and need start and end dates.
   The Self-Paced courses allow students
   to take the course at any time. In these
   courses the instructor needs to provide a
   suggested duration for the course.

3. Enter the New Course Settings:
   - Enter your Course Name, Institution,
     and Department.
   - Enter the expected duration of the class
     for the Self-Paced classes and the start
     and end dates for the In-Session classes.
   - Enter the description for the course.
     This description will appear inside the
     iTunes U Catalog.
   - Upload a square image for the course.
     It should be something that grabs
     attention, since it is shown in the iTunes
     U Store if the class is public.
   - Select the license for your content. This
     can range from All Rights Reserved to
     Attribution.

4. After you've entered all the course information, you will see your dashboard that lists all your courses. Select the course that you want to edit, or add posts, materials, and assignments to.

5. You can now build your course using the Overview, Outline, and Instructor pages.

   • Overview page: The information on this page is taken from the Course Settings, but you can edit it here at any time.

   • Outline page: This is where you enter the course syllabus. For the In-Session classes, you can add the outline topics as you go; for the Self-Paced classes, you should enter the entire course outline in the beginning. Every post and assignment will be associated with topics in your outline. You can include up to two sublevels for each topic.

   • Instructor page: The Instructor page is information from the Instructor profile but can be edited here to closely match the course.

   • You can add a new page if needed— for example, course policies, prerequisites, or anything else that can be useful to students.

6. Add Posts, Assignments, and Materials:

   • Posts allow you to communicate directly with the students. These posts could be instructions, explanations, or even a summary of the material.

   • You can create Assignments on any post. The Assignment is a task that needs to be completed by the student. For the In-Session courses, you select a due date for the assignment.

   • Materials: This is where it gets really cool. You can include a ton of different materials, including video, audio, presentations, web links, and even the new iBooks textbooks. You can add content from the App Store or the iBookstore, or upload you own material. You can even add a link directly into a certain chapter of a book or a spot in a video.

7. Once you have everything set up you can publish your course, which gives you a URL that can be used for in-classroom use or you can send it to your institution's iTunes U administrator to publish it to your institution's iTunes U site.

SPECIAL EDUCATION

While I don't believe that Apple went out to develop a device for special education needs, they certainly have excited the special education teachers that I have spoken to. The iPad is great for kids who can't use a traditional mouse but instead can just use their fingers. The iPad can read text aloud in a very natural voice and can also help noncommunicative kids talk by using the iPad's voice.

One of the leaders in this app category is one of the more expensive apps available in the iTunes Store. The app is called Proloquo2Go and costs $189.99. This may seem very expensive in an ecosystem where app prices usually range from free to $9.99, but compared to the thousands of dollars that an AAC (augmentative and alternative communication) device usually costs it is inexpensive and accessible. In a nutshell, the Proloquo2Go app enables people who have difficulty speaking to communicate by tapping on icons in the app.

There is another bonus to using the iPad for kids with special needs and that is the "cool factor." The iPad is everywhere and most people either have one or want one. So when a child or teen with special needs carries one around, there isn't a stigma attached to it. On the contrary, the iPad enables them to fit in more than ever before.

The Proloquo2Go app can be customized, making the device useful to a wider range of people. The current version of the app includes the North American English male and female voices, but those can be switched to British-English voices from inside the app.

This use of the iPad was featured on the October 23, 2011, 60 *Minutes* episode that was about research that had been done with autistic children who are starting to communicate using the apps on the iPad. There is still a long way to go, but compared with spelling out words by pointing to letters on a plastic sheet, the iPad is opening up communication channels that were previously closed.

This is a very new and exciting use for the iPad and the advances that have been made since the device was released are impressive, but it will take a few more years to see what the long-term use of iPads in special education can achieve.

PART 4

Photo and Video

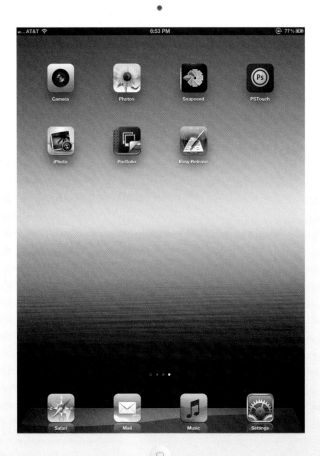

10

Photography

The Skim

I'm a photographer and when I'm not working on iPad books, I am out photographing concerts and events. The iPad is a fantastic device for photographers and I don't know of any photographers who don't already have one (or don't want one). The original iPad did not come with a camera, so you couldn't take photos with the device but you could still edit them and view them on the great iPad screen. The iPad 2 and the new iPad both have built-in cameras and built-in photo editing capabilities, and with the higher resolution screen on the new iPad your photos will look amazing. For more details on the iPad cameras, see Chapter 1.

TAKING PHOTOS

Taking photos with the iPad is simple—just launch the iPad Camera app and fire away. When you launch the Camera app the whole iPad screen turns into the viewfinder, making it easy to compose your image.

Across the bottom of the screen are four buttons:

- The first is the last photo taken. Tap on it to view the last photos taken without leaving the Camera app. Tap Done on the top right edge to go back to the Camera app.

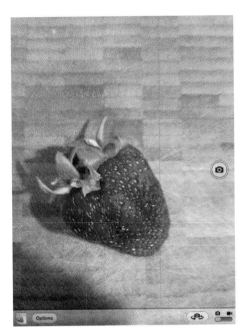

Figure 10-1
The iPad Camera app, showing the
Shutter Release button on the right side
of the screen and the Options button in
the bottom left corner.

- The second button is the Options button,
  which when tapped allows you to turn a
  grid on or off. The grid overlay is used to
  help with composition by showing the Rule
  of Thirds grid. The idea is that if you place
  the subject of the photo where the lines
  intersect, the photo will be better. If you
  want more information on photography
  composition, check out my *Composition
  Digital Field Guide*. I can only hope that
  there will be more options in a future
  release, since the idea that you have to tap
  Options to just get a single option seems
  like an extra unnecessary step.

- The next button allows you to switch
  between the front- and rear-facing cameras.

- The final button switches the camera from
  still to video mode.

There are also some features of the Camera
app that seem hidden at first but make it
easier to use. The first is that you can zoom
in and out when taking a photo. Just put two
fingers on the screen and move them apart to
zoom in or pinch them together to zoom out.
When you do this, a zoom bar appears on the
screen and you can move the slider to adjust
the zoom as well. You can also look at the last
photos taken by just swiping a finger across
the screen from left to right, and then go back
to the Camera app by swiping right to left.

To take a photo, just tap on the Shutter
Release button, which is one the right edge
of the screen. If you are used to the iPhone,
which has the Shutter Release button on the
bottom edge, this could take you a while to
get used to. There is also a second Shutter
Release button and that is the volume up
button. You can press the volume up button
to take photos, which works really well when
holding the iPad in portrait mode but doesn't
work well in landscape mode since to reach
the button you will most likely cover the camera lens with your left hand. You also need to
turn the rotation lock off when shooting in
landscape mode so that the Shutter Release
button stays on the right edge no matter the
device orientation.

Since the iPad is controlled by a touch screen,
the focus and exposure controls are just a
touch away. Just tap on the screen where you
want the camera to focus and a little white
box appears. The camera will automatically
focus on this spot and adjust the exposure
as best as it can. Tap on a bright area in
your photo and the scene automatically gets
darker, tap on a dark area and the scene
lightens up.

TRANSFERRING PHOTOS TO AND FROM A COMPUTER

Since the original iPad had no camera, the only thing you had to worry about was transferring your photos from the computer to the iPad. But with the release of the iPad 2 the new iPad, not only do you need to be able to transfer your existing photos from your computer to the iPad, you also need to be able to transfer the images from the iPad to the computer.

The easiest way to transfer images from your computer to the iPad is to use iTunes on the computer. Just follow these steps:

1. Turn on the computer.

2. Launch iTunes on the computer.

3. Plug the iPad into the computer using the supplied USB cable.

4. In iTunes, select the iPad from the device list on the left side of the iTunes window.

5. When the iPad Summary window opens, click on Photos at the top of the screen.

6. Click on Sync Photos in the tab and use the drop-down menu to pick the source of the images to be copied. You can pick only one source at a time, and if you change sources the older images will be deleted. For example, if you select to copy the photos from iPhoto and the next time you pick Aperture, the photos you synced from iPhoto will be removed.

7. Click on Sync on the bottom right side of the screen.

The images are now on the iPad and you can view them in the Photos app. You can use any data transfer program to transfer photos off of your iPad. All you need to do is attach the iPad to the computer using the supplied USB cable and choose a program to use for importing the images.

For example, if you are a photographer and you use Adobe Lightroom, you can import the photos as if you were getting them from any camera that was attached to the computer. On the Mac side of things, you can always use iPhoto to transfer the photos. All you need to do is use the supplied USB cable to attach the iPad to the computer and launch iPhoto on the computer. You will see the iPad listed in the device list and the import image window will open. You can now download the images taken with your iPad to your computer.

TRANSFERRING PHOTOS FROM A CAMERA

No matter how good the iPad camera is, taking photos with it can still be a little awkward. So, there are many times I want to use my iPad to show off or edit photos I took with my other cameras, especially the smaller point-and-shoot I carry all the time. Apple knows this and offers a simple solution in the form of the Camera Connection Kit. This kit costs $29 and is available directly from Apple—either at the Apple store or at apple.com.

Figure 10-2
The Camera Connection Kit with an SD card inserted.

Figure 10-3
The iPad screen with the word Camera on the top of the screen, showing that the images are on the camera, not the iPad.

The kit comes with two connectors; both plug into the dock connector of the iPad and allow you to transfer supported photo and video files into the Photo app on the iPad. The difference between the two connectors is that one allows you insert a SD card directly into the adaptor, while the other allows you to plug in a USB cord to the connecter and your camera into the other end. This is for cameras that use formats other than SD cards.

To transfer image files to your iPad using the Camera Connection Kit, follow these steps:

1. Turn on the iPad.

2. Unlock the iPad by sliding your finger across the bottom of the iPad.

3. Plug the Camera Connection Kit into the dock connector of your iPad.

4. Insert the SD card or plug the camera in using the USB cord, depending on the camera. The Photo app opens automatically.

5. The images from the card appear on the screen. You will know they are from the camera because you'll see the word Camera on the top of the screen.

6. Tap on Import All at the bottom of the screen or tap on the individual photos, and then tap on Import.

7. You are asked if you want to Import All or just Import Selected, tap on either one to continue.

8. After the images have been imported the Import Complete message appears and asks if you want to Delete the images from the camera/memory card or keep the images on the card. Tap either one to continue.

The images are now on the iPad and you can unplug the Camera Connection Kit.

SORTING PHOTOS AND USING ALBUMS

The Photo app on the iPad is where the photos are stored, edited, and viewed. Across the top of the app is a series of tabs that allow sorting, and then an Edit button over to the right (the Edit button is available only when in the Album view).

When you tap on the Edit button, a New Album button appears on the right. Tap it and a New Album Name window opens in the middle of the screen.

Type in the name of the album and tap Save. The next thing you see is a screen with thumbnails of all the photos on your iPad, allowing you to either add all the photos to the new album or select individual images. Tap on the photos you want to add; a blue check mark appears at the bottom right of the each thumbnail you select. When you are done, tap the Done button on the top right.

You've just created a new album! (Remember that the images are also still on the Camera Roll album and the Camera Roll album cannot be deleted.) If you want to add more photos to the album later, it's really easy. Just tap on the album and then tap on the Export button—you will see an Add Photos button appear. Tap it to see thumbnails of all the photos on your iPad, allowing you to add individual images or all photos to the album.

Figure 10-4
In the Photos app, you can create and name a New Album.

You can also remove images from the albums you create: Tap the Export button, tap on the image(s) you want to remove, and then tap the Remove button. You are not deleting the image from your iPad, as it remains in the original album, but it will no longer be a part of the current album. If you are in the Camera Roll album (the default album for the iPad) and you delete an image, it is removed from the iPad. If you go to delete an image from the Camera Roll and it is part of another album, you are warned that by deleting it, it will be deleted everywhere on the iPad.

EDITING PHOTOS

Many times you want to edit your photos before showing them off, I know I do. The

Figure 10-5
The built-in editor has four controls across the bottom of the screen that give you limited image editing capability.

good news is that the iPad 2 and the new iPad both have built-in photo editing (unlike the original iPad), and if that app doesn't have the power to make the edits you want there are numerous other great editing options, including Snapseed, Photoshop Touch, and the new iPhoto for the iPad.

The Built-In Photo Editor

The iPad's built-in photo editing tools are really basic, but may be good enough to help save an otherwise unusable image. All you have to do is open an image, launch the Photos app, and tap on the Edit button. You will see four controls appear across the bottom:

- **Rotate:** Tapping this rotates the photo counterclockwise with each tap.

- **Enhance:** Tap this button to turn on or off auto-enhance.

- **Red-Eye:** The red-eye removal tool works fairly well most of the time. Tap each eye in the image that has red-eye to try to remove it.

- **Crop:** This is the most useful tool in the built-in editing controls as it allows you to crop your images easily. Once the image is cropped you can save the image that way, but this is a destructive crop and cannot be undone once the image is saved.

These built-in editing tools are better than nothing, but not much. There are a great many other image editing tools available for the iPad, but the three best right now are Snapseed by Nik Software, Photoshop Touch by Adobe, and the new iPhoto for the iPad.

Snapseed

There is good reason that Apple named Snapseed the iPad App of the Year in 2011—it's really fun to use and, instead of trying to make a desktop application fit the iPad, Nik Software developed the app specifically for the tablet first. The Snapseed app is now

available for the desktop as well, but it really shines on the iPad.

The photo editing capabilities of Snapseed can be broken down into two types: Adjustments and Creative Enhancements. The Adjustment settings include:

- **Auto Correct:** The Auto Correct tool analyzes your photo and automatically adjusts the color and exposure. You can fine-tune the correction until you are happy with it.

- **Selective Adjust:** This brings the power of the Nik control points right to the iPad, allowing you to adjust specific areas of your images instead of the whole image. Just tap the Add button at the bottom of the screen, and then tap on the screen where you want to place the control point.

  You can increase or decrease the size of the control point by placing two fingers on the screen and pinching your fingers together or spreading them apart. Then, swipe up and down to pick Brightness, Saturation, or Contrast, and then swipe left or right to increase or decrease the amount of the effect. This is a very powerful editing feature, especially since you can add eight control points to each image.

- **Tune Image:** The Tune Image setting allows you to adjust the White Balance, Saturation, Contrast, Brightness, and Ambience. Swipe up and down to pick which setting to adjust, then swipe left or right to increase or decrease that setting.

- **Rotate/Straighten:** You can easily straighten or rotate your image, making sure it looks exactly like you want it to.

- **Crop:** This allows you to quickly adjust the composition by cropping your image. This setting also allows you to crop using the standard aspect ratios, such as 1:1, 3:2, 4:3, 5:4, and 16:9.

Figure 10-6
On the Snapseed opening screen you can open an image and then choose one of the editing options.

- **Details:** You can easily adjust the sharpness of your image by either adjusting the traditional sharpening or the structure in your image. (The structure adjustment helps to bring out the details in the image, but too much can make the image look really processed.) Swipe your finger up and down to change between Sharpening and Structure, then swipe your finger left or right to add or subtract the amount the image is adjusted.

The fun part of Snapseed is its set of Creative Enhancements:

- **Black & White:** Tap this menu to convert the image to Black & White, but that's not all. You also get to pick one of six styles

that subtly changes the conversion by tapping on the Style button and picking one of the styles from the pop-up menu. You can also adjust the look of the photo by swiping up and down on the image to pick choose Brightness, Contrast, or Grain. Then swipe left to right to adjust the selected setting.

- **Vintage Films:** This set of styles creates a nostalgic look to your images and includes nine different styles. First, tap on the Style button on the bottom of the screen, and then pick one from the styles from the pop-up menu. Then tap on the Texture button and pick one of the four textures to overlay on your photo. You can then

159

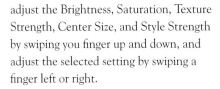

Figure 10-7
Punch up the details of your image
using Snapseed.

Figure 10-8
I love adding borders to my images and
Snapseed makes it easy to do so.

adjust the Brightness, Saturation, Texture
Strength, Center Size, and Style Strength
by swiping you finger up and down, and
adjust the selected setting by swiping a
finger left or right.

- **Drama:** Add a little mood and style with
  the Drama setting, where you can pick
  from six distinct settings. Tap on the
  Style button on the bottom of the screen,
  then swipe your finger up or down to pick
  between Filter Strength and Saturation,
  and swipe left or right to adjust.

- **Grunge:** There are 1,501 styles and 5
  textures available here, and when you add
  adjustments for Brightness, Contrast, Texture Strength, and Saturation, the creative
  possibilities are endless.

Tap on the Textures button on the bottom
of the screen to pick a Texture, then swipe
down on the screen to pick the Style menu,
and then swipe left or right to pick the style.
Swipe up or down on the screen to pick
Brightness, Contrast, Texture Strength, and
Saturation, and swipe left or right to adjust.

- **Center Focus:** Center Focus allows you
  to draw attention to a specific part of your
  photo by blurring the surrounding areas.
  When you tap on Center Focus a small
  blue dot appears in the middle of the
  screen. You can make the area you want
  to focus on bigger or smaller by placing
  two fingers on your screen and pinching together to make the area smaller, or
  spreading the fingers apart to make the
  area bigger.

160

You can also tap the Style button and pick one of the six styles, and then adjust the Center Size and Filter Strength by swiping up and down and then swiping left to right to adjust the selected setting.

- **Organic Frames:** This is one of my favorites—I think most images can use a little framing after the rest of the editing is done. Tap on the Style button and pick one of the eight frames or tap on Shuffle Properties to get a random frame. You can also swipe up and down to pick between Frame Width and Frame Offset, and then swipe left or right to adjust.

- **Tilt-Shift:** This helps recreate the look used when shooting with a large format camera that can tilt and swing. You can tap on the Style button to bring up the Linear or Elliptical style, and then you see a blue dot in the middle of the screen that you can move to get the focus point where you want it. Then you can rotate the area by placing two fingers on the screen and sliding one of the fingers. You can also make the selection larger or smaller by placing two fingers on the screen and pinching together or moving apart. Swipe up or down to select the following edits: Transition, Blur Strength, Brightness, Saturation, and Contrast. Then, swipe left or right to adjust.

At the bottom of every screen you can tap on the Back button, which takes you back to the main screen. There is also a Compare button that, when pressed, shows the original photo so you can quickly see the changes that you have made. There is also an Undo button and an Apply button. One of the really cool features is the meter across the bottom of the screen that shows the strength of the current

adjustment for those of us who like to have numbers associated with the adjustments.

The main screen of the Snapseed app is really simple. It allows you open an image; compare the changes you have made; revert back to the original; save the image back onto the iPad; and share the photo via e-mail, Print, Flickr, Facebook, or Twitter.

Adobe Photoshop Touch

When it comes to photo editing, there is one company (and product) that comes to everyone's mind. Adobe Photoshop has been the standard for image editing software since its release over 20 years ago. For the first time, Adobe has brought the power of Photoshop to the iPad. This photo editing app is the real deal, and not just a minimal set of editing tools with the Photoshop name slapped on it. This app does not work on the original iPad—it needs to have a camera, which the original iPad doesn't have.

Adobe has finally brought the power of Photoshop to the iPad, and it's only $9.99. In the iPad world where many apps are free or cost just $0.99, an app that costs $9.99 might

Figure 10-9
The opening window of the Adobe Photoshop Touch app. Pick either one of the cool tutorials or open an image to start your own project.

seem expensive. But if you compare the app price tag to the Adobe Photoshop applications for the computer, you'll see that at $9.99 it is a bargain.

When you first launch the Adobe Photoshop Touch app you are presented with two choices—you can either Begin a Tutorial or Begin a Project. This is really great because like most apps, Photoshop Touch doesn't come with a user manual, so the tutorials can really help get you up to speed on what the app can do. There are 13 tutorials that cover the following diverse subjects:

- Add dramatic flare
- Paint with effects
- Replace colors
- Create camera layers
- Make a pencil sketch
- Create a photo frame
- Add a tattoo
- Make a painting
- Add people to images
- Drop shadow text
- Antique photos
- Clean up a background
- Smooth image blending

If you take the time to go through these tutorials, you will have a much better understanding of what this app can do. Each of the tutorials walks you through, step-by-step, allowing you to do the steps yourself. I suggest that you start by doing at least a couple of the tutorials first to get used to the controls, but you can always just tap on Begin a Project and jump right in.

The first step is to open an image that you want to edit. The interface here is very intuitive and lets you easily access the images stored not only on your iPad but also those stored on the Adobe Creative Cloud, Google, and Facebook—and you can also access the iPad's built-in cameras.

On the left side of the screen, tap on the source for your photos and the images will appear on the right. It also lets you sign into your Adobe Creative Cloud account (or set one up) and sign in to your Facebook account. To use the images on the Creative Cloud, Google, or Facebook you need to be connected to the Internet either over Wi-Fi or over the cellular network.

Once you have selected the image you want to edit, tap the Add button to open the main editing window, as shown in Figure 10-10.

The main screen of the app has four separate parts:

- a menu bar across the top
- a tool menu on the left
- a layers palette on the right
- the main image in the middle of the screen

The menu bar has the following choices:

- The back arrow opens the Save/Don't Save menu.
- The Add Image allows you to add an image as a new layer to the original image. You can adjust exactly how the new layer is placed over the original layer.
- The pencil icon brings up the Cut/Copy menu that allows you to Cut, Copy, Copy Merged, Paste, Clear, Extract, and show Pointer.
- The Select icon brings up the Select menu, allowing you to Select all, Deselect, Select pixels, Inverse the selection, Feather the selection, Resize the selection, and Refine Edge.

Figure 10-10
The main screen of the Adobe Photoshop Touch app.

- The Hide Menu button slides the whole menu bar up and out of the way.
- The Resize menu allows you to intuitively resize the currently selected layer. Once you are done, tap the Done button to go back to the main editing window.
- The Adjustment icon opens the Adjustment menu. This is where you can make the following adjustments.
  - **Black and White:** This is a one-tap adjustment that turns the image to black and white.
  - **Saturation:** This opens the saturation slider on the bottom of the screen, allowing you to add or remove saturation.
  - **Auto Fix:** This is a one-tap fix for your images.

- **Brightness/Contrast:** This allows you to adjust both the contrast and brightness from -100% to +100%.
- **Temperature:** This allows you to adjust the color temperature from cooler (more blue) to warmer (more red).
- **Replace Color:** This adjustment allows you to pick a current color and a replacement color, and adjust the amount of change and the threshold of the color. It also allows you to pick the colors from the current image or from a color palette.
- **Shadows/Highlights:** This menu allows you to adjust the Highlights, Lights, Shadows, and Darks. Each of the sliders goes from -100% to +100%.

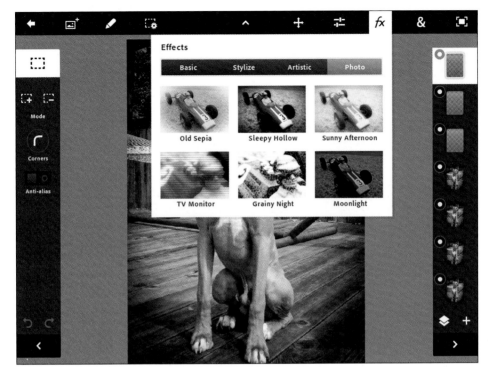

Figure 10-11
The FX menu gives you access to 28 different effects that you can use to edit your images.

- **Color Balance:** This adjustment allows you to adjust the reds, greens, and blues in your image.

- **Reduce Noise:** Digital noise is introduced into your images when you shoot in low-light conditions and this feature allows you to reduce some of that in your images. The more you reduce the noise the more there is a chance of slightly blurring the image.

- **Invert:** This is a one-tap trick that inverts the colors in your image. It gives you a negative image.

- **Levels:** This one of the most powerful editing tools in Photoshop and it is just as powerful here in Photoshop Touch.

You can adjust the endpoints and the light, dark, and midpoint for the whole image and for the individual red, green, and blue channels.

- **Curves:** You can adjust the curves with up to 11 points on each channel and on the overall image as well. This gives you a total of 44 different points to adjust the curves in your image.

• The FX menu has a 28 different effects divided into 4 basic categories:

- **Basic:** There are nine basic effects. Each opens an adjustment window. The Basic adjustments are: Gaussian Blur, Directional Blur, Sharpen, Drop Shadow, Glow, Bevel, Edges, Tint, and Lighting.

Figure 10-12
The tool bar gives you access to the tools and the tool options.

- **Stylize:** The Stylize menu allows you to apply the following effects: Multi Gradient Map, Halftone Pattern, Threshold, Glass, Posterize Color, and Old Photocopy.

- **Artistic:** There are seven different Artistic effects—Graphic Pen, Chalk & Charcoal, Pencil, Comic, Color Drops, Scratches, and Acrylic Paint.

- **Photo:** There are six different photo effects that you can add to your photos—Old Sepia, Sleepy Hollow, Sunny Afternoon, TV Monitor, Grainy Night, and Moonlight.

- The & icon gives you access to the following tools: Crop, Image Size, Fill & Stroke, Add Text, Add Gradient, Add Fade, Warp, and Add Camera Fill.

- The Full Screen button allows you to view your image without any of the menus.

The Tool menu on the left side of the screen gives you options for the selected tool and allows you to pick between the Marquee Selection Tool, Circle Selection Tool, Lasso Selection Tool, Magic Wand Tool, Scribble Selection Tool, Brush Selection Tool, Paint Tool, Spray Tool, Clone Stamp Tool, Healing Brush Tool, Eraser Tool, Blur Tool, and Smudge Tool. When the editing window first opens, the Marquee Selection tool is open; to change the tool, tap on the icon on the menu, then tap the desired tool.

The Layers Palette is where the full power of Photoshop is available on the iPad. You can

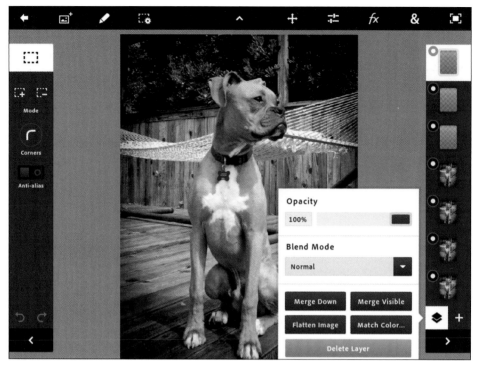

Figure 10-13
The Layer Palette showing the Layer options.

stack one layer on top of another, change the blending modes between the layers, add empty layers, and merge the layers together in a variety of ways.

Tap on the Layer menu button on the bottom of the Palette to bring up the layer options. From there you can adjust the opacity of the selected layer or change the blend mode. The blend mode choices are: Normal, Darken, Multiply, Lighten, Screen, Linear Dodge, Overlay, Difference, and Subtract. You can Merge Down, Merge Visible, Flatten the image, Match the color, and Delete the layer. You can also add a layer by tapping the + sign on the bottom of the palette. This allows you to open an Empty Layer, Duplicate Layer, Photo Layer, and Layer from Selection.

With all these tools, you can finally really edit your images easily on the iPad. Once you are done editing your image, you can save it. The image is saved in the Photoshop Touch file interface, which allows you to decide where to send the image file. This window has a menu bar across the top that allows you to do the following: Upload to Creative Cloud/ Launch the Creative Cloud website, Save the image to the camera roll, Share on Facebook, Share by e-mail, or Send to the printer. You can also Create new folders and move the images to the folders, Duplicate projects, Delete projects, and Sign in to Facebook.

There is also a Settings menu that allows you to sign in and out of your Adobe account, Change your preferences, Sign in to Face-

Figure 10-14
The Photo view in the new iPhoto app showing all the images on the iPad. It would be nice to be able to change the size of the thumbnails, but the screen is so good that the images are crystal clear even when shown at this size.

book, access the online Help forum, and get info about the app.

This is by far the best image editing app on the iPad, especially if you are used to using Photoshop on the computer. And for $9.99 it is an absolute steal.

iPhoto

When Apple released the new iPad in 2012 they also released the iPad version of iPhoto, the image sorting and editing application that has been part of the iLife computer suite for years. It joins the other two iLife components—GarageBand and iMovie—on the iPad and is the first true image editing app

from Apple. The app costs $4.99 and is really powerful and easy to use.

When you launch iPhoto the first screen shows you the photos that are available on your iPad for editing in the Album view. This is very slick looking, as it shows you the images in albums sitting on glass shelves. You can tap on Photos, Events, and Journals to get a different view of your images, or tap on the Settings button, which looks like a little gear on the top right corner of the screen. Over on the top left corner of the screen is a Help button, which brings up a manual for the app.

BEAMING AN IMAGE

You can send or Beam a photo right out of the iPhoto app to any other device running iOS and iPhoto. So, I can send an image to a friend's iPhone or iPad. Here's how to do that: The first step is to make sure that both devices are on the same Wi-Fi and that iPhoto is open and running on both devices. You also need to make sure that both devices are set up to beam photos. In the main iPhoto screen, tap on the Settings menu (the little gear icon) and then make sure that Wireless beaming is turned on. With all those things turned on, and the image you want to stream on the screen, follow these steps:

1. Tap on Export.
2. Tap on Beam.
3. You can now either beam the Selected, Flagged, All, or Choose by tapping the thumbnails.
4. A list of available devices is shown; select the one you want to beam the images to and tap on Beam.
5. On the receiving device, you will be asked to accept the image, and once you do the image will be sent and you'll see a confirmation on the iPad.

Figure 10-15
The image was beamed from my iPad to my iPhone.

To edit a photo, just tap on it to open it in the Edit window. You see the selected image in the middle of the screen with thumbnails either on the left or on the bottom, depending on the iPad orientation. You can now either choose to edit the selected image, or pick another one by tapping on the thumbnail or by swiping across the main image to the left or right. You will notice that on the top of the screen there is a little icon that looks like a grid. Tap it and the thumbnails disappear; tap it again and the thumbnails reappear.

Next to the grid icon is the ? icon. Tap it and helpful hints appear on the screen; tap it again and they disappear. These hints are really useful when learning how to use the app. The next button is the Undo/Redo button. Tap it once to undo something; tap and hold to redo. The next button is the Export/Share button where you can export your image into a Journal, save it back to the Camera Roll, share it in iTunes, send it via e-mail, beam it to another device (more on this in the Sidebar) print the image, share via Twitter, export it to Flickr or Facebook, or start a slideshow.

Next to the Export/Share button is the Info button, which gives you data about the image, including the camera make and model and the exposure settings. There is also a Comments section here, which shows comments from Facebook and Flickr if you've uploaded the image to either of these services.

The last two buttons are the Compare Photos button and the Edit button. Use the Compare Photos button to see the difference between the original photo and the edited photo. This button works only if the photo has been edited, otherwise the button is grayed out. The Edit button opens the editing function of the app. Tap it and the editing bar opens across the bottom of the image.

Across the bottom of the screen are the editing tools. The first five are the main editing tools:

- **Crop and Straighten:** This is where you can crop a photo to change the composition. Tap on this tool and tool handles appear on the image. Adjust the frame to get the composition that you want. You can also reposition the image inside the frame by moving it around using two fingers. If you want to constrain the crop to a specific size, tap on the gear on the bottom right corner of the screen to see your options.

  You can straighten the photo by using the dial across the bottom of the screen, which shows the angle of change. You can also rotate the image by tapping the dial on the bottom and tilting the iPad.

  One of those great little features is that if there is a horizon line in the image the app can locate it automatically and straighten your image for you. A line automatically appears over the horizon with an arrow on the right end. Just tap the arrow that appears in the image.

- **Adjust Exposure:** Tap on the Adjust Exposure button and the middle section brings up five sliders. The first adjusts the dark areas, the second and fourth adjust the contrast, the third adjusts the brightness, and the fifth adjusts the bright areas. You can just use the sliders to adjust the exposure of the image. You can also make the adjustments on the image itself. Tap on an area you want to adjust and then, without removing your finger from the screen, slide up and down to adjust the brightness and left or right to adjust the contrast.

- **Adjust Color:** You can easily adjust the hue and saturation of your photo, and you can adjust the overall color casts and help fix images taken under less than optimal lights (like fluorescent bulbs) by adjusting the white balance of the photo.

There are four main adjustments (listed from left to right on the screen) that can be adjusted individually: Overall Saturation, Blues, Greens, and Skin Tones. You can also change the color saturation by tapping on the screen and sliding your finger up and down to adjust the overall saturation, or left to right to adjust the color under your finger.

To adjust the white balance of your image tap on the WB button and then tap on one of the presets. They are, from left to right, Sun, Cloud, Flash, Shade, Incandescent, and Fluorescent. You can also set a custom white balance based either on skin tone or a neutral area of your photo by tapping on the icon and then tapping on the part in the image to use.

- **Enhance with Brushes:** You can use the brushes to paint on edits to certain parts of the photo. All you do is pick a brush by tapping on it and then using your finger to paint the selected effect on the image. There are eight brushes that you can use:

  - **Repair:** Paint over an area and it tries to use pixels from the surrounding areas to patch missing spots.

  - **Red Eye:** This works best if you zoom in so that the affected eyes are big on the screen. Then, select the Red Eye tool and tap on each of the affected pupils.

Figure 10-16
The photo editing tools showing the effects available in the menu options.

- **Saturate:** Increases the colors in the areas that this brush is applied.
- **Desaturate:** This decreases the colors in the areas where this brush is applied.
- **Lighten:** This lightens the areas of the photo where it is applied.
- **Darken:** This darkens the areas of the photo where it is applied.
- **Sharpen:** This increases the clarity of your image by making the harder edges stand out more.
- **Soften:** This is used to blur the edges in a photo.

• **Add Effects:** There are a lot of special effects that you can add to a photo, from Artistic, to Vintage, Black & White, and Duotone. They appear as a fan of effect strips. Click on a strip and it opens across the bottom of the screen. You can now pick the effect you want from the strip. Have fun with this one and experiment. You can always remove it by tapping on the little gear on the bottom right of the screen and tapping Remove Effect.

The next section (on the middle section of the bottom of the screen) changes depending on what tool you picked from the five previously listed tools. When the edit window first opens and none of the five editing tools (mentioned earlier) is selected there are basic tools present.

These basic tools are the Auto-Enhance tool, the Rotate 90 Degrees tool (hold your finger on this button and you can pick the direction of the rotation), the Flag tool (hold your finger on this and you can pick from Flag All, Unflag All, Last 24 Hours, Last 7 Days, or Choose the images from the thumbnails), Mark as Favorite, and the Hide Photo tool. The next two buttons will scroll through your

Figure 10-17
When you have applied any of the edits, you will see a little blue light above the tool that has been used. You can see here that all the tools have been used.

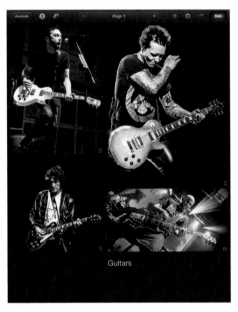

Figure 10-18
You can move photos around in a Journal page to make it look just the way you want.

images, and then there is the Copy and Paste menu. The gear on the bottom right corner of the image allows you to copy and paste the edits made in one photo to another photo or a set of photos.

You can share the images that you have edited by creating a Journal. This allows you to group images together and show them off on your iPad. When you have a single photo on the screen, tap on Export, and then tap on Journal. You can then choose either the Selected image (the one on the screen) or any flagged photos, All the photos, or you can choose the images to add. Then you can choose a new Journal and name it or choose an existing Journal. Then you can swipe left to right or right to left over the themes. Next, tap on Create Journal. You can now edit the journal by adding Headers, Text, Notes, More Pages, and other elements.

Once you've completed the Journal, it is automatically shared on all of your devices using the iCloud service. This is like scrap-booking right in the iPhoto app and is a great way to create albums that you can show off from right inside iPhoto.

SHARING PHOTOS

It's great to take and keep photos on your iPad, it's great to take photos with your iPhone, and it's great to take photos with your digital camera—but it's even better to always have access to all of your photos no matter where they are stored. That means that your images need to be shared between all the devices easily. Apple's solution is the Photo Stream service that uses iCloud to keep all the images synced between devices, but there is also another option—the Adobe Revel service.

Photo Stream

Photo Stream is an ambitious part of iCloud that allows all your images to be shared among your iOS devices (iPhone, iPad, and iPod Touch) and iPhoto and Aperture auto-matically. Take a photo with your iPhone and it appears on the iPad and in iPhoto or Aperture; take a photo with the iPad and the

Figure 10-19
The Settings app showing the iCloud service and the Photo Stream On/Off button.

photo appears on the iPhone and in iPhoto or Aperture. If you are not a Mac user, you can still use this because the photo will be synced to your Pictures Library. No need to export or import or sync, it just happens automatically. Now, for this to work you need to be signed up for Apple's iCloud service. For more on the iCloud service, check out Chapter 3.

To set up the Photo Stream on your iPad you first need to set up the iCloud service. Look in Chapter 3 for directions to set up the iCloud service. Once you have iCloud set up, you can turn on the Photo Stream easily by doing the following:

1. Tap on the Settings app.

2. Tap on iCloud in the list on the left.

3. The iCloud settings allow you to turn on or off parts of the app.

4. Turn Photo Stream on.

On the Mac side of things you now have to turn on Photo Stream in the iPhoto application. This only works with iPhoto 9.2

(also called iPhoto '11) or later. Here's how to turn it on:

1. Open iPhoto.
2. Click on iPhoto > Preferences.
3. Click on Photo Stream.
4. Check the box to Enable Photo Stream and then you can also decide if you want to:
   • Check Automatic Import.
   • Check Automatic Upload.

You can also turn the Photo Stream on or off using the System Preferences on the Mac. Just open System Preferences and click on the iCloud tab, then turn off Photo Stream in the list. That's all you have to do to get Photo Stream working on your Mac using iPhoto.

To set up Photo Stream on a PC running Microsoft Windows, do the following:

1. Download the iCloud Control Panel for Windows (Works with Vista Service Pack 2 and Windows 7) from support.apple.com/kb/DL1455.
2. From the Windows Stat menu, choose Control Panel > Network and Internet> iCloud.
3. Enter your Apple ID, and then select the Photo Stream service and turn it on.

Now that Photo Stream is on all your devices, the photos you take with your iPad will automatically be transferred over to other devices that have Photo Stream turned on. There is nothing else you have to do.

There are some downsides to this technology and hopefully they will be fixed by Apple in the future, because as it stands right now the service is really useful until you want to keep some photos private. I want to make this perfectly clear: with Photo Stream turned on,

ALL the photos that you take will be automatically uploaded to the Photo Stream. Let's put that into perspective. Say that I am shopping for a gift for my wife and take some photos with my iPad so that I can look at them later and decide which I like more. At the same time, those images are now in iPhoto on the home computer, where my wife sees them and it ruins the surprise. There is no way to decide which photos to share and which photos not to share—it is an all or nothing choice right now.

Deleting Photos from the Photo Stream

You can delete photos from the Photo Stream gallery on the iPad pretty easily, so long as you know where to look. First, open the Photos app and then open the Photo Stream tab, as you can see in Figure 10-20.

To delete any of the images, tap on the Export/Share button on the top right corner. You can now select the images that you want to either Share, Copy, or Delete. Just tap on the images and then tap on Delete. The image is now deleted from all the iOS devices, and from any iPhoto library. If you are in iPhoto and delete and image from the Photo Stream, it will be deleted from any of the devices that have that Photo Stream.

You can reset the Photo Stream service at any time. You need to do this using a browser on your computer, not on your iPad. Open an Internet browser on your computer and go to www.icloud.com. Sign in using your Apple ID and then click on your Account Settings button. The button is really well hidden—it is your user name on the top right corner of the screen. Clicking on your name opens up the Account Settings; then, you need to click on the Advanced button. This opens the Reset Photo Stream Page. All you have to do now

Figure 10-20
Here's a photo I took with my iPhone, showing up automatically on my iPad in the Photo Stream album. You can see that it's in the Photo Stream by the album name on the top left.

Figure 10-21
The sign in screen for Revel.

is click on the Reset Photo Stream Button. This removes the photos from the cloud but does not remove any of the photos from the individual devices.

Adobe Revel

The idea that to have automatic access to all of your photos, no matter which device you use to take them, is something that Adobe was working on at the same time that Apple was working on the Photo Stream functionality of iCloud. The Adobe solution was originally called Carousel while in beta, but is now formally called Adobe Revel.

Adobe Revel is not a free service. In fact, it costs $5.99 a month or $59.99 a year. The

good news is that you can try the service for free for 30 days.

The service allows you to upload your photos from the iPad (or the other devices running Revel) and access them any time you are connected to the Internet.

The basic steps to using Revel are as follows:

1. Turn on the iPad.

2. Open the App Store.

3. Search for Revel.

4. Download the Adobe Revel app. (The app is free.)

5. Tap on the Adobe Revel app.

6. Log in with your Adobe ID. (If you don't have an Adobe ID, you can create one easily when signing in to the app.)

7. Import the photos into Revel by tapping on the + in the Adobe Revel app.

8. Tap Choose Existing Photos and then select an album.

9. Select the photos you want to import, or tap Select All to import everything to the Revel service.

You can now access the photos everywhere, and more than that, you can actually share and edit the photos right in the Revel app, which updates them automatically. The real downside to this is the cost. $60 a year is a lot to spend compared to the free iCloud service.

PORTFOLIO FOR iPAD ($9.99)

The original iPad changed the way photographers showed off their work. The device seemed like a perfect way to show off photos, and with the higher resolution Retina display on the new iPad that ability has only improved.

The problem with the original was that although the built-in Photo Viewer app showed the photos off, it was limited in its ability to sort the photos on the iPad. Although you can now create albums and move photos on the iPad, there are still some better options for those who want to show off their images in a more controlled environment.

The app that I use to show off my photos on the iPad is the same one that I have been using since the iPad came out and it has remained my favorite portfolio app. The app is called Portfolio for iPad.

This is the perfect app for photographers who have more than one iPad and want to keep the same portfolio on all of them. You can

create a portfolio on one iPad and transfer the same portfolio to any other iPad as long as it is using the same Apple ID. (A little more on that later on.) First, let's look at the basics of the app and why of all the portfolio apps on my iPad, this is the one that I still use.

The Portfolio for iPad app allows you to have a custom opening page, giving you a place to include your own branding. You can create a custom landscape or portrait opening page, and you can also create a custom opening page for when you have your iPad connected to an external screen. To create a custom image you just need to format your logo image as follows:

- For Landscape, format the image at 657 pixels by 748 pixels.
- For Portrait, format the image at 493 pixels by 1004 pixels.
- For External Monitors, format the image at 1024 pixels by 768 pixels.

I expect that these format requirements might change when the app is updated for the new iPad and the new higher screen resolution. The Customize Appearance page will have the most up-to-date sizes needed.

You can also set custom colors for the Viewer Background, the Thumbnail Strip, the Slideshow Background, and the Gallery List Background. The best part is that customizing the interface is really easy. When you first open the app, you see the following message: "Tap here to place your logo." Tap it to open the Customize Appearance menu, as shown in Figure 10-22.

To load a photo, tap on the corresponding spot and a menu pops up with the following choices:

- **Clear Image:** This clears the current image.

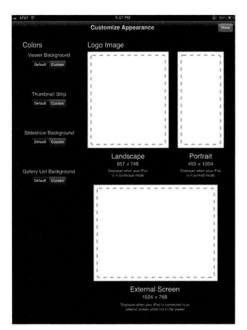

Figure 10-22
The Customize Appearance screen in
the Portfolio for iPad app.

Tap on Manage Galleries to open the Galleries menu. To start setting up a gallery, tap the + button, enter the gallery name, and tap Enter. The gallery now shows up on the left side of the app.

Now it's time to add photos to the gallery. To do that, tap on the Download button, which looks like a folder with a downward-facing arrow. When you tap on it, you get the following options to load photos into your gallery:

- Load from iPad Media
- Load from File Sharing
- Load from URLs
- Load from Dropbox
- Load from a Mac

Once you've loaded the images into the gallery, you can configure the gallery by tapping the Settings button, which looks like a small gear and is located on the right corner of the screen. This allows you to:

- Renumber All Items
- Sort All Items
- Configure Slideshow
- Configure Metadata
- Configure Gallery
- Repair Gallery

Now that a gallery is all set, you can hand your iPad over to people to check out your images—but before you do, you can lock the app so that the people looking over your images can't access the Settings control. From the main page, tap on the Configure menu and tap the Lock button. The first time you do this, the app will ask you to enter a passcode. From now on you will need to enter that passcode to access the settings of the app.

- **Load from iPad Media:** This lets you pick the image from photos that are already loaded onto your iPad.
- **Load from File Sharing:** This opens a file sharing window and allows you to get your image into the Portfolio for iPad app.
- **Load from URL:** This allows you to enter a URL for an image to import.
- **Load from Dropbox:** This allows you to connect to your Dropbox account and browse your Dropbox for images to use.

Once you've set up the portfolio with your branding, it is time to set up the portfolio. This is easily done by tapping on the Configure button, which looks like a little gear and is located at the top of the page next to the word Portfolio.

MODEL RELEASES

Model releases are a fact of life for working photographers and usually mean carrying a lot of papers around and making sure you get the signatures in the right places. I know it might not sound like a lot of work, but if you forget the forms at home it can be a real problem.

The solution is to have the model release on your iPad—and don't worry, there is an app for that. The app that I keep on my iPad is called Easy Release. It retails for $9.99 and is well worth the money.

Easy Release replaces the traditional paper model and property release forms and works on the iPad, iPhone, and iPod Touch. The app allows you to create a model or property release easily.

The Easy Release app allows you to enter all the information needed and even use the built-in camera to take a photo of the model and use the current location. Once you've entered all the information, the model can sign the release with her finger. You can then create a PDF of the form and e-mail it right from the app.

Seriously, if you are a photographer who works with models and needs a model release, this is the app for you. The app is with you at all times and can be modified as needed.

Figure 10-23
Tap on the + in the top right corner to get started.

Figure 10-24
A completed model release, ready to be signed.

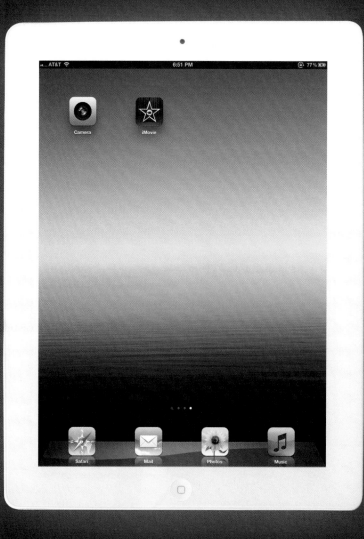

Video

The Skim

I find it awkward to shoot video with the iPad, but that might just be me. My wife shoots great video with the iPad and doesn't seem to have any of the problems holding it steady like I do. The iPad 2 and the new iPad both have two cameras that can shoot still images and video. Both devices have a front-facing camera and a rear-facing camera, and although the front-facing camera is the same on both devices, the rear-facing camera is not. The rear-facing camera in the new iPad is superior to the camera in the iPad 2. This affects the quality of the video captured by the device, but other than that the actual capture and editing of the video remains the same.

SHOOTING VIDEOS

Taking videos with the iPad is simple—just use the built-in camera. There are some slight changes to the layout of the video controls in the new iOS5.1 compared to the controls in the earlier version. The main change is the position of the Shutter Release button/Record button. It is no longer on the bottom edge of the screen; it is now on the right side of the screen and, even better, you can use the volume up button on the side of the iPad to start and stop the video recording. This allows you to hold the iPad steadier and still touch the Shutter Release button or the Volume buttons.

Here's how to use the video cameras to shoot video:

1. Turn on the iPad.

2. Tap on the Camera button.

3. To switch between still camera and video camera use the slide button on the bottom right. Slide the switch to the right to use the video camera.

4. You can also switch between the front- and rear-facing cameras by tapping on the Switch Camera button on the bottom right corner of the screen. Once you start to film you can't switch cameras.

5. Tap once on the Record button to start recording, tap it again to stop recording. You can also start recording by pressing the volume up button once to start recording and then tap it again to stop recording.

There is no zoom function when using the video camera but you can change the focus point by tapping on the screen. This focus point also controls the exposure, so each tap on the screen could change the way the video looks. Tap on a very bright part and the rest of the screen goes dark. Tap on a very dark part of the scene and everything gets brighter.

The video is automatically saved into the Camera Roll folder in the Photo app. It is marked differently from the still images; it has a small video camera icon and time on the bottom of the thumbnail. Tap the icon to open it and then tap the Play button in the middle of the screen to play it back. Once the video is in the iPad, you can edit it.

Figure 11-1
The video recording screen. Notice that the Record button is on the right.

EDITING VIDEOS WITH iMOVIE

With the release of the new iPad in 2012, Apple also updated the iMovie video editing app. What started out as a great app has become even better and the good news is that it only costs $4.99, or if you had the previous versions it is a free upgrade. The app works only on the iPad 2 and the new iPad. It will not run on the original iPad (since it doesn't have a camera).

When you first launch the iMovie app you are greeted with an old-style movie marquee. Go ahead and tap the + on the bottom of the screen to start your first project or trailer. You now have a choice between a full-blown iMovie Project and the new iMovie Trailer. I'm going to start with Trailers and will cover Projects a little later.

iMOVIE TRAILERS

With the release of the new iPad in 2012, Apple updated the iMovie app, allowing users to create short movie Trailers. Creating a Trailer can be broken down into five parts:

- Choose a Trailer
- Edit the Outline
- Customize the Titles

NOTE

All directions for iMovie assume that the iPad is in horizontal position.

- Add Video from Your Video Library
- Record Video

This is one of the coolest things I have ever seen on the iPad. I was able to create a really cool Trailer about my 2 dogs in about 30 minutes.

Choose a Trailer

When you first tap on the + sign and pick New Trailer, you get to pick a theme for your video. There are nine choices for themes:

- **Bollywood:** The Bollywood theme runs 1 minute and 7 seconds, and is based on the Bollywood style from the Indian movie industry.

- **Expedition:** This theme runs 62 seconds. It can have 2 to 6 cast members and looks a lot like the *Indiana Jones* adventure movies.

- **Fairy Tale:** This theme is great for little kids and runs 62 seconds. It has the feel of a Disney live action movie.

- **Narrative:** This is one of the longest themes, at 1 minute and 34 seconds, and has the feel of an epic movie like *Out of Africa*.

- **Retro:** This theme runs just under a minute and looks like a movie created in the sixties. Bold colors and clean lines make this theme a lot of fun to use.

- **Romance:** At 1 minute and 23 seconds, this theme is on the long side and is set up to have just two main stars.

- **Scary:** This is one of my favorite themes, not because I love scary movies, but because I think it is really well done. The Trailer is 61 seconds long and does a good job of emulating the feel of classic scary movies like *The Exorcist*.

- **Superhero:** As a huge comic book fan, I think this theme is very cool. It needs 2 to

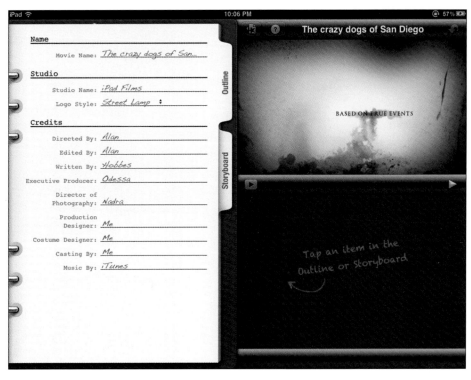

Figure 11-2
The Outline view of my masterpiece Trailer. I picked the Scary theme since I really like the look of it.

6 people and matches the current Hollywood superhero movie style.

- **Swashbuckler:** At just over a minute long, this theme is reminiscent of *Treasure Island* or *Pirates of the Caribbean.*

To pick a theme, use your finger to scroll through the choices across the bottom of the screen and then tap the Play button in the middle of the screen to see the Trailer in action. Once you have one you like, tap on the blue Create button on the top right.

Edit the Outline

The first view that opens is the Trailer Outline view, which allows you to enter the information about the movie. Tap any of the placeholders to enter the text you want. You can enter the name of the movie, the name of the studio, the logo style, and the credits. If the Trailer has a place to put in a cast, then you can enter their names here as well.

Customize the Titles

The next step is to look at the storyboard for your Trailer by tapping on the Storyboard tab in the middle of the screen. You can tap on any of the blue bars and edit the text.

As you type in the new text, you will see it update on the preview screen on the right.

Figure 11-3
The Storyboard view allows you to change the text in your Trailer.

Add Video from Your Video Library

Now you get to add video to the Trailer in the Storyboard view. There are placeholders (called wells) that you can fill easily with your video clips. Just do the following while in the Storyboard view:

1. Tap on an empty video placeholder. (Each placeholder has a label that suggests the best video for that spot.)

2. In the video browser over to the right, tap on the video that you want to insert. (If you don't see any video, tap the Video button on the bottom of the screen—it looks like a little film strip). You also need to make sure that the Location Services is turned on for iMovie. Turn it on in Location Services in the Settings App.

3. The selected portion of the video is outlined in yellow. To preview the selection, hold your finger on it until you see a red vertical line, and then drag your finger over the selection to watch it in the preview window.

4. Tap the blue arrow to add the selected video clip to the storyboard placeholder and iMovie automatically adjusts the length of the video to fit the placeholder.

5. Repeat for all the placeholders.

Record Video

If you don't have the video clip that you need in the video library, you can record right from the placeholder. To do that, just follow along from inside the Storyboard view:

183

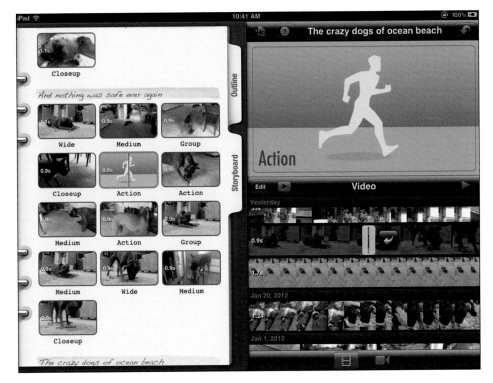

Figure 11-4
Adding video is pretty easy, just choose the clip and tap the blue arrow.

1. Tap to select an empty video template spot.

2. Tap the Camera icon on the bottom of the screen, which opens the camera in the preview window.

3. Tap the Record button and iMovie starts a 3-second countdown, and then begins recording.

4. Tap the Record button to stop the recording or let the app stop the recording automatically, which will be 3 seconds longer than the placeholder.

5. The newly filmed clip will be displayed in the edit window where you can do fine adjustments and control the audio.

That's it! Your Trailer is now complete. Tap on the Project button at the top of the preview window to go back to the main screen of the app and there you will see your new Trailer. From this window you can Start Another Project, Play the Current Project, Share the Movie (sharing the movie is covered later in this chapter), or Import Projects from iTunes. You can also toss the Trailer away if you want by tapping on the trash can.

CREATING AN iMOVIE PROJECT

iMovie Project allows you to create any type of movie, and although there are themes it isn't quite as quick and easy to use as the Trail-

Figure 11-5
You can access the camera from right inside the Trailer storyboard screen.

ers. The real difference is that iMovie Project enables you to create full movies and you are not limited to the 60 seconds or so that the Trailer gives you. You can also add your own titles, decide the length of your clips, and have fine controls over the transitions.

Click on the + on the front page and select New Project to open the project workspace. This workspace has three sections:

- The media library, on the top left
- The preview window, on the top right
- The timeline, across the bottom half of the screen

The basics are simple—just use clips from the media library to create a movie.

With the main editing screen open, tap on the icon that looks like a small film strip located on the left side of the screen in the middle. This brings up the video clips that are on your iPad that you can use with the iMovie app.

Tap on a clip and it becomes outlined in orange with little orange dots on the top left and bottom right, and a blue arrow in the middle. The orange dots allow you to trim the clip before entering it into the editing timeline. Put your finger on either of the orange dots and the preview window will show the selected clip. Now, just slide the dot to the left or right to trim the selected clip. The video in the preview window will show you exactly where you

Figure 11-6
The main project editing window.

are in the clip so that you can make the edits exact. Once the video start and stop points are set, tap on the blue arrow to insert the video clip into the editing timeline.

Before adding another clip, let's look at what we can do in the main editing widow to that just-imported clip.

- Tap on the clip once and the two orange dots appear again, allowing you to fine-tune the clip. Slide the orange dots to edit the start and end of the clip. For good transitions, keep in mind you should leave a little space at the start and end of the clips.

- Double tapping on the clip brings up the Clip Settings menu. This is where you can add a Title Style, add a location, and adjust

the volume. You can also delete the clip if you want. This won't delete it from the iPad, just from the timeline.

You can just keep adding clips to the timeline now to create your movie. Once you add a second clip, a transition icon appears between the two clips. Every time you add a clip a transition box will appear.

These transitions are what makes a home movie look more professional and are automatically applied when you add a second (or third, fourth, etc…) clip to the movie timeline. You can edit the transitions anytime; I usually wait until I am done adding clips before adjusting the transitions.

Figure 11-7
The Transition Editor.

To adjust the transitions:

- Single tapping on the transition brings up the transition editor, which looks like two little arrows pointing at each other. Tap these arrows and the transition editor expands allowing you to edit where the transition starts and ends. You get to use those orange dots to move the transition around. You can zoom in to make picking the right spot easy. Just place two fingers on the timeline and slowly move them apart. This will zoom in, making it easier to make good edits. Moving the fingers closer together will zoom out, allowing you to see the whole movie at a single glance.

- Double tap the transition to bring up the Transition Setting menu. This is where you can control the length of the transition and the style. The default is Cross Dissolve, but it can also be set to None or it can use the Theme transition. You can set the length fro 0.5 sec to 2 sec

There are times when you want to add a still photo to your movie—I mean Ken Burns has made an entire career using still images in his fantastic documentaries. You can add any still photos that are on your iPad to your movie quickly and easily.

Right next to the Video button is a Still Photo button (it looks like two frames overlapping); tap on it and the video files on the top left are replaced with the photos stored on your iPad, sorted by folders. Tap on a folder to see the images in that folder. Hold your finger on

187

Figure 11-8
Adding photos to your movies is pretty easy and you can adjust the image by double-tapping on it in the timeline to bring up the Photo Settings menu.

an image to preview it, and then tap on it to insert it into the timeline.

The default setting when you add a still image to the timeline is that the image will be there for three to five seconds, depending on the transitions. You can adjust the length of time of the photo by using the orange dots to either trim or expand the clip. The photos all have the Ken Burns effect applied automatically. To edit the clip just do the following:

1. In the timeline, tap the photo you want to adjust.

2. In the preview window you will see Start and End buttons that are used to set where the image movement begins and ends.

3. To set the start of the Ken Burns effect, tap the Start button and it will dim.

4. In the image viewer, position the image by dragging it around with your finger and use your fingers to zoom in.

5. Set the End button to show how the Ken Burns effect will end up. Tap the End button to select it, and then drag the image around the viewer and pinch to zoom in or out on a specific portion of it.

6. Tap Done.

If you set the start and end to look the same there will be no effect on the image.

Sound is really important to movies and iMovie has you covered here. iMovie allows you to add music, special effects, and voice-overs to your movie. You can add the following types of music/sounds to a movie project:

- **Background Music:** There are two types of background music: theme music, which changes depending on which theme you use, and your own songs that are in the iTunes library on your iPad. To add background music:

  1. In iMovie with a Project open, tap the Music button (it looks like a musical note).

  2. Tap Theme Music to choose any of the built-in theme music or tap any one of the other categories to find your music that is loaded on the iPad.

  3. Tap on the song/music you want as background music. It will show up as a green bar behind the video clips.

  4. To adjust the volume of the music, double tap the green bar to open the Audio Clip Settings window, and move the volume slider to the right or left.

  5. You can turn the music looping on or off by tapping the Project Settings button and turn Loop Background Music on or off.

- **Sound Effects:** iMovie comes loaded with sound effects. Adding them to the movie is the same as adding background music, but instead of a green bar that runs behind the clip you get a small audio clip on your timeline. Tap it once and you can adjust the length of the clip, tap it twice and you can adjust the volume of the clip or you can just delete it.

- **Voice-over:** There is a Microphone button that when tapped allows you to record

NOTE

You can have only one music track in your project with background music looping turned on. If you want more than one background music track, you must turn off looping.

any sound through the iPad's built-in microphone or one of the headphones with the built-in microphone plugged into the headphone jack on the iPad. The recorder comes up with a volume display showing that you are ready to record. Tap the Record button and you get a 3-second countdown to start recording, and then once it is done you can discard, retake, review, or accept the recording. Once you've accepted the recording it is entered into the timeline.

To move the audio clips around the timeline just hold your finger on the audio clip until it pops off the background and move the clip with your finger to the new spot, then drop it.

Other aspects of great movies are the titles and text. Apple has you covered there as well. You can add titles to any video clip or photo in the iMovie timeline. The text will be on the whole clip or photo—there is no way to adjust how long the title is present. It's either the whole clip or nothing.

To add a title, just follow these steps:

1. With iMovie open and the clip or photo visible, double tap the clip to open the Clip Settings Menu.

Figure 11-9
The audio editor allows you to adjust the audio in your movies.

THEMES

iMovie comes with themes to help you create good-looking movies. Each Theme is a set of coordinated transitions, music, and titles. There are eight built-in themes in iMovie, with the Modern Theme being the default. When you change the theme, any previous theme elements in your project are changed to the new theme, including any theme music if the theme music is turned on. To access the Theme Settings, you need to open the Project Settings menu. It is located on the top right and looks like a little gear. There are five settings in the Project Setting menu: Theme Chooser, Theme Music On or Off, Loop Background Music On or Off, Fade in from Black On or Off, and Fade Out to Black On or Off.

2. Tap on Type Style to bring up the Type Style menu.

3. Pick a style and you will see the preview on the preview window.

4. Tap on the Title Text Here in the preview window to change the title.

5. Tap Done on the keyboard to go back to editing.

Remember that you can apply only one title to each clip.

Movies are saved automatically as you create them, which means that they are ready to play at any time. When you are done creating and editing your movie, tap on the My Projects button. This takes you back to the My Projects screen. You can scroll through your saved Projects and Trailers by flicking your finger either left or right to scroll sideways. The first thing I like to do is change the name of the iMovie project to something more descriptive than "My Project." It's easy to do—just tap on the title on the movie marquee. You can't change the date or time that is under the name but that's ok, it's the date of the last edit and the running time of the movie.

SHARING VIDEOS

You can play the Projects and Trailers that you create in the iMovie app not only right on the device, but you can also share them with others on You Tube, Facebook, Vimeo, and CNN iReport, or export them to the iPad Camera Roll and iTunes.

You can add projects created with the iMovie app on your computer that are in iTunes. Attach the iPad to your computer and open iTunes, and then follow these directions:

1. On the computer, click on the iPad in the device list on the left side.

Figure 11-10
The Sharing window in iMovie.

2. Click on the Apps tab on the top.

3. Scroll down the page until the File Sharing window appears.

4. Click on iMovie in the apps list.

5. Click on Add at the bottom of the window and navigate to the project you want to copy over to your iPad.

6. On the iPad, open iMovie and tap on the Import button. You'll see a list of compatible iMovie projects; just tap on the one you want to import.

Lifestyle

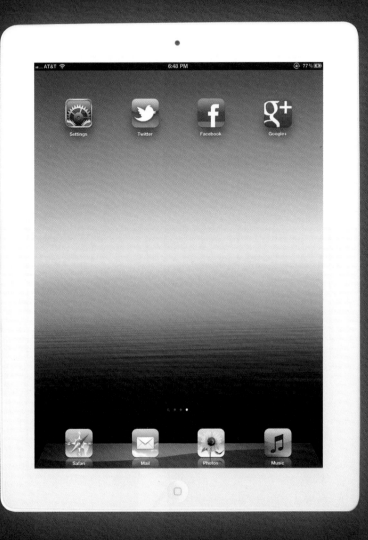

12

Social Media

The Skim

Twitter • Facebook • Google+

Social media has changed the way we interact and keep in contact with each other. Facebook now has over 800 million active users, with more than 50% of them (that's 400 million users!) logging on every day. Facebook is available in more than 70 different languages and there are now more users outside the United States than in the United States. The statistics for Facebook users on mobile devices are also quite impressive, with more than 350 million users actively accessing Facebook through their mobile devices, including iPads.

The Twitter numbers, while not quite as high as Facebook, are also really impressive, with more than 300 million Twitter users generating more than 300 million Tweets and 1.6 billion searches a day.

A new player in the game is Google+, bursting on the scene in 2011 and gaining more than 62 million users in just the first few months. It looks to be on track to have over 400 million users by the end of 2012, according to analyst Paul Allen.

Many companies believe that the future of interacting with their clients is tied to social media and many now have both a Facebook page and a Twitter account. This method of interaction can make the company seem more personable and it does seem to be working. For example, a few weeks ago I was trying to find out if my computer backup system could use the new software a company released. Instead of going though a long e-mail contact form, I just sent the company a Tweet and got an answer within 30 minutes. It was great customer service and it made my interaction with the company feel way more personal.

The iPad is a great device for keeping up with the social networks, and with the new iPad, Apple has built Twitter integration right into the operating system. Facebook has an official Facebook app and Google+ is trying to catch up.

TWITTER

Twitter allows you to send out short messages that can be read by anyone following you. These 140 character–long messages, or "Tweets," are like text messages sent out on the Internet. You get to read the messages, or Tweets, of the people you follow.

When Twitter first started, the messages were just plain text, but now you can Tweet out images, videos, and web links. Twitter also has a built-in messaging system called Direct Message, which works like e-mail between two people who follow each other. Twitter also uses the #, or hashtag, to facilitate searching of topics, but more on that in little later on. There are quite a few good Twitter apps for the iPad including a pretty good official Twitter app.

Built-in Twitter Functions

The reason I discuss Twitter first in this chapter is because it is integrated right into the iPad operating system, which allows you to use it without an actual app. Let me clarify that—you need to have a Twitter account but you don't need to have the official Twitter app or any of the third-party Twitter apps installed to send out some Tweets. You can simply use the Share menus in built-in apps—you can Tweet images directly from the Photos app and web links directly from the Safari apps. You cannot, however, create regular Tweets (those not generated inside of the Photos or

Figure 12-1
The Twitter options in the Settings app on the iPad.

Safari app) without the official Titter app or one of the third-party apps.

The first step is to go to the Settings app and tap on Twitter in the list on the left. You are now faced with four options:

- Download the official Twitter app if you haven't done so yet
- Sign in with your Twitter username and password
- Click on a link to get more info on Twitter
- Click on link to Create New Account

If you don't have a Twitter account, you need to sign up for one and you can do this right on the iPad. Once you have signed up for Twitter you can sign into your Twitter account in the Twitter settings, and then you get the option to Tweet from the Share menu (without running any Twitter apps). For example, you can

Figure 12-2
The User Name and Password entered, but no Twitter app installed.

Figure 12-3
The Tweet option when you want to export a photo.

Tweet links directly from Safari, photos from the Photos or Camera apps, movies from the YouTube app, or maps from the Maps app—and you can add the location information right to the Tweets.

If you want to Tweet a photo from your iPad, just go into the Camera app, take a photo, tap on the Export button (also called the Share button), and you will see a list of options that includes Tweet. Tap on Tweet and a message window opens allowing you to add text and/or a location to your Tweet. Press send and the Tweet is Tweeted out to the world.

Even though you can Tweet from different built-in apps, to unleash the real power of Twitter you need to have a Twitter app so that you can see the Tweets of the people you follow.

Figure 12-4
Once you tap Tweet you can add text, and the photo is attached to your Tweet.

The Twitter App

The official Twitter app is free and you can download it from the App Store or right from the Twitter settings in the Settings app. Once you've installed it on your iPad, tap on the Settings app and then on Twitter on the left. A list of apps appears on the right—choose the ones that you want to allow to use your Twitter account information.

Launch the Twitter app and you will see that the layout is a simple two-column affair. The left column allows you to pick what information is displayed on the right column. There are six choices:

- **Timeline:** This is where you see the Tweets from the people you follow. You can tap on a single post and everything slides neatly to the left. If the Tweet that you click on has a photo, link, or any attached info you will see it here.

- **Mentions:** This is where you see Tweets that mention your username. They can be Tweets that are directed to you or Tweets that you wrote that have been reTweeted by others.

- **Messages:** These are where you find the direct, private messages from other people on Twitter. You can send messages only to people who follow you.

- **Lists:** You can create different lists of people, making it easier to sort the incoming Tweets. This is especially useful if you follow a lot of people.

- **Profile:** This is how the other people on Twitter see you.

- **Search:** You can search Twitter here and can access saved searches when needed.

On the bottom of the left column there are two buttons: the first, which looks like a pen and paper, is used to create a new Tweet, and

Figure 12-5
The Twitter app showing the timeline.

the second, which looks like a gear, is a Settings button. The new Tweet button allows you to write a Tweet and send it out, and the Settings button allows you to set the notifications and add additional Twitter accounts if you have more than one. (Some folks like to have both a business and a personal Twitter account, for example.) It is here that you can set which services deal with images and videos; what app (if any) you want to use to read tweets that you save for later; and image quality and sound effects.

Other Twitter Apps

If you search for Twitter in the App Store you will find a good selection of apps with names like Echofon for Twitter, Tweetcaster for Twitter, and HootSuite for Twitter—and they are free. All of these apps give you the same information but in different ways. I like these

Figure 12-6
Tap on a Tweet in the timeline to see the details of the Tweet, including any attachments.

Figure 12-7
The Tweetcaster app plays ads on the bottom of the screen, but the interface is so well done that it has become one of my favorite apps.

apps and the different ways they look, but there is a hidden cost at times. For example, the very slick Tweetcaster plays advertisements across the bottom of the app. For these apps to work, you have to allow then access to your Twitter account.

Many of the Twitter apps allow you to post to multiple accounts at the same time and even allow you to post to your different social networks at the same time. This means that you can post to Twitter and Facebook from the same app.

FACEBOOK

Facebook is the largest social media network on the planet and is probably going to keep growing. Facebook finally released an

official Facebook app for the iPad in 2011, and although it has a nice look and feel, you might just find it easier (and faster) to check your Facebook account using Safari. If you don't have a Facebook account and want to set one up, go to www.facebook.com on a computer or on Safari on the iPad and follow the directions for setting up an account.

The Facebook App

Once you have loaded the official Facebook app on your iPad, tap it to open and you will see the Log In screen where you can enter your e-mail and password to access your Facebook account. There is also a Sign Up for Facebook button on the bottom of the screen if you don't have a Facebook account yet. If

Figure 12-9
Video post on the Facebook app.

Figure 12-8
The Facebook Log In screen.

Figure 12-10
Video post on the Facebook website
on Safari.

you tap on the Sign Up button, the app opens Safari and sends you to www.facebook.com, where you can sign up for an account.

After you have entered your information and tapped the Log In button you will see your Facebook stream. Well, you will after a while. Here is one of the main problems with the Facebook app and one of the reasons that I still use Safari more than the app to check Facebook: The Facebook app is slow. In my unofficial time trials, my Facebook stream took about 12 seconds to load with the app, but took about half that time when I opened it with Safari. Now, I know that a 6 second difference is not a whole lot of time, but when you are staring at the iPad waiting for it to do something, 6 seconds can seem like forever.

The real advantage to the Facebook app is that the interface looks a little better than the

website and each post is easier to see, especially when it comes to videos. If you look at Figures 12-9 and 12-10 you can see the same post on the Facebook app and the Website, and it's clear that the video on the app is much easier to see.

The layout of the Facebook app is very clean, with the main controls located across the top of the screen. The first button is the Menu button, and tapping it brings up the list of items that can be displayed on the main part of the app. This includes your News Feed, Messages, Friends, and Photos. Just a single tap on any of them and the main window changes to show the selected data. The iPad is a great device to show off your photos and Facebook knows this, so it has worked hard to make photo viewing on the iPad app really slick.

Figure 12-11
The photo galleries on my Facebook account.

Figure 12-12
The Facebook Log In page in Safari.

Tap on the Menu button, then tap on Photos and the screen shows you all the galleries you have on Facebook. Tap on a gallery and then on one of the photos to view it full size. Swipe across the screen to get to the next image, or tap to bring up the controls.

As I mentioned before, although the Facebook app is well done it does tend to be a little slow, especially when first starting up. Thankfully, it runs faster on the new iPad compared to the older iPads, but that is to be expected since the new iPad has a faster processor and more memory. Also, the new iPad can download the data faster when on a 4G network compared to the older generations of iPads.

Using Facebook in Safari

There is another way to use Facebook on the iPad that is really easy, especially for those of us who use Facebook on a computer regularly. You can use the built-in web browser Safari to access your Facebook account as if you were on a computer. There are a few tiny layout glitches, but on the whole it works great. Here's how to do it:

1. Open the Safari app.

2. Navigate to www.facebook.com.

3. Either log in to Facebook if you have an account or sign up for an account.

Checking the Keep me logged in box will show your Facebook page every time you navigate to Facebook.com on your iPad. Once you have logged in, you'll see that the Facebook page doesn't quite fit the screen properly. This is the one drawback to using the Facebook website over the Facebook app—some things just don't look right. If that bothers you then the app is a better way to go.

One cool thing that you can do is create a link to the Facebook website that is accessible from the Home Screen, making it a one-tap job to get into Facebook. All you have to do is the following:

1. Open the Safari app.

2. Navigate to www.facebook.com.

3. Log in if you need to.

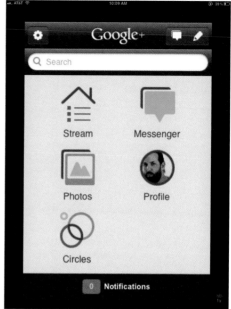

Figure 12-13
The Export menu showing the Add to Home Screen menu choice.

Figure 12-14
The Google+ app home screen.

4. Tap the Export button at the top of the screen.

5. Pick Add to Home Screen.

6. Name the link (Facebook, or anything else you want).

7. Tap Add.

That's it! You now have a link that looks just like an app icon and will take you right into your Facebook account in Safari.

GOOGLE+

It seems that Google is everywhere. Many people use Google not only for their Internet searches, but also for their e-mail (Gmail) and now Google+ for their social network. Google+ went public in the middle of 2011 and has grown quickly. Google continues to

try to make the service better and has added features not found on the other social networks, including the ability to have a video "hangout" with a group of friends and really easy photo sharing. There is also a unique and easy way of sorting the people you follow into circles. What Google+ doesn't have is an iPad app, and there is a problem using it on the built-in Safari web browser. So why did I include it here? I believe that the service will continue to grow, and grow quickly.

There are two ways to access a Google+ account on the iPad. Neither is great, so I hope that Google puts out an iPad app soon. Now I know that Google is the force behind the Android mobile device operating system that competes with Apple, but they also see the large number of people using the iPad. There is an iPhone version of the Google+

app, and since it can be used on the iPad that is the first and best choice right now for accessing your Google+ account on the iPad.

Google+ iPhone App

When you install the Google+ app on the iPad and first run it, you are asked to sign in or create a new Google Account. If you tap on Create a New Google account, you are taken to Safari and the Google account page opens. If you have any type of Google account, including a Gmail account, you can instantly sign up for Google+. After you have signed up for a Google account, you can now sign in and start to use Google+ on your iPad.

On the sign in screen, you can check the box that allows the app to remember the account so that you don't have to sign in each time. The Google+ app main screen has four sections:

- **Top menu bar:** This bar across the top of the app has three buttons: Settings, Messenger, and New Post.

  - **Settings:** The Settings menu allows you to sign out of your Google+ account, set up the push notifications that show up on the bottom of the main screen, choose the stream views, set up who can message with you, and provide feedback to Google. There are also the Google Privacy Policy and the Terms of Service agreements.

  - **Messenger:** This part of the app allows you to start a conversation with up to 50 people. Just type the name, e-mail, or circle to get started. Then just type the message and the recipients will be notified that you have started a conversation with them.

  - **New Post:** To create a post, tap on the New Post icon on the top right of the screen. This allows you to create a post and pick which circles you want to share it with, add a location, and even add photos.

- **Search bar:** This allows you to quickly search for posts or people. Just tap the search bar and the screen changes, bringing up the option to search for posts or people with a search bar across the top. Tap Cancel to go back to the main screen.

- **Main Menu:** The main part of the screen has five menu choices: Stream, Messenger, Photos, Profile, and Circles. Each of these is covered in more detail a little later on in the chapter.

- **Notifications:** The notifications count across the bottom of the screen allows you to quickly see how many unread notifications you have. This includes comments that have been made on your posts and who has added you on Google+.

The main section of the Google+ app is broken down into the following five sections:

- **Stream:** This is where you go to see people's posts (including your own). The stream is updated in real time, so it shows the most current first and then the older posts. Use your finger to scroll up and down through the posts and if you see one that you want to comment on, just tap it. The post will open up and you can comment or let the author know you like the post by tapping on the +1 in the upper right corner.

- **Messenger:** Tapping on Messenger opens up all the conversations you have going. You can also start a new conversation by

Figure 12-15
The Photos tab in the Google+ app.

Figure 12-16
Google+ on Safari using the desktop view settings.

tapping on the New Conversation button on the top right of the screen.

- **Photos:** One of the really great parts of Google+ is how it deals with photos, and that is evident here. Tap on the Photos button and you get a list of photos from different sources. The photos start with those from your circles, then photos of you, photos from your phone, followed by profile photos, and then photos from any of the photo galleries that you have created.

- **Profile:** This is where you can enter the information that people who follow you get to see, including a profile photo and website address.

- **Circles:** Circles are the way that Google+ organizes the people that you follow. You can set up as many circles as you want

and people can be in multiple circles. For example, I follow a lot of photographers and have them all in a circle called "Photographers;" some of them are also close friends and so are also in the "Friends" circle. If you tap on a circle to see all the people in it, look across the bottom of the screen—you can look at the circle by the People, the Posts, or the Photos.

Google+ on Safari

You can also access Google+ on your iPad using Safari. Tap on Safari and enter plus.google.com into the address bar to load the mobile browser version of Google+. That's right. Even though most websites treat the iPad Safari browser as a desktop version, Google+ doesn't.

The first thing that you have to do is sign in, but then the mobile web browser version works very much like the app, with a menu divided by stream, photos, circles, profile, and notifications. Tap on any of them and you get the same options as with the app.

Now you might be tempted to change the view to the desktop version from the mobile version, since the iPad has a lot more screen space than the smart phones that the mobile version of the browser was meant for. You can do that—just scroll to the bottom of the page and where it says view in: Mobile | Desktop, just tap on Desktop.

A word of warning: This view doesn't seem to be all that stable and can cause the screen to freeze and Safari to crash. I'm not saying that it does that for everyone, but it has done it to me so many times that I find using the app, even though it was designed for the iPhone and not the iPad, to be a better experience than using Safari and the desktop view.

A word in general about social networks and the iPad: It's a good idea to keep the iPad locked with a password if you plan on making any social media posts with the iPad. Just think of the sheer amounts of information about you that you would not want others to have. Tap on the Settings app, then tap on the General tab, then turn the Passcode on. You're protected!

13

Finance

The Skim

Like many of you, I use my iPad for everything from watching movies to checking my e-mail, and I also use it for banking, accepting payments when on the job, accessing my bank accounts, and even as a calculator. When I am not writing, I earn a living as a photographer and that means dragging a lot of gear around. If I can substitute an iPad instead of a laptop to take care of the business side of things I will do it every time.

CREDIT CARD APPS

Running a small business is tough, especially in these times of economic uncertainty. One of the ways that I stay competitive is to accept credit cards for the work I do as a photographer. In the past this would have been quite an ordeal, as I would have had to sign up for a merchant account with a credit card processing company that charges monthly fees and a transaction fees. With the advent of some new apps, though, all that has changed …

The service that I use is called Square. The Square app not only allows me to accept credit cards on my iPad (and iPhone) wherever I am, the app is free and so is the card reader. Recently, PayPal announced that they are releasing a credit card reader for mobile devices called PayPal Here™. The idea is the same as Square and I'm sure I'll try it out when the service is launched, but for right now I offer clients the option of paying with a credit card via the Square service.

Square (Free)

Square is both an accessory and an app and has changed my life. This little plastic credit card reader turns your iPad into a cash register, allowing you to accept credit card payments anywhere. The best part is that the card reader is free and so is the Square account, and the fee is 2.75% per swipe for most major credit cards.

I was first introduced to Square about a year ago when I was given one of the card readers at a trade show. I put the reader in my pocket and forgot about it. I recently had a client who wanted to pay on-site with a credit card and I remembered the Square reader, so I signed up for an account. It was super easy and the product works exactly as advertised. It allows me to accept payments by credit card on my iPad easily and securely.

Figure 13-1
You can sign up for information on the PayPal Here™ service at the PayPal website: www.paypal.com/webapps/mpp/credit-card-reader.

The first step is to sign up for an account and get a free credit card reader. So it really is just a one-step process to get going.

Visit the Squareup website at squareup.com to get started:

1. The sign up form is on the home page. Enter your e-mail address, create a password, and tap on the Sign Up For Square.

2. Enter your address so that they can send you a free credit card reader. If you have a reader already, just check the "I have a card reader." button and tap Continue.

3. Verify how you will use Square and enter the required Business (or Personal) information asked for. Tap Continue.

4. Go to the App Store and download the Square app. Just search for Square and you see it listed for free.

Or you can just download the Square App for the iPad and sign up or sign in right from the App's opening page. Since I had already signed up on the website, I went directly to the sign in screen when I opened the app. Just enter your e-mail address and password. A pop up opens the first time asking if you will allow Square to use your current location. I recommend agreeing to this because it

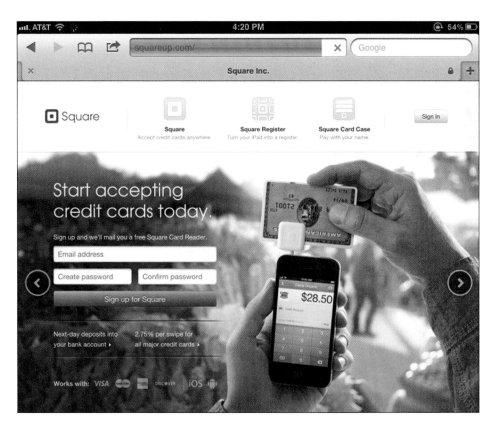

Figure 13-2
To sign up for the Square service, visit squareup.com right on your iPad.

"Square" Would Like to Use
Your Current Location

To protect buyers and sellers,
Square requires location information
for every payment.

Don't Allow   OK

Figure 13-3
I allow the Square app to record my
location so that if there is a question
later about a payment, I have the
location recorded.

records the location when a payment is made, making it easier to troubleshoot if there are any questions later.

There is a lot you can do from within the Square app, but to set up the account preferences you must visit the website. Go to squareup.com and sign in to your account. Click on the Account link, and then click on Edit Profile. Now you can add a logo, name, address, Twitter name, and phone number.

You can start using the Square app to accept payment even while you wait for the card reader to arrive in mail, but instead of swiping a card you have to enter the sale manually. You can do this by entering the amount of the sale, and then tapping on the Charge button

on the top right corner of the screen. This opens a menu on the screen where you can enter the credit card number or you can enter a cash sale. Just follow the screen prompts to accept payments.

The free card reader usually shows up within a few days; mine arrived two days after I signed up for the service. Tap on the Square app to open it and you see a page that allows you to enter a sale. Tap on the Account button on the top left to open the Account page. Here you will find the following:

- **Sales History:** This shows you your sales history. Tap on any of the charges to bring up a detailed list for that transaction. You can also send a receipt or issue a refund from the detail view of any of the transactions.

- **Items:** You can create items for sale. Just Tap the big + sign to set up an item. You can enter the Item Name, Item Description, and Price; turn the Sales Tax on or off; and even add a photo. You can also add the item to a shelf or create a new shelf, which keeps your products or services organized.

- **Tax:** Add the sales tax for your state here.

- **Tipping:** Turning this on allows your customers to add a tip when signing for their payments.

- **Signature:** You can turn Skip Signature on or off here. All payments over $25 require signatures.

- **Receipt:** The app supports the Star TP143LAN and the TSP650 printers (which are dedicated receipt printers) and you can set them up here if you have them. I don't have these printers, and since I use the device out on the road I just text or e-mail receipts.

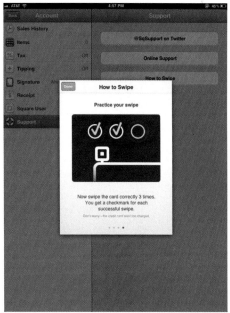

Figure 13-4
Turn on Add Sales Tax and enter the state or local tax rate in Square.

Figure 13-5
It took me a lot of practice to get this right, but once you get the hang of it swiping credit cards is easy.

- **Square User:** You can sign out of your account here, which is a good idea if you are not in possession of your iPad at all times.

- **Support:** There are three options here: Follow Square on Twitter, Access the Online Support, or view the How to Swipe instructions.

Once the card reader arrives, I suggest practicing swiping credit cards. The card reader plugs right into the headphone jack of your iPad. You can always go to the Account Settings, tap on Support, and then tap on How to Swipe. This brings up the instructions on card swiping and even lets you do practice swipes until you get it right three times.

When you want to take a payment, do the following:

1. Tap on the Square app.

2. Type in an amount, or swipe your finger across the entry pad from right to left to bring up the product list and tap on a product to automatically get the accompanying price. To get back to the manual price entry screen just swipe left to right across the bottom of the screen.

3. Tap on the + to add another line to the charge if needed.

4. Make sure the card reader is plugged into the headphone jack on the top of the iPad.

5. When you are ready to charge the credit card, just swipe it.

211

Figure 13-6
Get the customer to sign with his finger right on the iPad screen.

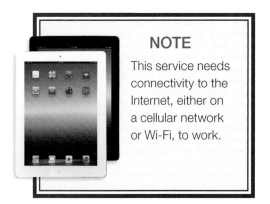

NOTE

This service needs connectivity to the Internet, either on a cellular network or Wi-Fi, to work.

6. If you don't have the card with you, then tap on the Charge button on the top right. You can tap Cash or tap Card Number to manually enter the credit card number or accept cash payment.

7. The credit card is charged and the customer signs the iPad screen with her finger.

8. Tap Continue.

9. You can send the customer a receipt to her cell phone or e-mail, print the receipt if you have a supported printer, or skip the receipt altogether. That's all there is to it.

The money is usually deposited into your Square account within minutes and is usually transferred to your bank account within 24 hours. It might take a day longer if the transaction is made after business hours. For example, if you process a payment at 10:30 pm on Monday, the money will be transferred on Wednesday since it is after business hours and won't be processed until Tuesday morning.

There are few services that I consider life changing, but this one from Square really is. Anyone can now accept credit cards for payment, and at a very low cost.

Square Register (Free)

The Square Register app takes accepting credit card payments to a whole new level. You can use this app to accept payments, and a whole lot more. You still use the iPad with the Square card reader, which plugs directly into the headphone jack, and you can accept cash and credit cards through it. The customer still signs with his finger right on the iPad screen, and you still use your Square account.

Right now you are probably asking yourself, "What is different about this app compared to the basic Square app?" For starters, you can set up a lot of different items for sale and organize them easily. You can also add names and photos for items, and can customize the layout of the screen. This app turns your iPad into a virtual cash register, making it a lot easier to quickly take payments—especially if you offer a wide variety of services or products.

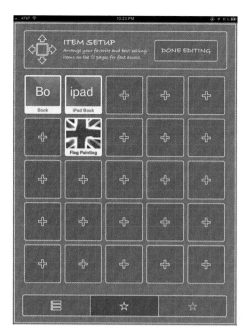

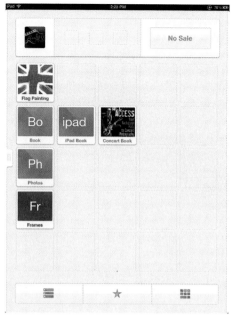

Figure 13-7
The Item Setup screen, where you can add items and move them around on the screen.

Figure 13-8
The Square Register app showing a few of the products that I created. Now all I do is tap on one of them to add it to the bill.

You can download the Square Register app from the App Store and if you have a regular Square account, you can just log right in using your regular Square information. Think of Square Register as an additional app that you can use with your Square account any time. When you first log into your Square account on the Square Register app, all the transactions made under that account show up.

Now it is time to start setting up the features of the Square Register app so that it works for you. Tap on the Settings button and you can edit your Public Profile; turn on the required signature; and turn on whether to apply Sales Tax to the transactions and, if so, the tax rate. (You can always turn off the tax for individual items or disable tax on the current sale for

tax-exempt customers) You can turn on the tipping feature, which allows customers to leave a tip, and set up receipt printers if you have them.

Look in the middle of the screen to see a small tab with three vertical lines. The real fun starts when you place your finger on this tab and slide it to the left to close the menus and start creating items libraries. You will see that the tab is now over on the left edge of the screen; you can always slide it out again to make it visible.

Tap the Edit button next to the Item Library header to start adding items to your Register. Any items that you already created in the basic Square app show up here, but now you can add and arrange your items so that when you are done you can just tap on any item to add it to a sale.

After you are done entering all of the items you have for a sale, tap on the Charge button on the top right corner. You can either enter the cash amount or swipe a credit card. Once the card is swiped, have the customer sign the screen with her finger. This is a great cash register app—and it's free!

BANKING APPS

Most banks have jumped on the mobile banking bandwagon and have designed apps for the iPad and iPhone. Banking apps are easy and convenient, and they keep customers out of the actual banks, which seems to be part of the banks' plan. We're not going to discuss every bank's mobile banking app here, but instead I want to give you some tips on staying safe when using these apps.

iPad Network Security

The first thing is to make sure you are on a trusted Wi-Fi network. The iPad makes it easy to join Wi-Fi networks, but that doesn't always mean that you should. There are some bad people out there who would love to steal your private information, and one of the ways they do it is by getting you to enter your banking account information when you're not on a secure network.

In the Settings app on your iPad, tap on the Wi-Fi tab on the left side of the screen to open the Wi-Fi menu. It is here that you can turn the Wi-Fi on or off, but more importantly, you can set your iPad to Ask to Join Networks. Turning this option on makes it easier to join networks when in a new place, but that convenience also makes it much easier to join a network that you don't know the origin of.

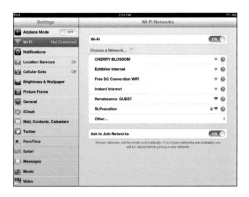

Figure 13-9
Here is a list of networks that are available to my iPad while I sit in a hotel room. The only one I trust is the locked one. (You can see the lock icon to the right of the name.)

When you turn your iPad on, it starts to look for available Wi-Fi networks to join. It first looks to see if there are any networks that you have previously used and will automatically join one of them if it is available. If there are all new networks, then the iPad opens a message screen showing you which networks are currently broadcasting in your area and asks if you want to join one of them.

If you turn off the Ask to Join Networks, the iPad will still join the networks it knows, but will not show you the list of other networks, nor will it give you the ability to join them with a single tap. Instead, you would have to manually select the network you want to join. The key to keeping safe here is to not join a network that you do not know.

Password Protecting Your iPad

Many people have passwords on their computers and smartphones, but forget to password protect the iPad. It's easy to do and can really save you if you leave your iPad somewhere or it gets stolen. Just do the following:

Figure 13-10
On the bottom of the Passcode menu is the ability to turn on the Erase Data function, which erases the data on your iPad after 10 failed passcode attempts.

Figure 13-11
You can activate the Remote Wipe ability at the iCloud website.

1. Tap on the Settings app.

2. Tap on General on the left side of the screen.

3. Tap on Passcode Lock.

4. Tap Turn Passcode On.

5. Enter the Passcode.

6. Re-enter the Passcode.

7. You can also set the iPad to Erase Data after 10 failed passcode attempts by turning on the Erase Data function.

If you do lose your iPad, you can remotely wipe the device. For this to work, you have to set the following up when you first get your iPad. The first thing to do is make sure that you are signed up for the iCloud service and have Find My iPad turned on. To do that, go to the Settings app, and then tap on iCloud and make sure that Find My iPad is turned on.

If you've lost your iPad, go to iCloud.com and sign in with your account info. Then, click on Find My iPad and choose your device in the list on the left. If the iPad is turned on and accessible then you will see it on a map; just click on the i to bring up the information for that device, which allows you to Remote Lock the device or Remote Wipe the device. If the device is not accessible then you can send a Remote Wipe that will happen the moment the iPad connects to the Internet.

There are some great reasons to use banking apps on the iPad and the big banks have some really good-looking apps. Many of the smaller and regional banks are starting to offer iPad apps, but the big banks have been doing it for a while. The following three all offer great views, navigations, and account access.

215

Figure 13-12
The Bank of America app allows you to not only sign into existing bank accounts, but you can also sign up for new bank accounts easily.

Bank of America for iPad (Free)

The Bank of America app allows you to sign up for a bank account or a Merrill Lynch Investment account right from the front page, or you can sign in to your existing bank account. The app interface is better than using the website because it gives you easy access to multiple accounts at the same time. You can pay bills and transfer funds all from inside the app. Just remember to log out when you are done.

Chase Mobile (Free)

Launch the Chase Mobile app and the first thing it asks for is your User ID and password. You can save the User ID so that you don't need to enter it every time you launch the

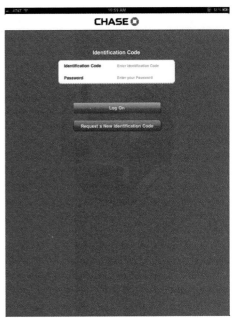

Figure 13-13
To activate the Chase Mobile app you must enter an Identification Code that you have received from Chase.

app. This is convenient but not secure, since it allows others to just try to guess the password.

One really cool feature of the Chase app is that when you first use your iPad to sign in to the Chase service, you have to register the device with an Identification Code. You can request the code right from the app. The Identification Code can be sent as an e-mail, a text message, or a phone call. You then need to enter the Identification code to get access to your Chase accounts. The app interface looks better than the banking website because it is designed for the iPad, but make sure you log out when done or your banking information will stay open and accessible to anyone who picks up your iPad.

Figure 13-15
The regular calculator screen has big buttons and a simple layout. If you use it in landscape orientation, you get a results tape that shows your data entry.

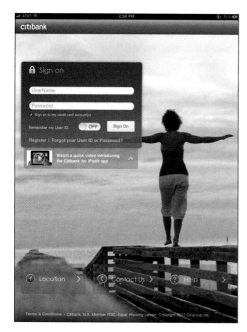

Figure 13-14
The Citibank app, like the other banking apps, allows you to store your username when signing into the app.

Citibank (Free)

The first thing that you see when you launch the Citibank app is the Terms & Conditions document that you must agree to before using the app. Next you must sign into the app with your ID, and right on the front page is a switch that allows the app to remember your ID. This option is great as long as you are the only one to ever use your iPad. Even though you need to enter the password each time you use the app, saving the username on an iPad that others can access is not very safe. If you don't have an account set up, tap on the Register button to enter your bank account number. When you are done with your banking, make sure you log out.

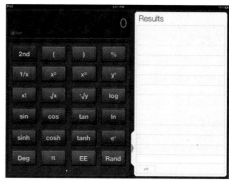

Figure 13-15
Swipe left to right to access the scientific calculator screen of the app. Again, in landscape orientation you get a results tape on the right.

CALCULATORS

There are 2,203 calculators in the iPad store as I write this and many of them are free or $0.99. My favorite calculator is the Calculator™ app, which sells for $0.99. This calculator has both a basic and a scientific

Figure 13-17
The Loan Calculator + app allows you to enter all the information about your loan or the loan you are considering.

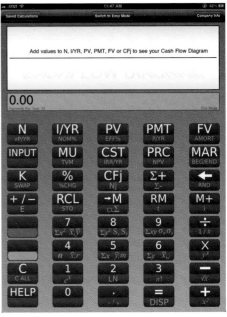

Figure 13-18
The Financial Calculator 10bii app can be intimidating, but this app has all the functions someone who needs them could want.

calculator that work in portrait and landscape modes. There is a history tape and you can swipe to edit. The Calculator app supports the iPad multi-tasking, so you can switch to another app and come back to all your calculations.

There are more than just basic calculators available on the iPad; you can also get some cool specialty calculators, like a loan calculator. My favorite is the Loan Calculator +, which costs $1.99. It has a nice interface and is easy to use. The app makes it simple to track multiple mortgages, and you can find out what would happen if you make extra payments and how much you can borrow.

There are also financial calculators for those who need more advanced functions, such as the 10bii Financial Calculator app, which retails for $5.99 and has all the bells and whistles of a much more expensive physical calculator. You can even save PDF amortization tables on it.

For Fun

The Skim

Games • In-App Purchases • Art • Making Music with GarageBand

The iPad is fun. I try to pretend that everything I do is serious and important, but playing games and having fun is so easy to do with the iPad. I know I am not alone because there are a lot of games and other purely recreational apps for the iPad. That's what this chapter is all about—having some fun with your iPad.

GAMES

If you pick up my iPad, you will see that I probably have more games on my iPad than anything else. I'm not proud of the hours I have spent flinging angry birds at egg-stealing pigs in the various Angry Bird games (yes, I have played them all) or trying to create words in W.E.L.D.E.R.

In all seriousness, gaming on the iPad is big business, and although this section covers a few specific games it also discusses the in-game purchases that developers are using to make giant profits on free games. More importantly, I'll tell you how to turn this function off so that users of your iPad don't inadvertently rack up huge charges on the credit card that's tied to the App Store.

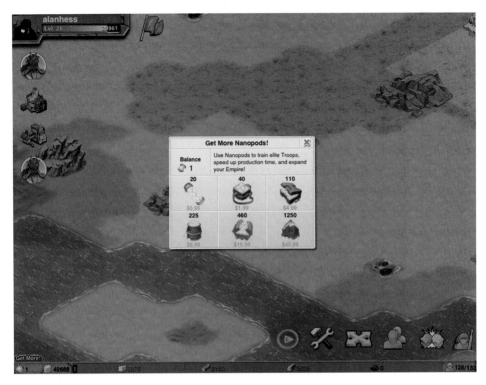

Figure 14-1
You can purchase extra Nanopods if you want them, but be careful because they cost real money.

In-App Purchases

You'll find in-app purchasing in both free and paid apps—and therein lies the problem. You can download a free game, but at some point the game might require you to purchase game currency, which costs real-world money. For example, the popular game Battle Nations is free to download. The gameplay is pretty fun—you get to build a city, train army troops, and expand your empire. The cost becomes a factor when you realize that you need more Nanopods to train the good troops, and those Nanopods cost real money—lots of real money—as shown in Figure 14-1.

Now there is nothing wrong with companies charging for their products, but many times parents let kids play games on the iPad it can comes as a great surprise that a "free" game actually cost them $49.99 in app purchases.

The good news is that you can turn off in-app purchases! Even better, you can password protect the setting so a password is required to turn it back on. Here's how to set up in-app purchase blocking:

1. Turn on the iPad.

2. Tap on the Settings app.

3. Tap on General on the left side of the screen.

IN-APP PURCHASES

There are four types of in-app purchases:

- **Non-replenishable:** These purchases require you to buy them only once and can be transferred from device to device without having to purchase them again. These types of purchases can include extra game levels or extra functionality for an app.

- **Replenishable:** These are items that you use up and then can't download again for free. This can include extra health in games. Be careful—you could really rack up the charges if you're not paying attention. More on this later on in the chapter.

- **Subscriptions:** These are one-time purchases that you must purchase again when the subscription runs out.

- **Auto-renewing subscriptions:** These are subscriptions that automatically renew unless you cancel them.

4. Tap on Restrictions on the right side of the screen.

5. Tap Enable Restrictions on the top right corner of the screen.

6. Enter a 4-digit restriction code, and then re-enter it.

7. Turn off the in-app purchases and set the require password to Immediately.

You can now also turn on any other restriction that you might want to, depending on who uses the iPad. Now when you go to make an in-app purchase, an error message appears as in Figure 14-2.

Angry Birds (free to $2.99)

It is impossible to discuss games on the iPad without talking about Angry Birds. This game is really simple to play and really hard to master. The idea is simple: You shoot, using different birds as ammunition, trying to knock out the pigs that have stolen your eggs. Each

Figure 14-2

After you've restricted in-app purchases, an error message pops up when you try to buy something.

Figure 14-3
The Angry Birds interface is simple, just pull back on the slingshot with your finger and let the bird fly.

of the birds has a different effect on the pigs' buildings, and you can score extra points by not using all the birds allotted in each level.

To play, load a bird into a catapult, pull back with your finger, and let go. Some birds have special effects that happen when you tap the screen while the bird is in the air. Simple ... and very addictive. There are currently four different Angry Birds games for the iPad: Angry Birds HD, Angry Birds Seasons HD, Angry Birds Rio HD, and Angry Birds Space HD. Both the regular Angry Birds HD and the Angry Birds Rio HD come in a free version so you can try before you buy. A word of warning—this game can be addictive.

The Angry Birds Space HD game (which sells for $2.99) changes the playing field once again. Angry Birds Space HD takes the bird-catapulting game and adds planets and gravity to the mix. This version allows you to shoot the birds from planet to planet, and the trajectory of the flying fowl is influenced by the gravity circles. There is also a guide that appears when you start to aim the birds that shows how the specific gravity will affect them in flight.

W.E.L.D.E.R ($0.99)

The W.E.L.D.E.R. game might sound like it has to do with construction, but the only things that you build are words. The idea

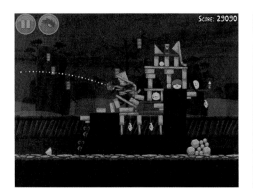

Figure 14-4
Newer versions of the game, like this image from Angry Birds Seasons, include themed backgrounds and story lines.

Figure 14-5
The Angry Birds Space gameplay allows the gravitational pull of the planets to affect the birds' flights.

Figure 14-6
The W.E.L.D.E.R. game screen is simple. To play, just move the tiles around to form words of at least four letters.

Figure 14-7
At the end of each round the remaining swaps are converted into points, and the more points you have the more swaps you start out with on the next level.

is to move the tiles around to create words that are four letters or longer. The longer the word, the more points you get, and if you use any of the special tiles, you get extra points for that as well.

The hard part of the game is that you get only a fixed number of tile swaps and when you run out, the game is over. For every 250 points you earn, you get more swaps, but with every level you clear the starting number of swaps is reduced. What I really like about this game is that you can take your time and study the game board, looking for the best way to make words. Once you have made a word, you can tap on it in the word list and see the definition. In case you were wondering, the name W.E.L.D.E.R stands for Word Examination Laboratory for Dynamic Extraction and Reassessment.

There are also blank tiles and, just like in Scrabble, you can use them as any letter—but using one costs you a swap and the tile isn't worth any points, so try to minimize using the blank tiles as much as possible for as long as possible. One key to the game is that at the end of the round, the number of swaps you have left helps you earn bonus swaps for start of the next round.

The Infinity Blade Series ($2.99 to $6.99)

If you are looking for a game that shows off the iPad, then the Infinity Blade series is for you. The graphics are stunning and the gameplay is smooth. Now this game might not be for everyone, since all you are doing is having multiple sword fights with a variety of stunningly ugly opponents and trying to earn better weapons, armor, and magic rings. This game is squarely in the sword and sorcery category that is much more likely to appeal to young men, or just men young at heart.

These games are built on the Unreal technology that powers many games for the PC, and the environments and characters are rendered very lifelike. The original Infinity Blade was released for the original iPad. Infinity Blade II came out for the iPad 2, but it also runs on the original iPad. Infinity Blade Dungeons was previewed at the new iPad announcement and was set for release in April 2012. It looks like it will change up gameplay once again, with an overhead view of the action instead of the first-person view of the first two games.

The original Infinity Blade sells for $2.99 and Infinity Blade 2 retails for $6.99. These games are not for little kids and are rated 9+ for violence. I am not sure why these get a 9+ and Batman (covered a little later in the chapter) gets a 12+, but just be aware that these games do show fights that are violent.

Where's My Water? ($.0.99)

The Where's My Water? game hooked me the first time I saw my nephew playing it. Created by Disney and available for the iPad and iPhone, the idea is simple. You need to create a path for the water to reach the shower so that Swampy the Alligator can get clean. Seems easy enough, but the great part about this game is that the levels get progressively harder, not in huge leaps but in small steps, so that by the time you are halfway through, the game has become a real thinker.

I feel comfortable recommending this game for all ages. Disney has created a great website with videos, photos, and even a meet the characters section; go to disney.go.com/wheresmywater and look around.

There is a free and a paid version of this app, which means you can try it before you buy it, but at $0.99 it is worth the price for 200+ levels of gameplay.

Figure 14-8
An Infinity Blade combat screen—the graphics are great.

Figure 14-9
Infinity Blade II
upped the ante
and the graphics
are even better
than the first game.

Figure 14-10
Great graphics and simple controls make the Where's My Water? game great for all ages.

Figure 14-11
Temple Run is all about running and staying ahead of the pursuers. Simple and addictive.

Temple Run (Free)

Want to kill a few minutes, or maybe half a day? Then check out this little doozy of a game. As far as concepts go, this game is the simplest of the bunch. Your character is running and you just need to make sure he doesn't run into a tree or off the path. Swipe left or right to change direction, swipe up to jump, swipe down to slide, and tilt the iPad left or right to collect the coins on the path. The idea is to go as far as possible. As far as I know, there is no end to the path, or at least in my extensive "testing" of this game I have never found one.

When you have amassed enough coins, you can buy new characters and power-ups, but the game really stays the same—you just

keep running. Now the little twist is that you are being chased, so if you bump into a lot of things you will slow down and get caught—and that means an end to your character until you start over and begin running again.

Batman: Arkham City Lockdown ($5.99)

I have been a Batman fan since I was a little kid and the opportunity to play a game as the caped crusader on my iPad was just too appealing to pass up. The game story is pretty standard Batman fare; the bad guys have escaped from prison and you (as Batman) need to round them up and put them back behind bars. All the great Batman villains are here, including Joker, Two-Face, and Harley Quinn.

For the Batman fan, the ability to buy costumes from different eras is appealing, but this is an in-app purchase that costs real money. The advantage is that each of the different costumes comes with a slightly different set of abilities for the Batman character.

For example, the standard Batman suit that the game starts with has a Health Rating of 100, a Damage Rating of 100, and a Speed Rating of 100, but if you buy the Dark Knight Returns Batman, you get a Heath Rating of 135, a Damage Rating of 110, and a Speed Rating of 90. The cost is $0.99 per costume and that might just be worth it if you want to play as your favorite version of Batman.

If there is one downside, it is that the controls can take a little getting used to and it is tough watching the villains win time and time again. At least they tend to win when I'm playing, as I am just not that great of a Dark Knight. Also a word of warning, this game is not for the little kids, as it is rated 12+, and does contain quite a bit of violence … actually the whole game is just Batman and his foes beating each other up.

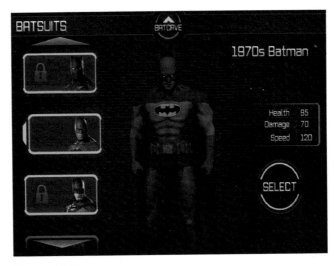

Figure 14-12

Feeling nostalgic? You can play Batman in the classic 1970s costume.

Figure 14-13

The gameplay on Batman is similar to the Infinity Blade series and that's because both games are built on the same platform.

Figure 14-14
The digital painting of a Golden Mantle Ground Squirrel done by Patrick
LaMontagne on an iPad using ArtStudio © Patrick LaMontagne.

ART

I am not an artist but luckily I know a few. My artistic ability tends to be more stick figure than anything else, so when I saw what artist Patrick LaMontagne (www.cartoonink.com) could do with his iPad, I was stunned.

Now Patrick was already an accomplished digital painter, so for him to be able to use the apps on the iPad to produce something that looks that good wasn't luck, but skill. The interesting part was that instead of listening to people who complained that the iPad wasn't pressure-sensitive enough or didn't have high enough resolution, Patrick just learned to be a better digital painter by learning to work around the limitations.

I asked Patrick to recommend some good art programs for the iPad and he suggested these two:

- Procreate
- ArtStudio

Procreate ($4.99)
The Procreate app puts the basic painting tools right at your finger tips. The controls are at the edge of the screen, which leaves most of the screen open for painting. Across the top of the screen you have:

- **Gallery:** Tap this to open the gallery, where you can see your artwork.

- **Settings:** This is where you can insert a photo into your work and control the eye-

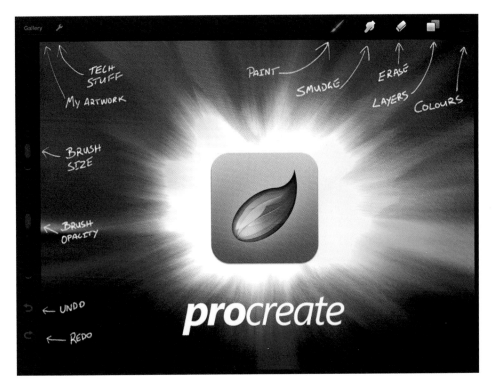

Figure 14-15
The Procreate screen showing the painting controls.

dropper and artwork orientation; and you can save a canvas to Photos, which then enables you to treat the image as a photo, meaning that you can use the Photos app to share it or e-mail it out.

- **Paintbrush:** There are 12 different brushes that you can pick here. Just grab the one that's right for the style you want.

- **Smudge:** You'll find the same brushes here as in the Paintbrush selection, but instead of painting it's all about smudging.

- **Erase:** Pick a brush style, but you'll use this tool to erase instead of paint.

- **Layers:** This is where you can control the layers in your image, including the order

Figure 14-16
I guess listening to the Kinks while playing with the Procreate app has its consequences.

Figure 14-17
The Settings menu in the ArtStudio app—and yes, that is another one of my fine Union Jack paintings. I think I need to stick to writing and photography.

and opacity. Tap the + in the upper right corner to add a layer or tap the trash can to get rid of one.

- **Colors:** This opens a color picker so you can get just the right shade in your piece.

And then down the left side of the iPad you have the brush size and opacity controls, along with the Undo and Redo buttons.

When you are in the Galleries view you can tap the + sign to start a new piece, tap the Share button to e-mail your artwork or duplicate the work, or send it to iTunes. You can also tap the trash can to delete it or open the Settings panel, where you can remember the tool size and opacity, and access the User Guide.

ArtStudio ($2.99)

When the ArtStudio app opens it looks like just a blank canvas. But if you look closely, you can see a little arrow in the bottom right corner. Tap it and the menu bar pops up from the bottom of the screen. It is clear from these controls that this is a very serious painting app. With a wide variety of tools and controls I found this app to be a little intimidating to use at first, but after a few minutes of experimenting I found it easy to navigate the menus and got a very fine control over the tools.

Across the bottom of the screen are the following:

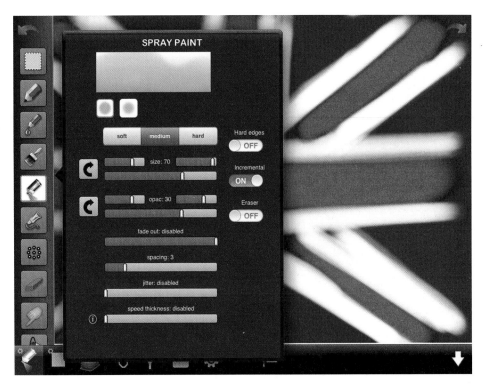

Figure 14-18
Check out the options you have for just the Spray Paint tool. Awesome.

• **Brush menu:** If you want drawing/painting tools, here they are. You get to pick between Pencil, Wet Paint Brush, Paint, Spray Paint, Paint Tube, Scatter, Eraser, Smudge, Fill, Gradient Fill, Text, Clone, Blur/Sharpen, Light Overlay (Dodge), Dark Overlay (Burn), Custom, and Saved Bushes. And each of these tools has a sub menu that gives you control over the brush. Just tap and hold on the Brush menu icon. Tap it again and the menu disappears.

• **Color Palette:** Tap on the color palette icon and the color swatches appear, tap and hold your finger on the icon and the color picker appears.

• **Layers menu button:** Tap on the Layers menu button and you see all the layers in your work on the left, but tap and hold the Layers menu button and the Layers control menu appears, allowing you to add, delete, duplicate layers, and more. You can even change the blending mode of the layer.

• **Shape tool:** This brings up the Shape tool with a cool mirror feature. On the top menu there is the choice for a single shape; next to it you can pick for the shape to be mirrored vertically or horizontally. This allows you to make a shape on one side that is then mirrored on the other. It's fun to use this to make patterns.

- **Effects menu:** This app has a full set of filters that allows you to change the Brightness and Contrast, Hue Saturation and Lightness, and more. You can even add a border to your art.

- **Import/Export menu:** This is where you can save you image, create a new image, import, export, or visit the online gallery.

- **Settings:** Want to offset the drawing or set the bottom layer type? Then this is the menu to use.

- **Lessons:** There are some really good lessons on painting, not so much how to use the app, but how to actually create a dog or cat. If these were interactive demos, then it would be even better.

- **Hide/Show:** Tap here to hide or show the menu.

Across the top of the screen are the Undo, Brush Size, Opacity, and Redo buttons. These are easy to access, but they can also get in the way when you're painting.

MUSIC WITH GARAGEBAND

Creating music on the iPad is fun and easy (even for people like me who are tone-deaf and have no real music ability at all) mostly due to Apple's GarageBand app. Apple released the GarageBand app at the same time it released the iPad 2, and it released an updated version to coincide with the new iPad release.

The key to the GarageBand app is the Smart Instruments. These gems allow anyone to create music that sounds pretty good. There are smart versions of the following instruments:

STYLUS FOR THE IPAD

If you go into the Apple store to buy a stylus for your iPad, you won't find one. That is not to say they don't exist, it's just that Apple doesn't think you need it. For most things you might not, but it is nice to have the option.

I have a Wacom Bamboo Stylus that works great on the iPad because it was designed for the iPad. Visit www.wacom.com/en/Products/Bamboo/BambooStylus.aspx to get more information. Targus also makes styluses that work on the iPad; you can find them at www.targus.com.

These styluses work just like your finger and allow you to have more control, especially if you have big fingers, long fingernails, or problems with your fingers. There is one other really good reason to use an iPad stylus and that is to avoid fingerprints on the iPad screen, especially when you use the tablet to show off your images. When you touch the screen, the oil in your skin can and will leave fingerprints on the iPad. This can be distracting to people looking at your images.

Figure 14-19
The Smart Strings interface, showing the helpful hints.

drums, strings, bass, keyboards, and guitar. Each of these five instruments works in a slightly different way but the technology enables you to create music that sounds good, even if you have very little musical ability:

- **Smart Drums:** With the Smart Drums tool you can play drums even if you don't have rhythm. You just place the drums by sliding them from the list on the right onto the smart pad, and your placement controls the volume and the complexity of the rhythm.

  Want to experiment? Just move the drums around or tap on the dice in the bottom left corner to get a random setup. You can also change the type of drums you are playing by tapping on the drum kit on the left side of the screen. GarageBand has six different drum kits—three traditional and three drum machines.

- **Smart Strings:** Added to the app in 2012, with this interface you have access to a complete string section that allows you to pick between controlling a whole orchestra string section or a solo string part. You get to control violins, violas, cellos, and even upright basses. You can choose whether you want to play actual cords for the orchestra as a whole, or if you want to play notes of a single instrument. If you play on the chords setting, you can also set the Autoplay between 1 and 5, or turn it off completely. Setting it on 5 makes even me sound like a I know what I am doing.

235

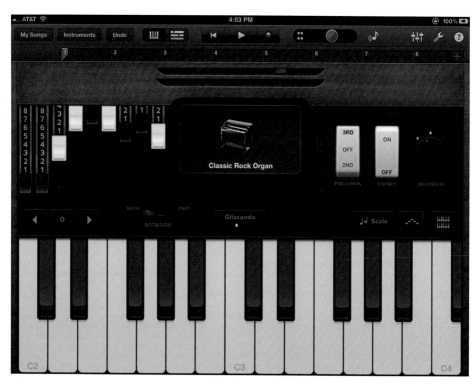

Figure 14-20
The touch keyboards showing the Classic Rock Organ.

- **Smart Bass:** You pick between four different basses, and you can play either chords or notes. If you need some help with getting the sound right, just turn on Autoplay.

- **Smart Keyboard:** This instrument gives you four different choices for your keyboarding needs. From a Grand Piano to a Classic Rock Organ, you can play them all. Turn on Autoplay to let the app help you out by playing along for you. Each of the keyboards has different controls. For example, you can control the rotation of the speaker horn from slow to fast in the Classic Rock organ, or turn on the sustain and control the Auto Wah and Phaser in the Smooth Clav.

- **Smart Guitar:** Ever want to play an acoustic guitar or maybe a Hard Rock guitar (looks suspiciously like a Gibson)? You can here. You get to strum the cords up and down or just tap to play each one separately. If you turn on Autoplay and pick a cord, the app does the rest and plays the guitar for you. My favorite part of using this app is watching the strings bend as they play, just like a real guitar.

There are also two touch instruments, the Drums and Keyboards. You play these instruments by just tapping on the iPad screen. The app knows if you are tapping hard or soft and the instruments respond accordingly. The touch instruments have all the same controls that the smart instruments have, just not an Autoplay mode, so you really need a bit of musical ability to be able to use them. The really fun part of using the touch drums is that you are playing a virtual drum kit. Tap on the edge of the drum and it sounds very different from banging in the middle of the drum, just like a real drum kit.

Playing the touch keyboards is like having eight different keyboards, including a Grand Piano, Classic Rock Organ, Whirly, and Heavy Metal Organ. If you choose the Classic Rock Organ, you can control the draw bars just like you would on a regular organ.

There are three ways to get music into the GarageBand app. The first is for those out there who play guitar.

- **Guitar Amp:** The Guitar Amp enables you to plug your real electric guitar right into the iPad. You need an adaptor, such as the Apogee JAM Guitar Input ($99), which has a 1/4-inch input for a guitar or bass and has a control knob to easily adjust the input.

  After you've plugged in the guitar, you have the option to use a variety of Guitar Amps—there are eight different combinations in each of four categories, and each of categories has eight different amps. That's a lot of musical choices.

  You can also add up to four stomp boxes to make your own custom pedal board. Tap on the pedal icon in the top right corner, and then add, remove, or adjust the pedals to your liking. There is also a nice way to tune your guitar; just tap on the tuning fork and get that axe in tune.

- **Audio Recorder:** You can record audio right into GarageBand through either

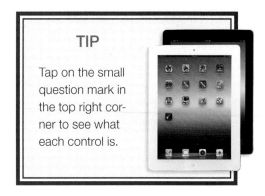

TIP

Tap on the small question mark in the top right corner to see what each control is.

the built-in microphone or an external microphone. Just watch the meter and make sure it doesn't go into the red too much because that will most likely distort the sound.

- **Sampler:** This allows you to record a sound and then play it back using the onscreen keyboard. The app comes with some samples already built in, but it's easy to create your own. Just tap on the New Sample button, tap the Start button, record the sound, and then tap the Stop button. Your sample is now ready to be used.

Just playing around with a tune is one thing, but GarageBand allows you to do much more—it is an eight-track recording studio. Follow these instructions and you'll have a good idea of how to create a song all on your own.

1. Open GarageBand and pick an instrument. It doesn't matter which one.

2. Tap on the My Song button on the top left corner of the screen.

3. You will see the screen where the songs you create are stored.

4. Tap on + in the top left corner and then tap New Song.

5. Now you can use the instrument in Step 1 or pick another one.

Figure 14-21
The Track view of a song shows the
instruments and the playback of the
song, you can adjust the volume of
each track on the fly.

6. Tap on the Instrument Settings button (it
    looks like a set of three sliders).

7. Adjust the Track Volume, Track Panning,
    Echo Level, Reverb Level, Quantization,
    Merge Recordings, and/or Master Effects.
    (The Master Effects controls the Echo and
    Reverb for the whole track.)

8. Tap on the wrench icon on the top right
    corner to open the Song Settings menu,
    giving you control over the Metronome,
    Count In, and Sound. You can also set the
    Tempo and the Key. This is also the loca-
    tion of the Help menu, which is very use-
    ful for finding out all about the bells and
    whistles in the GarageBand app.

9. Now you are ready to play, so tap the
    Record button and go for it.

10. Tap the Stop button when you're done
    laying down a track.

11. You can now play the track back using
    the Play button in the top middle of the
    screen.

12. You can also look at the track in the Mix-
    ing Board view; it's the icon at the top of
    the screen that looks like a set of parallel
    horizontal lines. Tap it and you can see
    your newly recorded track. More on the
    mixing a little later.

13. Tap on the Instrument button to get back
    to the Instrument view; it's the button
    next to the Track view.

14. You can now lay down another track using
    the same instrument or any of the others.

15. Just switch to another instrument, check
    your settings, tap Record, and start
    playing. You will hear your previously
    recorded tracks playing as you lay down
    your new track. You can record a total of
    eight tracks.

16. Once you are done recording your mas-
    terpiece, just tap on the My Songs but-
    ton. Your song will be saved and you can
    access it in the My Songs menu.

You can now edit your song using the mixing
controls. From the My Songs menu, tap on the
song you want to edit. If it is in the Instrument
view, tap on the Track view to see the individual tracks in your song. Swipe your finger from
left to right to open up the track controls.

For each of the tracks you can mute the
whole track, or send that track to the headphone jack. You can also control the volume
of each track to get a better mix. Double tap
on the track itself and you can Cut, Copy,
Delete, Loop, or Slip the track; you can
also adjust the placement and the start/stop
points by using the handles on the end of
the selected clip. If you have fewer that eight
clips, you can also use the + sign on the bottom to add another track.

After you are done, tap on the My Songs button to save your song and get back to the My Songs page. Once you are there and have a song selected you can change the name of your song by tapping once on the name and entering a new one. You can export the song by either sending it to iTunes or e-mailing the song.

From the My Songs page, you can also import songs from iTunes into the app, you can tap on the + sign to start a new song, or you can duplicate the current song. You can also delete the song if it just isn't up to your high standards. (I have deleted a lot of songs.) To delete or share a song, do the following:

1. When on the My Songs page, tap on the Edit button on the top right corner.

2. Tap on the song you want to delete or share.

3. Tap on the trash can icon on the top row to delete or tap on the Share button on the top row and choose one of the sharing options that appears.

Up until this point, everything has been a solo effort, but in the real world it is rare that all music is created by one person. The fine folks at Apple know this so they have come up with a brilliant solution. You can have a jam session with up to four different people on four different iPads at the same time. One user creates a Jam Session and the others join in. This is how to get your Jam Session started.

1. Open GarageBand.

2. Pick an instrument.

3. On the Menu bar at the top of the screen tap the Jam Session button; it looks like a music note with two curved lines next to it.

Figure 14-22
The Jam Session button opens the Jam Session menu where you can be the band leader and control the recording and playback of all the band members.

4. One person taps Create Session while the others tap Join Session.

5. The iPad that starts the session is the Bandleader and controls the recording and playback for the Jam Session.

Play away ... and you can even change instruments without having to exit and re-enter the Jam Session.

This is an amazing app for only $4.99 and if Apple keeps updating it every year, I cannot see a time when this app is not on my iPad. I can't wait to take my iPad over to a friend's place and see if we can live out our rock-n-roll fantasies and record a killer hit tune during our jam session.

APPS LIST

It's pretty easy to fill your iPad with tons of apps, but the reality is that you will probably use only a few of them all the time. I purchased all the apps mentioned in this book. None of them were given to me by the creators, nor did I receive anything from Apple. All the directions and walk-throughs in this book were done with hardware and software that were current as of March 18, 2012, as were the prices I paid for the apps.

iPADS APPS

App Name	Developer	Cost
10bii Financial Calc	In a Day Development	$5.99
Angry Birds HD	Chillingo Ltd.	$2.99
Angry Birds Rio HD	Chillingo Ltd.	$2.99
Angry Birds Seasons HD	Chillingo Ltd.	$1.99
App Store	Apple	Free (preloaded)
Artstudio	Lucky Clan	$2.99
Bank of America	Bank of America	Free
Batman: Arkham City Lockdown	Warner Bros. Entertainment	$5.99
Browser+ HD	Spreadsong, Inc.	$2.99
Calculator	Guise Calculator Converter Equipment Online	$0.99
Calendar	Apple	Free (preloaded)
Camera	Apple	Free (preloaded)
Chase	Chase	Free
Citibank	Citibank	Free
CloudOn	CloudOn, Inc..	Free
Contacts	Apple	Free (preloaded)
Dropbox	Dropbox, Inc.	Free
Easy Release	ApplicationGap	$9.99

 **Apps List**

App Name	Developer	Cost
Facebook	Facebook	Free
FaceTime	Apple	Free (preloaded)
Game Center	Apple	Free (preloaded)
GarageBand	Apple	$4.99
Google+	Google	Free
iAnnotate PDF	Aji, LLC	$9.99
iBooks	Apple	Free
iCab Mobile	Alexander Clauss	$1.99
Infinity Blade	Chair Entertainment Group, LLC	$5.99
Infinity Blade II	Chair Entertainment Group, LLC	$6.99
iMovie	Apple	$4.99
iPhoto	Apple	$4.99
iTunes	Apple	Free (preloaded)
iTunes U	Apple	Free
Keynote	Apple	$9.99
Kindle	Amazon	Free
Loan Calculator +	MH Riley	$1.99
Mail	Apple	Free (preloaded)
Maps	Apple	Free (preloaded)
Messages	Apple	Free (preloaded)
Music	Apple	Free (preloaded)
Newsstand	Apple	Free (preloaded)
Nook	Barnes & Noble	Free
Notes	Apple	Free (preloaded)
Numbers	Apple	$9.99
Pages	Apple	$9.99
PDF Expert	Igor Zhadanov	$9.99
Photo Booth	Apple	Free (preloaded)
Photos	Apple	Free (preloaded)
Photoshop Touch	Adobe	$9.99

App Name	Developer	Cost
Portfolio for iPad	Britton Mobile Development	$14.99
Procreate	Savage interactive	$4.99
Reminders	Apple	Free (preloaded)
Safari	Apple	Free (preloaded)
Settings	Apple	Free (preloaded)
Snapseed	Nik Software	$4.99
Square	Square, Inc.	Free
Square Register	Sqaure, Inc.	Free
Temple Run	Imangi Studios, LLC	Free
Twitter	Twitter, Inc.	Free
YouTube	Apple	Free (preloaded)
Videos	Apple	Free (preloaded)
W.E.L.D.E.R	Ayopa Games LLC	$0.99
Where's My Water?	Disney	$0.99

COMPUTER APPS

Handbrake	handbrake.fr	Free
iBooks Author	Apple	Free (Mac Only)
Printopia	ecamm	$19.95

There are two other apps that I covered in the previous versions of this book that I still use regularly—Hulu+ and Pandora.

When it comes to watching TV on the iPad, many cable companies are creating apps that allow you to watch TV shows right on your iPad. I'm a fan of Hulu+, which allows you access to a wide variety of TV and movies. The app is free but the subscription costs $7.99 a month, and you can cancel anytime.

For music, I still use the Pandora app that gives my iPad access to a huge online music library. This does need a Wi-Fi signal to work, but is a great way to find new music.

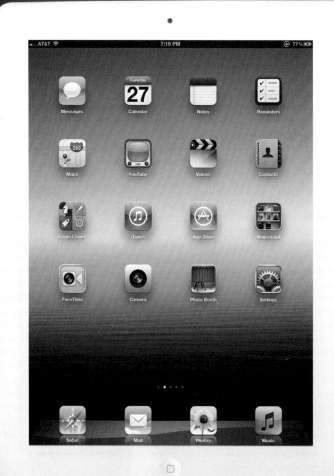

INDEX

■ ■ ▥ ◉ **Index**